PRINCIPLES OF FINANCIAL ECONOMICS

The subfield of financial economics is generally understood to be a branch of microeconomic theory and, more broadly, of general equilibrium theory. Finance methods are increasingly used to analyze problems involving time and uncertainty in such fields as monetary and environmental economics.

This book introduces graduate students in economics to the subfield. It stresses the link between financial economics and equilibrium theory, devoting less attention to purely financial topics such as valuation of derivatives. Because students often find this link hard to grasp, the treatment aims to make the connection explicit in each stage of the exposition. Emphasis is placed on detailed study of two-date models because almost all of the key ideas in financial economics can be developed in the two-date setting. The analysis aims to be comparable in rigor to the best work in microeconomics; at the same time, the authors provide enough discussion and examples to make the ideas readily understandable.

Stephen F. LeRoy is Professor of Economics at the University of California, Santa Barbara. He served as Carlson Professor of Finance at the Carlson School of Management, University of Minnesota, from 1991 to 1996 and taught at the University of Chicago, University of California, Berkeley, and California Institute of Technology. Professor LeRoy has published articles in eminent journals such as the *International Economic Review*, *American Economic Review*, *Journal of Political Economy*, *Econometrica*, *Journal of Economic Theory*, *Journal of Finance*, *Review of Financial Studies*, and *Economic Theory*.

Jan Werner is Associate Professor of Economics at the University of Minnesota. He taught at the University of Bonn and the Pompeu Fabra University, Barcelona. Professor Werner's research has been published in leading journals such as the *International Economic Review*, *Econometrica*, *Journal of Mathematical Economics*, *Journal of Economic Theory*, *Economic Theory*, and *Review of Economic Studies*.

PRINCIPLES OF FINANCIAL ECONOMICS

STEPHEN F. LEROY
University of California, Santa Barbara

JAN WERNER
University of Minnesota

Foreword by Stephen A. Ross

PUBLISHED BY THE PRESS SYNDICATE OF THE UNIVERSITY OF CAMBRIDGE
The Pitt Building, Trumpington Street, Cambridge, United Kingdom

CAMBRIDGE UNIVERSITY PRESS
The Edinburgh Building, Cambridge CB2 2RU, UK
40 West 20th Street, New York, NY 10011-4211, USA
10 Stamford Road, Oakleigh, VIC 3166, Australia
Ruiz de Alarcón 13, 28014 Madrid, Spain
Dock House, The Waterfront, Cape Town 8001, South Africa

http://www.cambridge.org

First published 2001

Printed in the United States of America

Typeface Times 11/14 pt.   *System* LaTeX 2_ε [TB]

A catalog record for this book is available from the British Library.

Library of Congress Cataloging in Publication Data
LeRoy, Stephen F.
Principles of financial economics / Stephen F. LeRoy, Jan Werner.
p.   cm.
ISBN 0-521-58434-5 – ISBN 0-521-58605-4 (pbk.)
1. Investments – Mathematical models.   2. Finance – Mathematical models.
3. Economics – Mathematical models.   4. Securities – Prices – Mathematical models.
5. Capital market – Mathematical models.   I. Werner, Jan.   II. Title.
HG4515.2.L47   2000
332 – dc21   00-028936

ISBN 0 521 58434 5   hardback
ISBN 0 521 58605 4   paperback

Contents

Foreword

For quite some time there has been a need for a modern treatment of the principles of finance suitable for the beginning Ph.D. graduate student. This rigorous, thoughtfully constructed, and thoroughly excellent text more than fills the bill. The ideas are carefully developed in a discrete time setting with both rigor and intuition – no easy pedagogic task since it requires an uncommonly sensitive balance between the Scylla of sterile formalism and the Charybdis of blowsy chat. The decision to work in a strictly discrete time setting is entirely appropriate for a beginning course and is to be much applauded; the seeming ease of analysis in continuous time comes at the expense of a deeper mathematical foundation that can obscure the underlying economic principles.

The order of development is natural. The text begins with the cornerstone of modern finance, the absence of arbitrage and the implications of this absence for pricing. It moves on to a careful development of risk and utility theory and from there goes naturally into the basic portfolio problem. Spanning and completeness are given a thorough airing and the authors share my view of the importance of this topic, which is seldom treated in the fullness it deserves. When the mean variance analysis and the CAPM are introduced, starting with a very nice tutorial on the Hilbert space approach, the student is ready for it as a special case of the more general development that has preceded. The beginning student will no doubt be pleasantly surprised by both the elegance and the generality of the structure, and this is all to the good; too many students of economics who have only a passing familiarity with finance fail to appreciate the value of the mean variance analysis. Intertemporal analysis and the martingale pricing approach ends the text, leaving the student perfectly positioned for advanced pricing courses and for the empirical world of modern finance.

The student who has gone through a course based on this book has been exposed to all of the tools and ideas necessary for a solid foundation in finance. From here it is an easy step to continuous-time valuation methods and that step will now seem very natural and make the ensuing mathematical requirements seem natural as well. The student is also well prepared to take advanced courses in empirical finance and in corporate finance. This tree structure beginning with a basic theory course and branching into subsequent courses in advanced pricing theory, i.e., continuous-time finance, empirical finance, and corporate finance, is emerging as the preferred model for Ph.D. sequences in finance.

This book is perfectly positioned for the first course of such a sequence. In fact, I teach such a course at MIT, and I have been searching in vain for an appropriate textbook. I will be assigning LeRoy and Werner in my class this term with enthusiasm and with a sigh of relief.

Stephen A. Ross
May 2000

Preface

Financial economics plays a far more prominent role in the training of economists than it did even a few years ago. This change is generally attributed to the parallel transformation in financial markets that has occurred in recent years. Assets worth trillions of dollars are traded daily in markets for derivative securities, such as options and futures, that hardly existed a decade ago. However, the importance of these changes is less obvious than the changes themselves. Insofar as derivative securities can be valued by arbitrage, such securities only duplicate primary securities. For example, to the extent that the assumptions underlying the Black–Scholes model of option pricing (or any of its more recent extensions) are accurate, the entire options market is redundant because by assumption the payoff of an option can be duplicated using stocks and bonds. The same argument applies to other derivative securities markets. Thus it is arguable that the variables that matter most – consumption allocations – are not greatly affected by the change in financial markets. Along these lines one would no more infer the importance of financial markets from their volume of trade than one would make a similar argument for supermarket clerks or bank tellers based on the fact that they handle large quantities of cash.

In questioning the appropriateness of correlating the expanding role of finance theory to the explosion in derivatives trading, we are in the same position as the physicist who demurs when journalists express the opinion that Einstein's theories are important because they led to the development of television. Similarly, in his appraisal of John Nash's contributions to economic theory, Myerson [13] protested the tendency of journalists to point to the FCC bandwidth auctions as indicating the importance of Nash's work. At least to those curious about the physical and social sciences, Einstein's and Nash's work has a deeper importance than television and the FCC auctions! The same is true of finance theory: its increasing prominence has little to do with the expansion of derivatives markets, which, in any case, owes more to developments in telecommunications and computing than to finance theory.

A more plausible explanation for the expanded role of financial economics is found in the rapid development of the field itself. A generation ago, finance theory was little more than institutional description combined with practitioner-generated rules of thumb that had little analytical basis and, for that matter, little validity. Financial economists agreed that, in principle, security prices ought to be amenable to analysis using serious economic theory. In practice, however, most did not devote much effort to developing economics in this direction.

Today, in contrast, financial economics is increasingly occupying center stage in the economic analysis of problems that involve both time and uncertainty. Many of the problems formerly studied using nonfinance methods now are seen as finance topics. The term structure of interest rates is a good example: formerly this was a topic in monetary economics; now it is a topic in finance. There can be little doubt that the quality of the analysis has improved immensely as a result of this change. Increasingly finance methods are used to analyze problems beyond those involving securities prices or portfolio selection, particularly when these involve both time and uncertainty. An example is the real options literature, in which finance tools initially developed for the analysis of options are applied to areas like environmental economics. Such areas do not deal with options per se, but do involve problems to which the idea of an option is very much relevant.

Financial economics lies at the intersection of finance and economics. The two disciplines are different culturally, more so than one would expect given their substantive similarity. Partly this reflects the fact that finance departments are in business schools and are oriented toward finance practitioners, whereas economics departments typically are in liberal arts divisions of colleges and universities and usually are not oriented toward any single nonacademic community. From the perspective of economists starting out in finance, the most important difference is that finance scholars typically use continuous-time models, whereas economists use discrete-time models. Students notice that continuous-time finance is much more difficult mathematically than discrete-time finance, leading them to ask why finance scholars prefer it. The question is seldom discussed. Certainly product differentiation is part of the explanation, and the possibility that entry deterrence plays a role cannot be dismissed. However, for the most part the preference of finance scholars for continuous-time methods is because the problems most distinctively financial rather than economic – valuation of derivative securities, for example – are best handled using continuous-time methods. The technical reason relates to the effect of risk aversion on equilibrium security prices in models of financial markets. In many settings risk aversion is most conveniently handled by imposing a certain distortion on the probability measure used to value payoffs. Under very weak restrictions, in continuous time the distortion affects the drifts of the stochastic processes characterizing the evolution of security prices, but not their volatilities

(Girsanov's theorem). This is evident in the derivation of the Black-Scholes option pricing formula.

In contrast, it is easy to show using examples that in discrete-time models distorting the underlying measure affects volatilities as well as drifts. Furthermore, given that the effect disappears in continuous time, the effect in discrete time is second-order in the length of time interval. The presence of these higher-order terms often makes the discrete-time versions of valuation problems intractable. It is far easier to perform the underlying analysis in continuous time, even when one must ultimately discretize the resulting partial differential equations in order to obtain numerical solutions. For serious students of finance, the conclusion from this is that there is no escape from learning continuous-time methods, however difficult they may be.

Despite this, the appropriate place to begin is with discrete-time and discrete-state models – the maintained framework in this book – where the economic ideas can be discussed in a setting that requires mathematical methods that are standard in economic theory. For most of this book (Parts One–Six) we assume that there is one time interval (two dates) and a single consumption good. This setting is most suitable for the study of the relation between risk and return on securities and the role of securities in allocation of risk. In the remaining parts (Parts Seven–Eight), we assume that there are multiple dates (a finite number). The multidate model allows for gradual resolution of uncertainty and retrading of securities as new information becomes available.

A little more than ten years ago the beginning student in doctoral-level financial economics had no alternative but to read journal articles. There are several obvious disadvantages to such sources. The ideas are not presented systematically, so that authors typically presuppose, often unrealistically, that the reader already understands prior material. Alternatively, familiar material may be reviewed, often in painful detail. Furthermore, typically notation varies from one article to the next. The inefficiency of this process is evident.

Now the situation is the reverse: there are about a dozen excellent books that can serve as texts in introductory courses in financial economics. Books that have an orientation similar to ours include Krouse [9], Milne [12], Ingersoll [8], Huang and Litzenberger [5], Pliska [16], and Ohlson [15]. Books that are oriented more toward finance specialists, and therefore include more material on valuation by arbitrage and less material on equilibrium considerations, include Hull [7], Dothan [3], Baxter and Rennie [1], Wilmott, Howison, and DeWynne [18], Nielsen [14], and Shiryaev [17]. Of these, Hull emphasizes the practical use of continuous-finance tools rather than their mathematical justification. Wilmott, Howison, and DeWynne approach continuous-time finance via partial differential equations rather than through risk-neutral probabilities, which has some advantages and some disadvantages. Baxter and Rennie give an excellent intuitive presentation of the mathematical ideas of continuous-time finance, but do not discuss the economic ideas at length. Campbell, Lo, and MacKinlay [2] stress empirical and econometric issues. The most authoritative text is Duffie [4]. However, because Duffie presumes a very thorough mathematical preparation, that source may not be the place to begin.

Several excellent books exist on subjects closely related to financial economics such as the introductions to the economics of uncertainty by Laffont [10], and Hirshleifer and Riley [6]. Magill and Quinzii [11] is a fine exposition of the economics of incomplete markets in a more general setting than that adopted here.

Our opinion is that none of the finance books cited above adequately emphasizes the connection between financial economics and general equilibrium theory, or sets out the major ideas in the simplest and most direct way possible. We attempt to do so. However, we understand that some readers have a different orientation. For example, finance practitioners often have little interest in making the connection between security pricing and general equilibrium, and therefore want to proceed to continuous-time finance by the most direct route possible. Such readers might do better to begin with studies other than ours.

This book is based on material used in the introductory finance field sequence in the economics departments of the University of California, Santa Barbara, the University of Minnesota, and the Carlson School of Management at the University of Minnesota. The second author has also taught material from this book at Pompeu Fabra University and the University of Bonn. At the University of Minnesota the book is now the basis for a two-semester sequence, and at the University of California, Santa Barbara, it is the basis for a one-quarter course. In a one-quarter course it is unrealistic to expect that students will master the material; rather, the intention is to introduce the major ideas at an intuitive level. Students writing dissertations in finance typically sit in on the course again in years following the year they take it for credit, at which time they digest the material more thoroughly. It is not obvious which method of instruction is more efficient.

Our students have had good preparation in doctoral-level microeconomics, but have not had enough experience with economics to have developed strong intuitions about how economic models work. Typically they have had no previous exposure to finance or the economics of uncertainty. When that has been the case we have encouraged them to read undergraduate-level finance texts and the introductions to the economics of uncertainty cited above. Rather than emphasizing technique, we have tried to discuss results so as to enable students to develop intuition.

After some hesitation we decided to adopt a theorem-proof expository style. A less formal writing style might make the book more readable, but it would also make it more difficult for us to achieve the level of analytical precision that we believe is appropriate in a book such as this. We have provided examples wherever appropriate. However, readers will find that they will assimilate the material best if they make up their own examples. The simple models we consider lend themselves well to numerical solution using *Mathematica* or *Mathcad*. Although not strictly necessary, it is a good idea for readers to develop facility with methods for numerical solution of these models.

We are painfully aware that the placid financial markets modeled in these pages bear little resemblance to the turbulent markets one reads about in the *Wall Street Journal*. Furthermore, attempts to test empirically the models described in these pages have not had favorable outcomes. There is no doubt that much is missing from these models; the question is how to improve them. There is little consensus on the best method, so we restrict our attention to relatively elementary and noncontroversial material. We believe that when improved models come along, the themes discussed here – allocation and pricing of risk – will still play a central role. We hope that readers of this volume will be in a good position to develop these improved models.

We wish to acknowledge conversations about these ideas with many of our colleagues at the University of California, Santa Barbara, and the University of Minnesota. Jack Kareken read successive drafts of parts of this book and made many valuable comments. The book has benefited enormously from his attention. However, we do not entertain any illusions that he believes our writing is as clear as it could and should be. Our greatest debt is to several generations of Ph.D. students at the University of California, Santa Barbara, and the University of Minnesota. Comments from Alexandre Baptista have been particularly helpful. Students assure us that they enjoy the material and think they benefit from it. Remarkably, the assurances continue even after grades have been recorded and dissertations signed. Our students have repeatedly and with evident pleasure accepted our invitations to point out errors in the text. We are grateful for these corrections. Several ex-students, we are pleased to report, have gone on to make independent contributions to the body of material introduced here. Our hope and expectation is that this book will enable others whom we have not taught to do the same.

Bibliography

[1] Baxter, M. and Rennie, A. *Financial Calculus*. Cambridge University Press, Cambridge, 1996.

[2] Campbell, J. Y., Lo, A. W., and MacKinlay A. C. *The Econometrics of Financial Markets*. Princeton University Press, Princeton, NJ, 1996.

[3] Dothan, M. U. *Prices in Financial Markets*. Oxford U.P., New York, 1990.

[4] Duffie, D. *Dynamic Asset Pricing Theory, Second Edition*. Princeton University Press, Princeton, NJ, 1996.

[5] Huang, Chi-fu and Litzenberger, R. *Foundations for Financial Economics*. North-Holland, New York, 1988.

[6] Hirshleifer, J. and Riley, J. G. *The Analytics of Uncertainty and Information*. Cambridge University Press, Cambridge, 1992.

[7] Hull, J. C. *Options, Futures and Other Derivative Securities*. Prentice-Hall, 1993.

[8] Ingersoll, J. E. *Theory of Financial Decision Making*. Rowman and Littlefield, Totowa, NJ, 1987.

[9] Krouse, C. G. *Capital Markets and Prices: Valuing Uncertain Income Stream*. North-Holland, New York, 1986.

[10] Laffont, J.-J. *The Economics of Uncertainty and Information*. MIT Press, Cambridge, MA, 1993.

[11] Magill, M. and Quinzii, M. *Theory of Incomplete Markets*. MIT Press, 1996.

[12] Milne, F. *Finance Theory and Asset Pricing*. Clarendon Press, Oxford, UK, 1995.

[13] Myerson, R. Nash equilibrium and the history of economic theory. *Journal of Economic Literature*, **XXXVII**:1067–82, 1999.

[14] Nielsen, L. T. *Pricing and Hedging of Derivative Securities*. Oxford University Press, Oxford, UK, 1999.

[15] Ohlson, J. A. *The Theory of Financial Markets and Information*. North-Holland, New York, 1987.

[16] Pliska, S. R. *Introduction to Mathematical Finance: Discrete Time Models*. Oxford University Press, Oxford, 1997.

[17] Shiryaev, A. N. *Essentials of Stochastic Finance: Facts, Models, Theory*. World Scientific Publishing Co., River Edge, NJ, 1999.

[18] Wilmott, P., Howison, S., and DeWynne, H. *The Mathematics of Financial Derivatives*. Cambridge University Press, Cambridge, UK, 1995.

Part One

Equilibrium and Arbitrage

1

Equilibrium in Security Markets

1.1 Introduction

The analytical framework in the classical finance models discussed in this book is largely the same as in general equilibrium theory: agents, acting as price-takers, exchange claims on consumption to maximize their respective utilities. Because the focus in financial economics is somewhat different from that in mainstream economics, we will ask for greater generality in some directions while sacrificing generality in favor of simplification in other directions.

As an example of greater generality, it will be assumed that markets are incomplete: the Arrow–Debreu assumption of complete markets is an important special case, but in general it will not be assumed that agents can purchase any imaginable payoff pattern on securities markets. Another example is that uncertainty will always be explicitly incorporated in the analysis. It is not asserted that there is any special merit in doing so; the point is simply that the area of economics that deals with the same concerns as finance but concentrates on production rather than uncertainty has a different name (capital theory).

As an example of simplification, it will generally be assumed in this book that only one good is consumed and that there is no production. Again, the specialization to a single-good exchange economy is adopted only to focus attention on the concerns that are distinctive to finance rather than microeconomics, in which it is assumed that there are many goods (some produced), or capital theory, in which production economies are analyzed in an intertemporal setting.

In addition to those simplifications motivated by the distinctive concerns of finance, classical finance shares many of the same restrictions as Walrasian equilibrium analysis: agents treat the market structure as given, implying that no one tries to create new trading opportunities, and the abstract Walrasian auctioneer must be introduced to establish prices. Markets are competitive and free of transaction costs (except possibly costs of certain trading restrictions, as analyzed in Chapter 4), and

3

they clear instantaneously. Finally, it is assumed that all agents have the same information. This last assumption largely defines the term "classical"; much of the best work now being done in finance assumes asymmetric information and therefore lies outside the framework of this book.

However, even students whose primary interest is in the economics of asymmetric information are well advised to devote some effort to understanding how financial markets work under symmetric information before passing to the much more difficult general case.

1.2 Security Markets

Securities are traded at date 0, and their payoffs are realized at date 1. Date 0, the present, is certain, whereas any of S states can occur at date 1, representing the uncertain future.

Security j is identified by its payoff x_j, an element of $\mathcal{R}^S$, where x_{js} denotes the payoff the holder of one share of security j receives in state s at date 1. Payoffs are in terms of the consumption good. They may be positive, zero, or negative. There exists a finite number J of securities with payoffs $x_1, \ldots, x_J$, $x_j \in \mathcal{R}^S$, taken as given.

The $J \times S$ matrix X of payoffs of all securities

$$
X = \begin{bmatrix} x_1 \\ x_2 \\ \vdots \\ x_J \end{bmatrix}
\tag{1.1}
$$

is the *payoff matrix*. Here, vectors x_j are understood to be row vectors. In general, vectors are understood to be either row vectors or column vectors, as the context requires.

A *portfolio* is composed of holdings of the J securities. These holdings may be positive, zero, or negative. A positive holding of a security means a long position in that security, whereas a negative holding means a short position (short sale). Thus, short sales are allowed (except in Chapters 4 and 7).

A portfolio is denoted by a J-dimensional vector h, where h_j denotes the holding of security j. The *portfolio payoff* is $\sum_j h_j x_j$ and can be represented as hX.

The set of payoffs available via trades in security markets is the *asset span* and is denoted by $\mathcal{M}$:

$$
\mathcal{M} = \{z \in \mathcal{R}^S : z = hX \text{ for some } h \in \mathcal{R}^J\}.
\tag{1.2}
$$

Thus $\mathcal{M}$ is the subspace of $\mathcal{R}^S$ spanned by the security payoffs, that is, the row span of the payoff matrix X. If $\mathcal{M} = \mathcal{R}^S$, then markets are *complete*. If $\mathcal{M}$ is a proper subspace of $\mathcal{R}^S$, then markets are *incomplete*. When markets are complete, any date-1 consumption plan (that is, any element of $\mathcal{R}^S$) can be obtained as a portfolio payoff but perhaps not uniquely.

Theorem 1.2.1 *Markets are complete iff the payoff matrix X has rank S.*[1]

Proof: Asset span $\mathcal{M}$ equals the whole space $\mathcal{R}^S$ iff the equation $z = hX$, with J unknowns h_j, has a solution for every $z \in \mathcal{R}^S$. A necessary and sufficient condition for this is that X has rank S. □

A security is *redundant* if its payoff can be generated as the payoff of a portfolio of other securities. There are no redundant securities iff the payoff matrix X has rank J.

The prices of securities at date 0 are denoted by a J-dimensional vector $p = (p_1, \ldots, p_J)$. The price of portfolio h at security prices p is $ph = \sum_j p_j h_j$.

The *return r_j* on security j is its payoff x_j divided by its price p_j (assumed to be nonzero; the return on a payoff with zero price is undefined):

$$r_j = \frac{x_j}{p_j}. \tag{1.3}$$

Thus, "return" means gross return ("net return" equals gross return minus one). Throughout we will be working with gross returns.

Frequently the practice in the finance literature is to specify the asset span using the returns on the securities rather than their payoffs. The asset span is the subspace of $\mathcal{R}^S$ spanned by the returns on the securities.

The following example illustrates the concepts introduced above.

Example 1.2.2 Let there be three states and two securities. Security 1 is risk free and has payoff $x_1 = (1, 1, 1)$. Security 2 is risky with $x_2 = (1, 2, 2)$. The payoff matrix is

$$\begin{bmatrix} 1 & 1 & 1 \\ 1 & 2 & 2 \end{bmatrix}.$$

The asset span is $\mathcal{M} = \{(z_1, z_2, z_3) : z_1 = h_1 + h_2, \ z_2 = h_1 + 2h_2, \ z_3 = h_1 + 2h_2, \ \text{for some } (h_1, h_2)\}$ – a two-dimensional subspace of R^3. By inspection, $\mathcal{M} = \{(z_1, z_2, z_3) : z_2 = z_3\}$. At prices $p_1 = 0.8$ and $p_2 = 1.25$, security returns are $r_1 = (1.25, 1.25, 1.25)$ and $r_2 = (0.8, 1.6, 1.6)$. □

---

[1] Here and throughout this book, "A iff B," an abbreviation for "A if and only if B," has the same meaning as "A is equivalent to B" and as "for A to be true, B is a necessary and sufficient condition." Therefore, proving necessity in "A iff B" means proving "A implies B," whereas proving sufficiency means proving "B implies A."

1.3 Agents

In the most general case (pending discussion of the multidate model), agents consume at both dates 0 and 1. Consumption at date 0 is represented by the scalar c_0, whereas consumption at date 1 is represented by the S-dimensional vector $c_1 = (c_{11}, \ldots, c_{1S})$, where c_{1s} represents consumption conditional on state s. Consumption c_{1s} will be denoted by c_s when no confusion can result.

At times we will restrict the set of admissible consumption plans. The most common restriction will be that c_0 and c_1 be positive.[2] However, when using particular utility functions it is generally necessary to impose restrictions other than, or in addition to, positivity. For example, the logarithmic utility function presumes that consumption is strictly positive, whereas the quadratic utility function $u(c) = -\sum_{s=1}^{S}(c_s - \alpha)^2$ has acceptable properties only when $c_s \leq \alpha$. However, under the quadratic utility function, unlike the logarithmic function, zero or negative consumption poses no difficulties.

There is a finite number I of agents. Agent i's preferences are indicated by a continuous utility function $u^i : \mathcal{R}_+^{S+1} \to \mathcal{R}$, in the case in which admissible consumptions are restricted to be positive and $u^i(c_0, c_1)$ is the utility of consumption plan (c_0, c_1). Agent i's endowment is w_0^i at date 0 and w_1^i at date 1.

A *securities market economy* is an economy in which all agents' endowments lie in the asset span. In that case one can think of agents as endowed with initial portfolios of securities (see Section 1.7).

Utility function u is *increasing at date* 0 if $u(c_0', c_1) \geq u(c_0, c_1)$ whenever $c_0' \geq c_0$ for every c_1 and *increasing at date* 1 if $u(c_0, c_1') \geq u(c_0, c_1)$ whenever $c_1' \geq c_1$ for every c_0. It is *strictly increasing at date* 0 if $u(c_0', c_1) > u(c_0, c_1)$ whenever $c_0' > c_0$ for every c_1 and *strictly increasing at date* 1 if $u(c_0, c_1') > u(c_0, c_1)$ whenever $c_1' > c_1$ for every c_0. If u is (strictly) increasing at date 0 and at date 1, then u is (strictly) increasing.

Utility functions and endowments typically differ across agents; nevertheless, the superscript i will frequently be deleted when no confusion can result.

1.4 Consumption and Portfolio Choice

At date 0 agents consume their date-0 endowments less the value of their security purchases. At date 1 they consume their date-1 endowments plus their security

---

[2] Our convention on inequalities is as follows: for two vectors $x, y \in \mathcal{R}^n$,

$x \geq y$ means that $x_i \geq y_i$ $\forall i$; x is greater than y,
$x > y$ means that $x \geq y$ and $x \neq y$; x is greater than but not equal to y,
$x \gg y$ means that $x_i > y_i$ $\forall i$; x is strictly greater than y.

For a vector x, *positive* means $x \geq 0$, *positive and nonzero* means $x > 0$, and *strictly positive* means $x \gg 0$. These definitions apply to scalars as well. For scalars, "positive and nonzero" is equivalent to "strictly positive."

payoffs. The agent's consumption-portfolio choice problem is

$$\max_{c_0, c_1, h} u(c_0, c_1) \tag{1.4}$$

subject to

$$c_0 \leq w_0 - ph \tag{1.5}$$

$$c_1 \leq w_1 + hX \tag{1.6}$$

and a restriction that consumption be positive, $c_0 \geq 0$, $c_1 \geq 0$, if that restriction is imposed.

When, as in Chapters 11 and 13, we want to analyze an agent's optimal portfolio abstracting from the effects of intertemporal consumption choice, we will consider a simplified model in which date-0 consumption does not enter the utility function. The agent's choice problem is then

$$\max_{c_1, h} u(c_1) \tag{1.7}$$

subject to

$$ph \leq w_0 \tag{1.8}$$

and

$$c_1 \leq w_1 + hX. \tag{1.9}$$

1.5 First-Order Conditions

If utility function u is differentiable, the first-order conditions for a solution to the consumption-portfolio choice problem (1.4)–(1.6) (if the constraint $c_0 \geq 0, c_1 \geq 0$ is imposed) are

$$\partial_0 u(c_0, c_1) - \lambda \leq 0, \qquad [\partial_0 u(c_0, c_1) - \lambda]c_0 = 0 \tag{1.10}$$

$$\partial_s u(c_0, c_1) - \mu_s \leq 0, \qquad [\partial_s u(c_0, c_1) - \mu_s]c_s = 0, \qquad \forall s \tag{1.11}$$

$$\lambda p = X\mu, \tag{1.12}$$

where λ and $\mu = (\mu_1, \ldots, \mu_S)$ are positive Lagrange multipliers.[3]

---

[3] If f is a function of a single variable, its first derivative is indicated $f'(x)$ or, when no confusion can result, f'. Similarly, the second derivative is indicated $f''(x)$ or f''. The partial derivative of a function f of two variables x and y with respect to the first variable is indicated $\partial_x f(x, y)$ or $\partial_x f$.

Frequently the function in question is a utility function u, and the argument is (c_0, c_1), where, as noted above, c_0 is a scalar and c_1 is an S-vector. In that case the partial derivative of the function u with respect to c_0 is denoted $\partial_0 u(c_0, c_1)$ or $\partial_0 u$, and the partial derivative with respect to c_s is denoted $\partial_s u(c_0, c_1)$ or $\partial_s u$. The vector of S partial derivatives with respect to c_s, for all s is denoted $\partial_1 u(c_0, c_1)$ or $\partial_1 u$.

Note that there exists the possibility of confusion: the subscript "1" can indicate either the vector of date-1 partial derivatives or the (scalar) partial derivative with respect to consumption in state 1. The context will always make the intended meaning clear.

If u is quasi-concave, then these conditions are sufficient as well as necessary. If it is assumed that the solution is interior and that $\partial_0 u > 0$, inequalities (1.10) and (1.11) are satisfied with equality. Then Eq. (1.12) becomes

$$p = X \frac{\partial_1 u}{\partial_0 u} \tag{1.13}$$

with typical equation

$$p_j = \sum_s x_{js} \frac{\partial_s u}{\partial_0 u}, \tag{1.14}$$

where we now – and henceforth – delete the argument of u in the first-order conditions. Equation (1.14) says that the price of security j (which is the cost in units of date-0 consumption of a unit increase in the holding of the jth security) is equal to the sum over states of its payoff in each state multiplied by the marginal rate of substitution between consumption in that state and consumption at date 0.

The first-order conditions for problem (1.7) with no consumption at date 0 are as follows:

$$\partial_s u - \mu_s \leq 0, \qquad (\partial_s u - \mu_s)c_s = 0, \quad \forall s \tag{1.15}$$

$$\lambda p = X\mu. \tag{1.16}$$

At an interior solution, Eq. (1.16) becomes

$$\lambda p = X\partial_1 u \tag{1.17}$$

with typical element

$$\lambda p_j = \sum_s x_{js}\partial_s u. \tag{1.18}$$

Because security prices are denominated in units of an abstract numeraire, all we can say about security prices is that they are proportional to the sum of marginal-utility-weighted payoffs.

1.6 Left and Right Inverses of a Matrix

The payoff matrix X has an inverse iff it is a square matrix ($J = S$) and of full rank. Neither of these properties is assumed to be true in general. However, even if X is not square, it may have a *left inverse*, defined as a matrix L that satisfies $LX = I_S$, where I_S is the $S \times S$ identity matrix. The left inverse exists iff X is of rank S, which occurs if $J \geq S$ and the columns of X are linearly independent. Iff the left inverse of X exists, the asset span $\mathcal{M}$ coincides with the date-1 consumption space $\mathcal{R}^S$, and thus markets are complete.

If markets are complete, the vectors of marginal rates of substitution of all agents (whose optimal consumption is interior) are the same and can be inferred uniquely from security prices. To see this, premultiply Eq. (1.13) by the left inverse L to obtain

$$Lp = \frac{\partial_1 u}{\partial_0 u}. \tag{1.19}$$

If markets are incomplete, the vectors of marginal rates of substitution may differ across agents.

Similarly, X may have a *right inverse*, which is defined as a matrix R that satisfies $XR = I_J$. The right inverse exists if X is of rank J, which occurs if $J \le S$ and the rows of X are linearly independent. Then, no security is redundant. Any date-1 consumption plan c_1 such that $c_1 - w_1$ belongs to the asset span is associated with a unique portfolio

$$h = (c_1 - w_1)R, \tag{1.20}$$

which is derived by postmultiplying Eq. (1.6) by R.

The left and right inverses, if they exist, are given by

$$L = (X'X)^{-1}X' \tag{1.21}$$

$$R = X'(XX')^{-1}, \tag{1.22}$$

where the prime indicates transposition. As these expressions make clear, L exists iff $X'X$ is invertible, whereas R exists iff XX' is invertible.

The payoff matrix X is invertible iff both the left and right inverses exist. Under the assumptions thus far, none of the following four possibilities is ruled out:

1. Both left and right inverses exist.
2. The left inverse exists, but the right inverse does not exist.
3. The right inverse exists, but the left inverse does not exist.
4. Neither directional inverse exists.

1.7 General Equilibrium

An *equilibrium* in security markets consists of a vector of security prices p, a portfolio allocation $\{h^i\}$, and a consumption allocation $\{(c_0^i, c_1^i)\}$ such that (1) portfolio h^i and consumption plan (c_0^i, c_1^i) are a solution to agent i's choice problem (1.4) at prices p, and (2) markets clear; that is

$$\sum_i h^i = 0, \tag{1.23}$$

and

$$\sum_i c_0^i \le \bar{w}_0 \equiv \sum_i w_0^i, \qquad \sum_i c_1^i \le \bar{w}_1 \equiv \sum_i w_1^i. \qquad (1.24)$$

The portfolio market-clearing condition (1.23) implies, by summing agents' budget constraints, the consumption market-clearing condition (1.24). If agents' utility functions are strictly increasing so that all budget constraints hold with equality, and if there are no redundant securities (X has a right inverse), then the converse is also true. If, on the other hand, there are redundant securities, then there are many portfolio allocations associated with a market-clearing consumption allocation. At least one of these portfolio allocations is market clearing.

In the simplified model in which date-0 consumption does not enter utility functions, each agent's equilibrium portfolio and date-1 consumption plan are a solution to the choice problem (1.7). Agents' endowments at date 0 are equal to zero, and thus there is zero demand and zero supply of date-0 consumption.

As the portfolio market-clearing condition (1.23) indicates, securities are in zero supply. This is consistent with the assumption that agents' endowments are in the form of consumption endowments. However, our modeling format allows consideration of the case in which agents have initial portfolios of securities and there is positive supply of securities. In that case, equilibrium portfolio allocation $\{h^i\}$ should be interpreted as an allocation of net trades in securities markets. To be more specific, suppose (in a securities market economy) that each agent's endowment at date 1 equals the payoff of an *initial portfolio* $\hat{h}^i$ so that $w_1^i = \hat{h}^i X$. Using total portfolio holdings, one can write an equilibrium as a vector of security prices p, an allocation of total portfolios $\{\bar{h}^i\}$, and a consumption allocation $\{(c_0^i, c_1^i)\}$ such that the net portfolio holding $h^i = \bar{h}^i - \hat{h}^i$ and consumption plan (c_0^i, c_1^i) are a solution to the problem (1.4) for each agent i, and

$$\sum_i \bar{h}^i = \sum_i \hat{h}^i, \qquad (1.25)$$

and

$$\sum_i c_0^i \le \sum_i w_0^i, \qquad \sum_i c_1^i \le \sum_i \hat{h}^i X. \qquad (1.26)$$

1.8 Existence and Uniqueness of Equilibrium

The existence of a general equilibrium in security markets is guaranteed under the standard assumptions of positivity of consumption and quasi-concavity of utility functions.

Theorem 1.8.1 *If each agent's admissible consumption plans are restricted to be positive, his utility function is strictly increasing and quasi-concave, his initial endowment is strictly positive, and a portfolio with positive and nonzero payoff exist, then an equilibrium in security markets exists.*

Although the proof is not given here, it can be found in the sources cited in the notes at the end of this chapter.

Without further restrictions on agents' utility functions, initial endowments or security payoffs, there may be multiple equilibrium prices and allocations in security markets. If all agents' utility functions are such that they imply gross substitutability between consumption at different states and dates, and if security markets are complete, then the equilibrium consumption allocation and prices are unique. This is because, as shown in Chapter 15, equilibrium allocations in complete security markets are the same as Walrasian equilibrium allocations. The corresponding equilibrium portfolio allocation is unique as long as there are no redundant securities. Otherwise, if there are redundant securities, then there are infinitely many portfolio allocations that generate the equilibrium consumption allocation.

1.9 Representative Agent Models

Many of the points to be made in this book are most simply illustrated using *representative agent models*: models in which all agents have identical utility functions and endowments. With all agents alike, security prices at which no agent wants to trade are equilibrium prices, for then markets clear. Equilibrium consumption plans equal endowments.

In representative agent models, specification of securities is unimportant, for in equilibrium agents are willing to consume their endowments regardless of which markets exist. It is often most convenient to assume complete markets so as to allow discussion of equilibrium prices of all possible securities.

1.10 Notes

As observed in the introduction, it is a good idea for the reader to make up and analyze as many examples as possible in studying financial economics. The question of how to represent preferences arises. It happens that a few utility functions are used in the large majority of cases in view of their convenient properties. Presentation of these utility functions is deferred to Chapter 9 because a fair amount of preliminary work is needed before these properties can be presented in a way that makes sense. However, it is worthwhile to find out what these utility functions are.

The purpose of specifying security payoffs is to determine the asset span $\mathcal{M}$. It was observed that the asset span can be specified using the returns on the securities rather than their payoffs. This requires the assumption that $\mathcal{M}$ does not consist of payoffs with zero price alone, for in that case returns are undefined. As long as $\mathcal{M}$ has a set of basis vectors of which at least one has nonzero price, then another basis of $\mathcal{M}$ can always be found of which all the vectors have nonzero price. Therefore, these can be rescaled to have unit price. It is important to bear in mind that returns are not simply an arbitrary rescaling of payoffs. Payoffs are given exogenously; returns, being payoffs divided by equilibrium prices, are endogenous.

The model presented in this chapter is based on the theory of general equilibrium as formulated by Arrow [1] and Debreu [3]. In some respects, the present treatment is more general than that of Arrow–Debreu; most significantly, we assume that agents trade securities in markets that may be incomplete, whereas Arrow and Debreu assumed complete markets. On the other hand, our specification involves a single good, whereas the Arrow–Debreu model allows for multiple goods. Accordingly, our framework can be seen as the general equilibrium model with incomplete markets (GEI) simplified to the case of a single good. See Geanakoplos [4] for a survey of the literature on GEI models; see also Magill and Quinzii [8] and Magill and Shafer [9].

The proof of Theorem 1.8.1 can be found in Milne [11], see also Geanakoplos and Polemarchakis [5]. Our maintained assumptions of symmetric information (agents anticipate the same state-contingent security payoffs) and a single good are essential for the existence of an equilibrium when short sales are allowed. An extensive literature is available on the existence of a security markets equilibrium when agents have different expectations about security payoffs. See Hart [7], Hammond [6], Nielsen [13], Page [14], and Werner [15]. On the other hand, the assumption of strictly positive endowments can be significantly weakened. Consumption sets other than the set of positive consumption plans can also be included (see Nielsen [13], Page [14], and Werner [15]). For discussions of the existence of an equilibrium in a model with multiple goods (GEI), see Geanakoplos [4] and Magill and Shafer [9].

A sufficient condition for satisfaction of the gross substitutes condition mentioned in Section 1.8 is that agents have strictly concave expects utility functions with common probabilities and with Arrow–Pratt measures of relative risk aversion (see Chapter 4) that are everywhere less than one. A few further results on uniqueness exist. It follows from results of Mitiushin and Polterovich [12] (in Russian) that if agents have strictly concave expected utility functions with common probabilities and relative risk aversion that is everywhere less than four, if their endowments are collinear (that is, each agent's endowment is a fixed proportion (the same in all states) of the aggregate endowment) and security markets are complete, then equilibrium is unique. See Mas-Colell [10] for a discussion of the Mitiushin-Polterovich result and of uniqueness generally. See also Dana [2] on uniqueness in financial models.

As observed in the introduction, throughout this book only exchange economies are considered. The reason is that production theory – or, in intertemporal economies, capital theory – does not lie within the scope of finance as usually defined, and not much is gained by combining exposition of the theory of asset pricing with that of resource allocation. The theory of the equilibrium allocation of resources is modeled by including production functions (or production sets) and assuming that agents have endowments of productive resources instead of, or in addition to, endowments of consumption goods. Because these production functions share most of the properties of utility functions, the theory of allocation of productive resources is similar to that of consumption goods.

In the finance literature there has been much discussion of the problem of determining firm behavior under incomplete markets when firms are owned by stockholders with different utility functions. There is, of course, no difficulty when markets are complete: even if stockholders have different preferences, they will agree that firms should maximize profit. However, when markets are incomplete and firm output is not in the asset span, firm output cannot be valued unambiguously. If this output is distributed to stockholders in proportion to their ownership shares, the stockholders will generally disagree about the ordering of different possible outputs.

This is not a genuine problem – at least in the kinds of economies modeled in this book. The reason is that in the framework considered here – in which all problems of scale economies, externalities, coordination, agency issues, incentives, and the like are ruled out – there is no reason for nontrivial firms to exist in the first place. As is well known, in such neoclassical production economies the zero-profit condition guarantees that there is no difference between an agent's renting out his or her own resource endowment and employing other agents' resources if it is assumed that all agents have access to the same technology. Therefore, there is no reason not to consider each owner of productive resources as operating his or her own firm. Of course, this is saying nothing more than that if firms play only a trivial role in the economy, then there can exist no nontrivial problem about what the firm should do. In a setting in which firms do play a nontrivial role, these issues of corporate governance become significant.

Bibliography

[1] Arrow, K. J. The role of securities in the optimal allocation of risk bearing. *Review of Economic Studies*, **31**:91–6, 1964.

[2] Dana, R.-A. Existence, uniqueness, and determinacy of Arrow-Debreu equilibria in finance models. *Journal of Mathematical Economics*, **22**:563–79, 1993.

[3] Debreu, G. *Theory of Value*. Wiley, New York, 1959.

[4] Geanakoplos, J. An introduction to general equilibrium with incomplete asset markets. *Journal of Mathematical Economics*, **19**:1–38, 1990.

[5] Geanakoplos, J. and Polemarchakis, H. Existence, regularity, and constrained suboptimality of competitive allocations when the asset markets is incomplete. In Walter Heller and David Starrett, editors, *Essays in Honor of Kenneth J. Arrow, Volume III*. Cambridge University Press, 1986.

[6] Hammond, P. Overlapping expectations and Hart's condition for equilibrium in a securities model. *Journal of Economic Theory*, **31**:170–5, 1983.

[7] Hart, O. D. On the existence of equilibrium in a securities model. *Journal of Economic Theory*, **9**:293–311, 1974.

[8] Magill, M. and Quinzii, M. *Theory of Incomplete Markets*. MIT Press, 1996.

[9] Magill, M. and Shafer, W. Incomplete markets. In Werner Hildenbrand and Hugo Sonnenschein, editors, *Handbook of Mathematical Economics, Vol. 4*. North Holland, 1991.

[10] Mas-Colell, A. On the uniqueness of equilibrium once again. In William A. Barnett, Bernard Cornet, Claude d'Aspremont, Jean Gabszewicz, and Andreu Mas-Colell, editors, *Equilibrium Theory and Applications: Proceedings of the Sixth International Symposium in Economic Theory and Econometrics*. Cambridge University Press, 1991.

[11] Milne, F. Default risk in a general equilibrium asset economy with incomplete markets. *International Economic Review*, **17**:613–25, 1976.

[12] Mitiushin, L. G. and Polterovich, V. W. Criteria for monotonicity of demand functions, vol. 14. In *Ekonomika i Matematicheskie Metody*, 1978.

[13] Nielsen, L. T. Asset market equilibrium with short-selling. *Review of Economic Studies*, **56**:467–74, 1989.

[14] Page, F. On equilibrium in Hart's securities exchange model. *Journal of Economic Theory*, **41**:392–404, 1987.

[15] Werner, J. Arbitrage and the existence of competitive equilibrium. *Econometrica*, **55**:1403–18, 1987.

2

Linear Pricing

2.1 Introduction

In analyzing security prices, two concepts are central: linearity and positivity. Linearity of pricing, treated in this chapter, is a consequence of the law of one price. The law of one price says that portfolios that have the same payoff must have the same price. It holds in a securities market equilibrium under weak restrictions on agents' preferences. Positivity of pricing is treated in the next chapter.

2.2 The Law of One Price

The *law of one price* says that all portfolios with the same payoff have the same price. That is,

$$\text{if } hX = h'X, \text{ then } ph = ph', \tag{2.1}$$

for any two portfolios h and h'. If there are no redundant securities, only one portfolio generates any given payoff, and thus the law of one price is trivially satisfied.

A necessary and sufficient condition for the law of one price to hold is that every portfolio with zero payoff has zero price. If the law of one price does not hold, then every payoff in the asset span can be purchased at any price. To see this, note first that the zero payoff can be purchased at any price because any multiple of a portfolio with zero payoff is also a portfolio with zero payoff. If the zero payoff can be purchased at any price, then any payoff can be purchased at any price.

2.3 The Payoff Pricing Functional

For any security prices p we define a mapping $q : \mathcal{M} \to \mathcal{R}$ that assigns to each payoff the price(s) of the portfolio(s) that generate(s) that payoff. Formally,

$$q(z) \equiv \{w : w = ph \text{ for some } h \text{ such that } z = hX\}. \tag{2.2}$$

In general, the mapping q is a correspondence rather than a single-valued function. If the law of one price holds, then q is single-valued.

Further, it is a linear functional:

Theorem 2.3.1 *The law of one price holds iff q is a linear functional on the asset span* $\mathcal{M}$.

Proof: If the law of one price holds, then, as just noted, q is single valued. To prove linearity, consider payoffs $z, z' \in \mathcal{M}$ such that $z = hX$ and $z' = h'X$ for some portfolios h and h'. For arbitrary $\lambda, \mu \in \mathcal{R}$, the payoff $\lambda z + \mu z'$ can be generated by the portfolio $\lambda h + \mu h'$ with price $\lambda ph + \mu ph'$. Because q is single valued, definition 2.2 implies that

$$q(\lambda z + \mu z') = \lambda ph + \mu ph'. \tag{2.3}$$

The right-hand side of Eq. (2.3) equals $\lambda q(z) + \mu q(z')$, and thus q is linear.

Conversely, if q is a functional, then the law of one price holds by definition. $\square$

Whenever the law of one price holds, we call q the *payoff pricing functional*.

The payoff pricing functional q is one of three operators that are related in a triangular fashion. Each portfolio is a J-dimensional vector of holdings of all securities. The set of all portfolios, $\mathcal{R}^J$, is termed the *portfolio space*. A vector of security prices p can be interpreted as the linear functional (*portfolio pricing functional*) from the portfolio space $\mathcal{R}^J$ to the reals,

$$p : \mathcal{R}^J \rightarrow \mathcal{R}, \tag{2.4}$$

assigning price ph to each portfolio h. Note that we are using p to denote either the functional or the price vector as the context requires. Similarly, payoff matrix X can be interpreted as a linear operator (*payoff operator*) from the portfolio space $\mathcal{R}^J$ to the asset span $\mathcal{M}$,

$$X : \mathcal{R}^J \rightarrow \mathcal{M}, \tag{2.5}$$

assigning payoff hX to each portfolio h. Assuming that q is a functional, we have

$$p = q \circ X, \tag{2.6}$$

or, more explicitly,

$$ph = q(hX), \tag{2.7}$$

for every portfolio h.

If there are no redundant securities, then the right inverse R of the payoff matrix X is well defined. Then we can write

$$q(z) = zRp \tag{2.8}$$

for every payoff $z \in \mathcal{M}$.

2.4 Linear Equilibrium Pricing

The payoff pricing functional associated with equilibrium security prices is the *equilibrium payoff pricing functional*. If the law of one price holds in equilibrium, then, by Theorem 2.3.1, the equilibrium payoff pricing functional is a linear functional on the asset span $\mathcal{M}$. We have

Theorem 2.4.1 *If agents' utility functions are strictly increasing at date* 0, *then the law of one price holds in an equilibrium, and the equilibrium payoff pricing functional is linear.*

Proof: If the law of one price does not hold at equilibrium prices p, then there is a portfolio h_0 with zero payoff, $h_0 X = 0$, and nonzero price. We can assume that $ph_0 < 0$. For every budget-feasible portfolio h and consumption plan (c_0, c_1), portfolio $h + h_0$ and consumption plan $(c_0 - ph_0, c_1)$ are budget feasible and strictly preferred. Therefore, an optimal consumption and portfolio choice for any agent cannot exist. □

Note that Theorem 2.4.1 holds whether or not consumption is restricted to be positive. We will see in Chapter 4 that the law of one price may fail in the presence of restrictions on portfolio holdings.

If date-0 consumption does not enter the agents' utility functions, the strict monotonicity condition for Theorem 2.4.1 fails. In that case the law of one price is satisfied under the conditions established in the following:

Theorem 2.4.2 *If agents' utility functions are strictly increasing at date* 1 *and there exists a portfolio with positive and nonzero payoff, then the law of one price holds in an equilibrium, and the equilibrium payoff pricing functional is linear.*

Proof: If the law of one price does not hold, then, as in the proof of Theorem 2.4.1, we consider portfolio h_0 with zero payoff and nonzero price, and an arbitrary budget-feasible date-1 consumption plan c_1 and portfolio h. Let $\hat{h}$ be a portfolio with positive and nonzero payoff. There exists a number α such that $\alpha ph_0 = p\hat{h}$. But then portfolio $h + \hat{h} - \alpha h_0$ and date-1 consumption plan $c_1 + \hat{h}X$ are budget feasible and strictly preferred. Thus, an optimal consumption and portfolio choice for any agent cannot exist.   □

The following examples illustrate the possibility of failure of the law of one price in equilibrium if the conditions of Theorems 2.4.1 and 2.4.2 are not satisfied.

Example 2.4.3 Suppose that there are two states and three securities with payoffs $x_1 = (1, 0)$, $x_2 = (0, 1)$, and $x_3 = (1, 1)$. The utility function of the representative agent is given by

$$u(c_0, c_1, c_2) = -(c_0 - 1)^2 - (c_1 - 1)^2 - (c_2 - 2)^2. \qquad (2.9)$$

His or her endowment is 1 at date 0 and $(1, 2)$ at date 1. Because the endowment is a satiation point, any prices p_1, p_2, and p_3 of the securities are equilibrium prices. When $p_1 + p_2 \neq p_3$, the law of one price does not hold. Here the condition of strictly increasing utility functions is not satisfied.   □

Example 2.4.4 Suppose that there are two states and two securities with payoffs $x_1 = (1, -1)$ and $x_2 = (2, -2)$. The utility function of the representative agent depends only on date-1 consumption and is given by

$$u(c_1, c_2) = \ln(c_1) + \ln(c_2), \qquad (2.10)$$

for $(c_1, c_2) \gg 0$. His or her endowment is 0 at date 0 and $(1, 1)$ at date 1.

Let the security prices be $p_1 = p_2 = 1$. The agent's optimal portfolio at these prices is the zero portfolio. Therefore, these prices are equilibrium prices even though the law of one price does not hold. Here the condition of strictly increasing utility functions at date 1 is satisfied, but there is no portfolio with positive and nonzero payoff.   □

2.5 State Prices in Complete Markets

Let e_s denote the sth basis vector in the space $\mathcal{R}^S$ of contingent claims, with 1 in the sth place and zeros elsewhere. Vector e_s is the *state claim* or the *Arrow security* of state s. It is the claim to one unit of consumption contingent on the occurrence of state s. If markets are complete and if the law of one price holds, then the payoff pricing functional assigns a unique price to each state claim. Let

$$q_s \equiv q(e_s) \qquad (2.11)$$

denote the price of the state claim of state s. We call q_s the *state price* of state s.

Because any linear functional on $\mathcal{R}^S$ can be identified by its values on the basis vectors of $\mathcal{R}^S$, the payoff pricing functional q can be represented as

$$q(z) = qz \qquad (2.12)$$

for every $z \in \mathcal{R}^S$, where q on the right-hand side of Eq. (2.12) is an S-dimensional vector of state prices. Observe that we use the same notation for the functional and the vector that represents it.

Because the price of each security equals the value of its payoff under the payoff pricing functional, we have

$$p_j = qx_j, \qquad (2.13)$$

or, in matrix notation,

$$p = Xq. \qquad (2.14)$$

Equation (2.14) is a system of linear equations that associates state prices with given security prices. When the left inverse of the payoff matrix is used, it follows that

$$q = Lp. \qquad (2.15)$$

The results of this section depend on the assumption of market completeness because otherwise state claim e_s may not be in the asset span $\mathcal{M}$, and thus $q(e_s)$ may not be defined. In Chapter 5 we will introduce state prices in incomplete markets.

2.6 Recasting the Optimization Problem

When the law of one price is satisfied, the payoff pricing functional provides a convenient way of representing the agent's consumption–portfolio choice problem. Substituting $z = hX$ and $q(z) = ph$, the problem (1.4)–(1.6) can be written as

$$\max_{c_0, c_1, z} u(c_0, c_1) \qquad (2.16)$$

subject to

$$c_0 \le w_0 - q(z) \qquad (2.17)$$
$$c_1 \le w_1 + z \qquad (2.18)$$
$$z \in \mathcal{M}. \qquad (2.19)$$

This formulation makes clear that the agent's consumption choice in security markets depends only on the asset span and the payoff pricing functional. Any two sets of security payoffs and prices that generate the same asset span and the same payoff pricing functional induce the same consumption choice.

If markets are complete, restriction (2.19) is vacuous. Further, we can use state prices in place of the payoff pricing functional. The problem (2.16)–(2.19) then simplifies to

$$\max_{c_0, c_1, z} u(c_0, c_1) \qquad (2.20)$$

subject to

$$c_0 \le w_0 - qz \qquad (2.21)$$

$$c_1 \le w_1 + z. \qquad (2.22)$$

This problem can be interpreted as the consumption–portfolio choice problem with Arrow securities.

The first-order conditions for the problem (2.20) (at an interior solution) imply that

$$q = \frac{\partial_1 u}{\partial_0 u}. \qquad (2.23)$$

Thus, state prices are equal to marginal rates of substitution. Security prices can be obtained from state prices using Eq. (2.14). Equation (2.23) can also be obtained by premultiplying Eq. (1.13) by L and using Eq. (2.15).

The following example illustrates the use of state prices for determining equilibrium security prices in complete markets.

Example 2.6.1 Suppose that there are two states and two securities with payoffs $x_1 = (1, 1)$ and $x_2 = (2, 0)$. The representative agent's utility function is given by

$$u(c_0, c_1, c_2) = \ln(c_0) + \frac{1}{2} \ln(c_1) + \frac{1}{2} \ln(c_2), \qquad (2.24)$$

for $(c_0, c_1, c_2) \gg 0$. His or her endowment is 1 at date 0 and $(1, 2)$ at date 1. Equilibrium security prices are such that the agent's optimal portfolio is the zero portfolio. Through simple substitution of variables, the agent's problem (1.4)–(1.6) can be written

$$\max_{h_1, h_2} \ln(1 - p_1 h_1 - p_2 h_2) + \frac{1}{2} \ln(1 + h_1 + 2h_2) + \frac{1}{2} \ln(2 + h_1). \quad (2.25)$$

The first-order condition for problem (2.25) evaluated at $h_1 = h_2 = 0$ yields equilibrium security prices $p_1 = 3/4$ and $p_2 = 1$.

The same prices can be calculated by using the payoff pricing functional. Because markets are complete, the payoff pricing functional is given by the state prices which, by Eq. (2.23), are equal to the marginal rates of substitution at the equilibrium consumption plan. The equilibrium consumption plan is (1, 1, 2), and the marginal utilities are 1 for date-0 consumption, $1/2$ for state-1 consumption, and $1/4$ for state-2 consumption. Marginal rates of substitution are $(1/2, 1/4)$; hence,

$$q = \left(\frac{1}{2}, \frac{1}{4}\right). \tag{2.26}$$

Equilibrium security prices are $p_1 = qx_1 = 3/4$ and $p_2 = qx_2 = 1$. □

2.7 Notes

As an inspection of the proof of Theorem 2.4.1 reveals, linear equilibrium pricing obtains under nonsatiation of agents' utility functions at equilibrium consumption plans. Nonsatiation is a weaker restriction than strict monotonicity.

The linearity of payoff pricing is a very important result. It is much discussed in elementary finance texts under the name *value additivity*. One implication of value additivity is the Miller–Modigliani theorem (Miller and Modigliani [3]), which says that two firms that generate the same future profits have the same market value regardless of their debt–equity structure. Another implication is that corporate managers have no motive to diversify into unrelated activities: if a firm pays market value for an acquisition, then the value of the two cash flows together is the sum of their values separately, and no more. Thus, acquisitions do not create value by making the firm more attractive to stockholders via, say, reduced cash-flow volatility. It remains true, though, that if the summed cash flows increase owing to reduced costs or "synergies" of management, then value is created.

Other important implications of the law of one price are parity relations such as interest rate parity, put-call parity, and others.

For articles emphasizing the role of state prices in analysis of security pricing, see Hirshleifer [1], [2].

Bibliography

[1] Hirshleifer, J. Investment decision under uncertainty: Choice theoretic approaches. *Quarterly Journal of Economics*, **79**:509–36, 1965.
[2] Hirshleifer, J. Investment decision under uncertainty: Application of the state preference approach. *Quarterly Journal of Economics*, **80**:252–77, 1966.
[3] Miller, M. and Modigliani, F. The cost of capital, corporation finance and the theory of investment. *American Economic Review*, **48**:261–97, 1958.

3

Arbitrage and Positive Pricing

3.1 Introduction

The principle that there cannot exist arbitrage opportunities in security markets is one of the most basic ideas of financial economics. Whether there exists an arbitrage opportunity or not depends on security prices. We show in this chapter that, if security prices exclude arbitrage, then the payoff pricing functional is strictly positive. Further, exclusion of arbitrage is necessary (and sufficient, when consumption is restricted to be positive) for the existence of optimal portfolios for agents with strictly increasing utility functions. In particular, equilibrium prices exclude arbitrage opportunities when agents have strictly increasing utility functions.

Conditions on security prices under which there exists no arbitrage are derived in this chapter in special cases (complete markets or two securities). The complete characterization will be given in Chapter 5.

3.2 Arbitrage and Strong Arbitrage

A *strong arbitrage* is a portfolio that has a positive payoff and a strictly negative price. An *arbitrage* is a portfolio that is either a strong arbitrage or has a positive and nonzero payoff and zero price. Formally, a strong arbitrage is a portfolio h that satisfies $hX \geq 0$ and $ph < 0$, and an arbitrage is a portfolio h that satisfies $hX \geq 0$ and $ph \leq 0$ with at least one strict inequality.

It is possible for a portfolio to be an arbitrage but not a strong arbitrage:

Example 3.2.1 Let there be two securities with payoffs $x_1 = (1, 1)$ and $x_2 = (1, 2)$ and prices $p_1 = p_2 = 1$. Then, portfolio $h = (-1, 1)$ is an arbitrage but not a strong arbitrage. In fact, there is no strong arbitrage. □

If there exists no portfolio with positive and nonzero payoff, then any arbitrage is a strong arbitrage. Further, a strong arbitrage exists iff the law of one price does not hold, and it is a portfolio with zero payoff and strictly negative price.

Example 3.2.2 Suppose that the securities have payoffs $x_1 = (-1, 2, 0)$ and $x_2 = (2, 2, -1)$. A portfolio $h = (h_1, h_2)$ has a positive payoff if

$$-h_1 + 2h_2 \geq 0, \tag{3.1}$$

$$h_1 + h_2 \geq 0, \tag{3.2}$$

and

$$-h_2 \geq 0. \tag{3.3}$$

These inequalities are satisfied by the zero portfolio alone. Therefore, there exists no portfolio with positive and nonzero payoff. Because there are no redundant securities, the law of one price holds for any security prices. Consequently, there is no arbitrage for any security prices. □

3.3 Diagrammatic Representation

It is helpful to have a diagrammatic representation of the set of security prices that exclude arbitrage. Suppose that there are two securities with payoffs x_1 and x_2, and consider the payoff pairs (x_{1s}, x_{2s}) in each state. These pairs are denoted $x_{\cdot 1}, \ldots, x_{\cdot S}$. Figure 3.1 is drawn on the assumption that $x_{js} > 0$ for all j and s, but the analysis does not depend on this restriction.

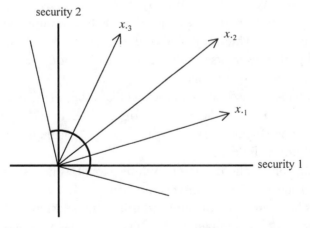

Figure 3.1 The rays labeled $x_{\cdot 1}$, $x_{\cdot 2}$, and $x_{\cdot 3}$ show payoffs of securities 1 and 2 in states 1, 2, and 3. The cone indicated by the arc shows portfolios that have positive payoffs in all states.

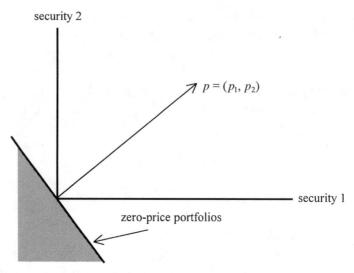

Figure 3.2 Portfolios in the shaded region have negative price.

Now interpret the coordinate axes as portfolio weights h_1 and h_2 so that any point in the diagram is associated with a portfolio (h_1, h_2). For each $x_{.s}$, construct a line perpendicular to $x_{.s}$ through the origin. The set of portfolios h with positive payoff in state s is the set of points northeast of this line. If this construction is performed in each state, the intersection of the indicated portfolio sets gives the set of portfolios with positive payoffs in all states. The indicated portfolios are those for which the ray through the point h intersects the arc.

Suppose that security prices are given by $p = (p_1, p_2)$, as shown in Figure 3.2. Then the set of zero-price portfolios consists of the line through the origin perpendicular to p. Figure 3.3, which combines Figures 3.1 and 3.2, shows that the set of positive-payoff portfolios intersects the set of negative-price portfolios only at the origin, and thus there is no arbitrage.

This conclusion is a consequence of the fact that p lies in the interior of the cone defined by the $x_{.s}$. If p lies on the boundary of the cone, then there is an arbitrage, but not a strong one (Figure 3.4), whereas if p lies outside the cone, then there exists strong arbitrage (Figure 3.5).

The preceding construction, being two-dimensional, is necessarily restricted to the case in which agents take nonzero positions in at most two securities. It is worth noticing that, if there are more than two securities, nonexistence of an arbitrage if portfolios are restricted to contain at most two securities is consistent with existence of arbitrage if portfolios are unrestricted. This is illustrated by the following example.

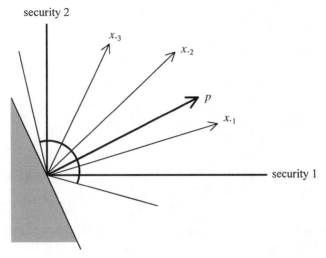

Figure 3.3 The portfolios in the cone have positive payoffs; the portfolios in the shaded region have negative price. These regions intersect only at the origin, indicating absence of arbitrage. This conclusion follows from the fact that p lies in the cone generated by the security payoffs.

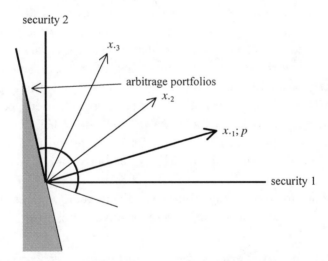

Figure 3.4 The ray p coincides with one of the boundaries of the cone generated by security payoffs. The interpretation is that there exists arbitrage, but not strong arbitrage.

Example 3.3.1 Consider three securities with payoffs $x_1 = (1, 1, 0), x_2 = (0, 1, 1)$, $x_3 = (1, 0, 1)$, and with prices $p_1 = 1$, and $p_2 = p_3 = 1/2$. No arbitrage exists with nonzero positions in any two of these securities, but portfolio $h = (-1, 1, 1)$ is an arbitrage. □

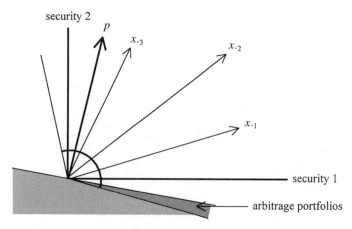

Figure 3.5 The ray p lies outside the cone generated by the security payoffs. The portfolios in the indicated region are arbitrages.

3.4 Positivity of the Payoff Pricing Functional

A functional is *positive* if it assigns positive value to every positive element of its domain. It is *strictly positive* if it assigns strictly positive value to every positive and nonzero element of its domain. Note that if there is no positive (positive and nonzero) element in the domain of a functional, then the functional is trivially positive (strictly positive). Our terminology of positive and strictly positive functionals is consistent with the terminology of positive and strictly positive vectors in the following sense: A linear functional $F : \mathcal{R}^l \to \mathcal{R}$ has a representation in the form of a scalar product $F(x) = fx$ for some vector $f \in \mathcal{R}^l$. Functional F is strictly positive (positive) iff the corresponding vector f is strictly positive (positive).

Absence of arbitrage or strong arbitrage at given security prices corresponds to the payoff pricing functional's being strictly positive or positive.

Theorem 3.4.1 *The payoff pricing functional is linear and strictly positive iff there is no arbitrage.*

Proof: The necessity of the condition is obvious. To prove sufficiency, note that exclusion of arbitrage implies satisfaction of the law of one price, which in turn implies that q is a linear functional (Theorem 2.3.1). If $z \in \mathcal{M}$, then $q(z) = ph$ for h such that $hX = z$. Exclusion of arbitrage implies that $q(z) > 0$, if $z > 0$, and thus q is strictly positive.   □

We also have

Theorem 3.4.2 *The payoff pricing functional is linear and positive iff there is no strong arbitrage.*

The proof is similar to that of Theorem 3.4.1.

3.5 Positive State Prices

In Chapter 2 we showed that if markets are complete, so that the asset span coincides with the date-1 contingent claims space, then the law of one price implies the existence of a state price vector q such that

$$p = Xq. \tag{3.4}$$

Because the payoff matrix X is left invertible under complete markets, the vector q that solves Eq. (3.4) is unique. In view of

$$q(z) = qz, \tag{3.5}$$

the absence of arbitrage is equivalent to state prices being strictly positive ($q \gg 0$), and the absence of strong arbitrage is equivalent to those prices being positive ($q \geq 0$).

We have demonstrated the role of state prices in characterizing security prices that exclude arbitrage in complete markets. It turns out that this characterization generalizes to the case of incomplete markets, but that requires separate treatment.

3.6 Arbitrage and Optimal Portfolios

If an agent's utility function is strictly increasing, absence of arbitrage is necessary for the existence of an optimal portfolio.

We have

Theorem 3.6.1 *If at given security prices an agent's optimal portfolio exists, and if the agent's utility function is strictly increasing, then there is no arbitrage.*

Proof: Suppose that there exists a portfolio $\hat{h}$ that is an arbitrage at given prices p. For every budget-feasible portfolio h and consumption plan (c_0, c_1), portfolio $h + \hat{h}$ is budget feasible. The resulting consumption plan $(c_0 - p\hat{h}, c_1 + \hat{h}X)$ is strictly preferred to (c_0, c_1) because the agent's utility function is strictly increasing. Therefore no optimal portfolio can exist.   □

If the agent's utility function is increasing but not strictly increasing, the conclusion of Theorem 3.6.1 may fail to hold.

Example 3.6.2 Consider two securities with payoffs in two states given by $x_1 = (1, 0)$ and $x_2 = (0, 1)$. An agent's utility function is given by

$$u(c_0, c_1, c_2) = c_0 + \min\{c_1, c_2\}. \tag{3.6}$$

His or her endowment is 1 at date 0 and $(1, 2)$ at date 1. At prices $p_1 = 1$ and $p_2 = 0$, the zero portfolio is an optimal portfolio. Security 2 is an arbitrage. Utility function u is increasing but not strictly increasing.   □

The absence of strong arbitrage is necessary for the existence of an optimal portfolio under a weaker monotonicity assumption.

Theorem 3.6.3 *If at given security prices an agent's optimal portfolio exists, and if the agent's utility function is strictly increasing at date 0 and increasing at date 1, then there is no strong arbitrage.*

The proof is the same as in Theorem 3.6.1.

The need for strict monotonicity in date-0 consumption is indicated by the following example.

Example 3.6.4 As in Example 2.4.4 there are two securities with payoffs $x_1 = (1, -1)$ and $x_2 = (2, -2)$. The utility function of the representative agent depends only on date-1 consumption and is given by

$$u(c_1, c_2) = \ln(c_1) + \ln(c_2) \tag{3.7}$$

for $(c_1, c_2) \gg 0$. His or her endowment is 0 at date 0 and $(1, 1)$ at date 1. At prices $p_1 = p_2 = 1$, portfolio $h = (-2, 1)$ is a strong arbitrage. However, there is an optimal portfolio: the zero portfolio. Utility function (3.7) is not strictly increasing at date 0 because date-0 consumption does not enter the utility function.   □

Theorems 3.6.1 and 3.6.3 require strictly increasing utility function at date 0 and therefore do not apply to settings with no date-0 consumption (see Example 3.6.4). As in Theorem 2.4.2, the assumption that the utility function is strictly increasing at date 0 can be replaced by the assumptions that there exists a portfolio with positive and nonzero payoff and that the utility function is strictly increasing at date 1.

If consumption is restricted to be positive, then the absence of arbitrage is also a sufficient condition for the existence of an optimal portfolio.

Theorem 3.6.5 *If at given security prices there is no arbitrage, and if the agent's consumption is restricted to be positive, then there exists an optimal portfolio.*

Proof: Absence of arbitrage implies that the law of one price holds. If there exist redundant securities, then their prices must equal the prices of the portfolios of other securities that have equal payoffs. A solution to the consumption and portfolio problem with a smaller subset of nonredundant securities is also a solution with the full set of securities. Therefore, we can assume without loss of generality that there are no redundant securities.

Because the agent's utility function is continuous, the Weierstrass theorem (which states that every continuous function on a compact set has a maximum) implies that it is sufficient to prove that the agent's budget set given by (1.5) and (1.6) is compact (that is, closed and bounded). It is clearly closed, and therefore we only have to demonstrate that it is bounded. Suppose, by contradiction, that it is not bounded. Then there exists an unbounded sequence of budget-feasible consumption plans and portfolios $\{c^n, h^n\}$. The inequalities $0 \leq c_0^n \leq w_0 - ph^n$ and $0 \leq c_1^n \leq w_1 + h^n X$ imply that the sequence of portfolios $\{h^n\}$ must be unbounded, for otherwise the sequences of prices $\{ph^n\}$ and payoffs $\{h^n X\}$ would be bounded, and consequently the sequence of consumption plans would be bounded as well.

Let $\|h^n\|$ denote the Euclidean norm of h^n. We have that $\lim \|h^n\| = +\infty$. Each portfolio $h^n / \|h^n\|$ has unit norm, and therefore the sequence $\{h^n / \|h^n\|\}$ is bounded, and, by switching to a subsequence if necessary, one can assume it to be convergent to a nonzero portfolio $\hat{h}$.

Through the use of positivity of consumption plan c^n, it follows from budget constraints (1.5) and (1.6) that

$$ph^n \leq w_0, \tag{3.8}$$

and

$$h^n X + w_1 \geq 0. \tag{3.9}$$

Dividing both sides of inequalities (3.8) and (3.9) by $\|h^n\|$ and taking limits as n goes to infinity, we obtain

$$p\hat{h} \leq 0, \tag{3.10}$$

and

$$\hat{h} X \geq 0. \tag{3.11}$$

Because portfolio $\hat{h}$ is nonzero and there are no redundant securities, its payoff is nonzero and inequalities (3.10) and (3.11) imply that $\hat{h}$ is an arbitrage. □

If consumption is unrestricted, exclusion of arbitrage does not guarantee existence of an optimal portfolio. This is illustrated by the following example.

Example 3.6.6 Suppose that there are two states and a single security with payoff $(1, 1)$. The agent's utility function is given by

$$u(c_0, c_1, c_2) = c_0 + c_1 + c_2. \tag{3.12}$$

If consumption is unrestricted, then there exists no optimal portfolio unless the price of the security equals 2 (in which case all portfolios are optimal). However, there is no arbitrage at any strictly positive price of the security. If consumption is restricted to be positive, an optimal portfolio exists for every strictly positive price.

3.7 Positive Equilibrium Pricing

Each agent's equilibrium portfolio is by definition an optimal portfolio. We can apply Theorem 3.6.1 to equilibrium security prices. Combining this result with Theorem 3.4.1, we obtain

Theorem 3.7.1 *If agents' utility functions are strictly increasing, then there is no arbitrage at equilibrium security prices. Further, the equilibrium payoff pricing functional is linear and strictly positive.*

Again, Example 3.6.2 demonstrates the need for strict monotonicity. The assumption of strictly increasing utility functions at date 0 in Theorem 3.7.1 can be replaced by assuming that utility functions are strictly increasing at date 1 and there exists a portfolio with positive and nonzero payoff.

Similarly, Theorems 3.4.2 and 3.6.3 imply

Theorem 3.7.2 *If agents' utility functions are strictly increasing at date 0 and increasing at date 1, then there is no strong arbitrage at equilibrium security prices, and the equilibrium payoff pricing functional is linear and positive.*

3.8 Notes

The assumption of no arbitrage plays a central role in finance. For example, in analyzing the valuation of derivative securities, the financial analyst takes security returns as primitives and derives prices of derivative securities in such a way that there is no arbitrage. Imposing the requirement of no arbitrage makes the analysis consistent with agents' having strictly increasing utility functions without explicitly specifying these functions. Thus, even though an equilibrium model of security markets is not explicitly employed, the requirement of no arbitrage makes the analysis consistent with an equilibrium.

The assumption of no arbitrage plays a much lesser role in economics than in finance. The reason is that in economics the focus is on equilibrium analysis. Accordingly, the economist takes preferences, endowments, and so on, to be the primitives. There is no need to make a separate assumption that there is no arbitrage because the assumption of strictly increasing utility functions, which is generally made explicitly, guarantees that there will be no arbitrage in equilibrium.

Thus the assumption of no arbitrage is the finance counterpart of the economic assumption of strictly increasing utility functions; one assumption is appropriate in the context of a valuation analysis, and the other in the context of an equilibrium analysis.

Arbitrage sometimes means "risk-free arbitrage": a portfolio with *state-independent* positive and nonzero payoff and a negative price or a zero payoff and strictly negative price. This notion of arbitrage is clearly much stronger than that defined in the text, and thus exclusion of risk-free arbitrage is a very weak restriction. In fact, if no nonzero risk-free claim is in the asset span, then a risk-free arbitrage cannot exist, and exclusion of risk-free arbitrage is equivalent to assuming satisfaction of the law of one price. Absence of arbitrage or strong arbitrage at given security prices corresponds to the payoff pricing functional being strictly positive or positive. If a nonzero risk-free payoff is in the asset span, then risk-free arbitrage is excluded as long as the sum of the state prices is strictly positive; this condition may be satisfied even if some state prices are negative, and thus there is arbitrage as we have defined it. The most interesting consequences of absence of arbitrage do not obtain if only risk-free arbitrage is excluded.

Financial analysts recognized the central role of the assumption of absence of arbitrage only gradually. Major papers developing the arbitrage theme were Black and Scholes [2] and Ross [5], [6]. A clear and intuitive discussion of arbitrage can be found in Varian [7], in which attention is restricted to what we call strong arbitrage. Werner [8] studied the relation between the absence of arbitrage and the existence of an equilibrium in a general class of markets.

The diagrammatic analysis of Section 3.3 is apparently attributable to Garman [3]. Theorem 3.6.5 is closely related to the results of Bertsekas [1] and Leland [4].

Bibliography

[1] Bertsekas, D. Necessary and sufficient conditions for existence of an optimal portfolio. *Journal of Economic Theory*, **8**:235–47, 1974.

[2] Black, F. and Scholes, M. The pricing of options and corporate liabilities. *Journal of Political Economy*, **81**:637–54, 1973.

[3] Garman, M. B. A synthesis of the pure theory of arbitrage. Reproduced, University of California, Berkeley, 1978.

[4] Leland, H. On the existence of optimal policies under uncertainty. *Journal of Economic Theory*, **4**:35–44, 1972.

[5] Ross, S. A. Risk, return and arbitrage. In Irwin Friend and James Bicksler, editors, *Risk and Return in Finance*. Ballinger, Cambridge, MA, 1976.

[6] Ross, S. A. A simple approach to the valuation of risky streams. *Journal of Business*, **51**:453–75, 1978.

[7] Varian, H. R. The arbitrage principle in financial economics. *Journal of Economic Perspectives*, **1**:55–72, 1987.

[8] Werner, J. Arbitrage and the existence of competitive equilibrium. *Econometrica*, **55**:1403–18, 1987.

4

Portfolio Restrictions

4.1 Introduction

So far we have assumed that agents can trade without explicit portfolio restrictions, meaning that they can choose any portfolio provided that the resulting consumption satisfies the agent's restriction on admissible consumptions (for example, positivity). In particular, the only limits on short selling were those implied by restrictions on consumption, if any were imposed.

Short sales restrictions and transaction costs are an important feature of real-world security markets. In this chapter we introduce explicit portfolio restrictions and discuss the validity of the results of Chapters 2 and 3 under such restrictions. The simplest example of an explicit portfolio restriction arises when short sales of securities are limited. The general treatment of portfolio restrictions in this chapter allows us to determine the consequences of short sales restrictions and also to model more complex portfolio restrictions such as bid-ask spreads.

4.2 Short Sales Restrictions

The most typical *short sales restriction* takes the form of a lower bound on holdings of a security. That is,

$$h_j \geq -b_j, \tag{4.1}$$

where b_j is a positive number and may be different for different agents. The short sales restrictions may apply to one or a few securities, not necessarily to all securities. The set of securities subject to short sales restrictions will be denoted by $\mathcal{J}_0$. The set of portfolios that satisfy restriction (4.1) for every $j \in \mathcal{J}_0$ is the agent's feasible portfolio set.

Our use of the term "short sales restriction" in regard to restriction (4.1) requires clarification. Strictly, the distinction between sales of a security and short sales is appropriate only when agents have nonzero endowments of the security. Suppose that agents' consumption endowments are interpreted as payoffs on initial portfolios. As in Section 1.7, we set $w_1 = \hat{h}X$, where $\hat{h}$ is an agent's initial portfolio. Assume that $\hat{h} \geq 0$. Any negative holding h_j of security j such that $h_j < -\hat{h}_j$ means that the agent sells more of the security than he initially owns. Consequently, the restriction (4.1) with the bound b_j set equal to $\hat{h}_j$ states that the agent is prohibited from selling more of security j than he or she is endowed with. With a bound b_j smaller than $\hat{h}_j$, the agent is permitted to sell only a fraction of his or her endowment of the security. With a bound that exceeds $\hat{h}_j$, the agent can sell more than his or her endowment of a security, but the size of the sale is limited. We will employ the term "short sales restriction" to denote any lower bound (4.1) on portfolios, and thus all these cases are covered.

Another case of a short sales restriction of the form (4.1) is as follows: Suppose that commitments to security holdings involving strictly negative payoffs in some states – these would result from short positions in securities with strictly positive payoffs in those states – are unenforceable in the absence of collateral. However, agents can precommit to fulfill the obligations implied by their security holdings by pledging their endowments as collateral. In such a setting an agent would divide his or her date-1 consumption endowment into collateral against each security position (that is, would choose w_{1j} for each j to satisfy $w_{1j} \geq 0$ and $\sum_j w_{1j} = w_1$) and would choose security holding h_j subject to

$$h_j x_j + w_{1j} \geq 0 \qquad\qquad (4.2)$$

for all j. It can easily be seen that if x_j is positive and nonzero such a restriction reduces to inequality (4.1) for some bound b_j.

Portfolio restrictions (4.2) are more stringent than the requirement that consumption be positive. Positivity of consumption can also be cast as a collateral requirement: an agent's date-1 endowment is a collateral against the payoff of his or her portfolio; consequently, the portfolio payoff must equal or exceed the negative of the agent's endowment. Clearly, restriction (4.2) implies that the payoff of portfolio h is equal to or exceeds $-w_1$, but the converse implication is not true.

Example 4.2.1 Suppose that there are two securities with payoffs $x_1 = (1, 0)$ and $x_2 = (1, 1)$. The restriction that consumption be positive imposes no limit on the long (positive) position the agent can take in portfolio $h = (-1, 1)$ because this portfolio's payoff is positive. In contrast, restriction (4.2) for security 1 requires that the holding of this security be limited by the agent's collateral in state 1 so that the agent cannot take an arbitrary position in portfolio h.   □

4.3 Portfolio Choice under Short Sales Restrictions

The agent's consumption-portfolio choice problem in the presence of short sales restrictions is

$$\max_{c_0, c_1, h} u(c_0, c_1) \tag{4.3}$$

subject to

$$c_0 \leq w_0 - ph \tag{4.4}$$

$$c_1 \leq w_1 + hX, \tag{4.5}$$

and

$$h_j \geq -b_j, \quad \forall j \in \mathcal{J}_0. \tag{4.6}$$

As usual, the agent's choice problem may involve an additional constraint on admissible consumption.

The presence of short sales restrictions in the consumption and portfolio choice problem (4.3) leads to first-order conditions that are slightly different from those of Section 1.5. In particular, if the optimal consumption plan is interior, we have

$$p_j \geq \sum_{s=1}^{S} x_{js} \frac{\partial_s u}{\partial_0 u}, \quad \forall j \in \mathcal{J}_0, \tag{4.7}$$

and

$$p_j = \sum_{s=1}^{S} x_{js} \frac{\partial_s u}{\partial_0 u}, \quad \forall j \notin \mathcal{J}_0. \tag{4.8}$$

Inequality (4.7) can be strict only if the short sale restriction is binding on the holding of security j at the optimal portfolio. If inequality (4.7) is strict, then the price of security j is greater than the sum over states of its payoff in each state multiplied by the marginal rate of substitution between consumption in that state and consumption at date 0.

When date-0 consumption does not enter the agent's utility function, the first-order conditions corresponding to expressions (4.7) and (4.8) are

$$\lambda p_j \geq \sum_{s=1}^{S} x_{sj} \partial_s u, \quad \forall j \in \mathcal{J}_0, \tag{4.9}$$

and

$$\lambda p_j = \sum_{s=1}^{S} x_{sj} \partial_s u, \quad \forall j \notin \mathcal{J}_0, \tag{4.10}$$

where λ is the Lagrange multiplier.

4.4 The Law of One Price

If there are no redundant securities – that is, if payoff matrix X has rank J – then the law of one price holds trivially with or without portfolio restrictions. We also saw in Theorems 2.4.1 and 2.4.2 that the law of one price holds in equilibrium in the absence of portfolio restrictions under weak monotonicity assumptions even if there exist redundant securities. This latter result fails in the presence of portfolio restrictions: there may exist two portfolios with the same payoff and different prices in an equilibrium.

Example 4.4.1 There are two states at date 1 and two agents who consume only at date 1 and have the same utility function

$$u\left(c_1^i, c_2^i\right) = \frac{1}{2}\ln\left(c_1^i\right) + \frac{1}{2}\ln\left(c_2^i\right), \tag{4.11}$$

for $i = 1, 2$. Their endowments are zero at date 0 and $(3, 0)$ and $(0, 3)$, respectively, at date 1. There are three securities with payoffs

$$x_1 = (1, 1), \qquad x_2 = (1, 0) \qquad \text{and } x_3 = (0, 1). \tag{4.12}$$

Note that the payoff of security 1 can be generated by a portfolio of one share each of securities 2 and 3. In the absence of short sales restrictions, we can calculate an equilibrium by first finding an equilibrium with security 1 deleted from the model. That equilibrium is an equilibrium for the model with three securities with agents' holdings of security 1 set at zero and the price of security 1 given by $p_1 = p_2 + p_3$ so that the law of one price holds. The equilibrium involves portfolio allocation $(0, -3/2, 3/2)$ for agent 1 and $(0, 3/2, -3/2)$ for agent 2, and security prices $p_1 = 2/3$, $p_2 = 1/3$, and $p_3 = 1/3$. This portfolio allocation gives both agents the same risk-free consumption $(3/2, 3/2)$. It can easily be checked that these portfolios and prices satisfy the first-order condition (1.18) that security prices be proportional to their payoffs multiplied by agents' marginal utilities summed over states.

Suppose now that agents can short sell at most one share of each security, and thus restriction (4.1) in the form $h_j \geq -1$, for each j, is imposed. Portfolios $(0, -3/2, 3/2)$ and $(0, 3/2, -3/2)$ are no longer feasible. We conjecture that portfolio allocation $(0, -1, 1)$ for agent 1 and $(0, 1, -1)$ for agent 2 and security prices $p_1 = 3/4$, and $p_2 = p_3 = 1/2$ are an equilibrium under the assumed short sales restrictions.

We can check that the first-order conditions (4.9) hold for both agents in the conjectured equilibrium with the Lagrange multiplier λ equal to 1. The portfolio $(0, -1, 1)$ generates the consumption plan $(2, 1)$ for agent 1; consequently, the vector of marginal utilities equals $(1/4, 1/2)$. The holdings of securities 1 and 3 in that portfolio are strictly greater than the bound -1, and thus inequality (4.9) holds with equality for these securities. Multiplying the payoffs of security 1 by agent 1's marginal utilities and summing over states, $1/4 \cdot 1 + 1/2 \cdot 1$, we obtain $p_1 = 3/4$. Similarly, $1/2 \cdot 1$ equals p_3.

Agent 1's holding of security 2 equals the bound -1. For that security, the payoffs multiplied by agent 1's marginal utilities and summed over states give $1/4$, which is strictly less than p_2, and thus inequality (4.9) is satisfied. Therefore, portfolio $(0, -1, 1)$ is optimal for agent 1 at prices $p_1 = 3/4$, $p_2 = 1/2$, and $p_3 = 1/2$ in the presence of short sales restrictions.

Checking that portfolio $(0, 1, -1)$ is optimal for agent 2 involves the same calculations as for agent 1 owing to the symmetry of payoffs, endowments, and utility functions across the states. Because we have

$$p_1 \neq p_2 + p_3, \tag{4.13}$$

the law of one price fails here. □

4.5 Limited and Unlimited Arbitrage

The fundamental result of Theorems 3.6.1 and 3.6.3 – that there exists no arbitrage in equilibrium under suitable monotonicity assumptions – does not extend to the case of portfolio restrictions. In Example 4.4.1, the portfolio $(1, -1, -1)$ has zero payoff and negative price and is therefore a strong arbitrage under the equilibrium prices.

In the presence of short sales restrictions it is necessary to distinguish unlimited arbitrage from limited arbitrage. An *unlimited arbitrage* is an arbitrage that involves a long (or zero) position in each of the securities that is subject to a short sales restriction; that is, a portfolio h such that $hX \geq 0$, $ph \leq 0$, with at least one strict inequality, and $h_j \geq 0$ for every $j \in \mathcal{J}_0$. Similarly, an *unlimited strong arbitrage* is a strong arbitrage that involves a long (or zero) position in each security that is subject to a short sales restriction; that is, a portfolio h such that $hX \geq 0$, $ph < 0$, and $h_j \geq 0$ for every $j \in \mathcal{J}_0$. A limited arbitrage (limited strong arbitrage) is an arbitrage that is not an unlimited arbitrage (strong arbitrage). In the absence of short sales restrictions, all arbitrages are unlimited arbitrages.

The reason for the distinction is that unlimited arbitrage (unlimited strong arbitrage) can be operated on any scale desired, whereas limited arbitrage (limited strong arbitrage) cannot. Portfolio $(1, -1, -1)$ is feasible under the short sales restrictions of Example 4.4.1, but scale multiples (with the scale parameter greater than one) of it are not. It is a limited strong arbitrage under equilibrium prices.

In the presence of short sales restrictions, under strict monotonicity the proof of Theorem 3.7.1 implies the nonexistence of unlimited arbitrage but does not rule out limited arbitrage. Similarly, under monotonicity the proof of Theorem 3.7.2 rules out unlimited strong arbitrage but does not rule out limited strong arbitrage.

4.6 Diagrammatic Representation

In Chapter 3 we presented a diagrammatic method of determining the set of security prices that exclude arbitrage when there are no short sales restrictions. In the presence of short sales restrictions we are interested in determining the set of security prices that exclude unlimited arbitrage.

The diagrammatic treatment is readily extended to this case. Suppose that there are two securities and that short selling of security 2 is restricted. If a vector of security prices $p = (p_1, p_2)$ lies in the convex cone generated by $x_{\cdot 1}$ and $x_{\cdot 2}$, as in Figure 3.3, then there is no limited or unlimited arbitrage portfolio. However, if p is as shown in Figure 4.1, then there is no unlimited arbitrage portfolio, but the portfolios in the shaded region are limited arbitrages. These portfolios involve a long position in security 1 and a short position in security 2. As the figure suggests, the set of security prices excluding unlimited arbitrage is larger than the set of prices excluding arbitrage.

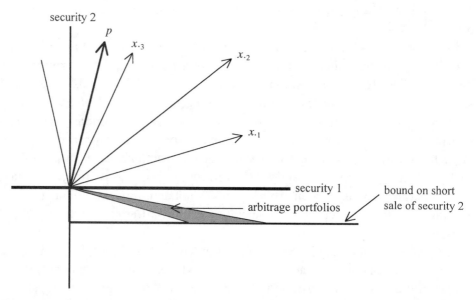

Figure 4.1 The arbitrage indicated by portfolios in the shaded region is implemented via a short sale of security 2. If unrestricted short sales of security 2 are prohibited, then the arbitrage is a limited arbitrage.

If short sales of both securities 1 and 2 are restricted, then any positive p excludes unlimited arbitrage.

4.7 Bid-Ask Spreads

In most real-world financial markets each traded security has two prices, a bid price and an ask price. These two prices are quoted by a specialist who matches buying and selling orders on each security. Agents buy securities from the specialist at ask prices (the prices the specialist is asking) and sell securities to the specialist at bid prices (the prices the specialist is bidding). The difference between the two prices is the bid-ask spread.

We can use the foregoing analysis of short sales restrictions to analyze bid-ask spreads. We will not attempt to formulate a full analysis of bid-ask spreads, which would include an explanation of why they exist, but rather discuss (here and in Chapter 7) some implications of the absence of arbitrage opportunities.

Let p_{bj} denote the bid price and p_{aj} the ask price of security j. It is convenient to describe an agent's portfolio choice by two portfolios: portfolio $h_a \in \mathcal{R}^J$, $h_a \geq 0$ purchased by the agent from the specialist at ask prices and portfolio $h_b \in \mathcal{R}^J$, $h_b \geq 0$ sold by the agent to the specialist at bid prices. The agent's consumption-portfolio choice problem is

$$\max_{c_0, c_1, h_a, h_b} u(c_0, c_1) \tag{4.14}$$

subject to

$$c_0 \leq w_0 - p_a h_a + p_b h_b, \tag{4.15}$$

$$c_1 \leq w_1 + (h_a - h_b)X, \tag{4.16}$$

$$h_b \geq 0, \qquad h_a \geq 0. \tag{4.17}$$

Security markets with bid-ask spreads can be viewed as markets with short sales restrictions. One only needs to consider each security j as two securities, each with a distinct price: one with payoff x_j and price p_{aj}, the other with payoff $-x_j$ and price $-p_{bj}$. Agents' holdings of such securities are limited by zero short sales restrictions $h_{aj} \geq 0$ and $h_{bj} \geq 0$.

A *strong unlimited arbitrage* under bid and ask price vectors p_b and p_a is a portfolio (h_b, h_a) satisfying $h_b \geq 0$, $h_a \geq 0$ and such that $p_a h_a - p_b h_b < 0$ and $(h_a - h_b)X \geq 0$. An *unlimited arbitrage* under bid and ask price vectors p_b and p_a is a portfolio (h_b, h_a) satisfying $h_b \geq 0$, $h_a \geq 0$ that is either a strong unlimited arbitrage or is such that $p_a h_a - p_b h_b = 0$ and $(h_a - h_b)X > 0$. The exclusion of strong unlimited arbitrage implies that

$$p_{aj} \geq p_{bj}, \tag{4.18}$$

that is, the bid-ask spread is positive for every security. To see this, note that if $p_{bj} > p_{aj}$, then a simultaneous purchase and sale of security j would constitute a strong unlimited arbitrage.

4.8 Bid-Ask Spreads in Equilibrium

Suppose that there are I agents whose portfolio-consumption decisions are as described in problem (4.14). The specialist who matches buying and selling orders for each security and imposes bid and ask prices earns a profit equal to the sum over all securities of the quantity of traded shares multiplied by the bid-ask spread. Suppose that the specialist consumes his profit at date 0.

An *equilibrium* for given bid-ask spreads $\{t_j\}$ consists of bid and ask security prices (p_b, p_a) that satisfy $p_{aj} - p_{bj} = t_j$ for each j, a portfolio allocation $\{h_b^i, h_a^i\}$, and a consumption allocation $\{c^i\}$ such that portfolio (h_a^i, h_b^i) and consumption plan c^i are a solution to agent i's choice problem (4.14) at prices (p_b, p_a) and markets clear. The market-clearing conditions are

$$\sum_i h_b^i = \sum_i h_a^i, \tag{4.19}$$

$$\sum_i c_0^i \le \sum_i w_0^i - \sum_j \left[t_j \left(\sum_i h_{bj}^i \right) \right], \tag{4.20}$$

and

$$\sum_i c_1^i \le \sum_i w_1^i. \tag{4.21}$$

Condition (4.20) reflects the assumption that the specialist consumes his or her profit at date 0. Note that the market-clearing conditions (4.20) and (4.21) follow from condition (4.19) and the budget constraints (4.15)–(4.17).

The bid-ask spreads are exogenously given, but one could specify an objective function for the specialist and derive his or her optimal choice of bid-ask spreads.

Example 4.8.1 There are two states at date 1 and two agents who have the same utility function

$$u(c_0^i, c_1^i, c_2^i) = \ln(c_0^i) + \frac{1}{2} \ln(c_1^i) + \frac{1}{2} \ln(c_2^i), \tag{4.22}$$

for $i = 1, 2$. Agent 1's endowment is $(1, 2, 0)$, and agent 2's endowment is $(1, 0, 2)$. The securities traded have payoffs $x_1 = (1, 0)$ and $x_2 = (0, 1)$. The bid-ask spread is set exogenously at t for both securities; that is, $p_{1a} - p_{1b} = p_{2a} - p_{2b} = t$.

If $t = 0$, so there is no bid-ask spread, agents will exchange one unit of each security so as to reach the risk-free consumption $(1, 1, 1)$ for each agent. When t is strictly positive, agents will not eliminate individual risk completely owing to the transactions cost.

To determine the equilibrium prices and portfolios, write agent 1's portfolio choice problem as

$$\max_{h_{1b}^1, h_{2a}^1} \ln\left(1 + p_{1b}h_{1b}^1 - p_{2a}h_{2a}^1\right) + \frac{1}{2}\ln\left(2 - h_{1b}^1\right) + \frac{1}{2}\ln\left(h_{2a}^1\right). \quad (4.23)$$

Here the notation anticipates that agent 1 will set $h_{1a}^1 = h_{2b}^1 = 0$ (that is, he or she will not sell security 2 or buy security 1). The first-order conditions are

$$1 + p_{1b}h_{1b}^1 - p_{2a}h_{2a}^1 = 2\left(2 - h_{1b}^1\right)p_{1b} \quad (4.24)$$

and

$$1 + p_{1b}h_{1b}^1 - p_{2a}h_{2a}^1 = 2h_{2a}^1 p_{2a}. \quad (4.25)$$

By a similar calculation, the first-order conditions of agent 2 are

$$1 - p_{1a}h_{1a}^2 + p_{2b}h_{2b}^2 = 2h_{1a}^2 p_{1a} \quad (4.26)$$

and

$$1 - p_{1a}h_{1a}^2 + p_{2b}h_{2b}^2 = 2\left(2 - h_{2b}^2\right)p_{2b}. \quad (4.27)$$

The symmetry of payoffs, endowments, and utilities across the states implies that equilibrium prices satisfy

$$p_{1b} = p_{2b} \equiv p_b \quad (4.28)$$
$$p_{1a} = p_{2a} \equiv p_a, \quad (4.29)$$

and equilibrium portfolios satisfy

$$h_{1b}^1 = h_{2b}^2 \qquad h_{2a}^1 = h_{1a}^2. \quad (4.30)$$

Market-clearing Eq. (4.19) implies that $h_{1b}^1 = h_{1a}^2$ and $h_{2a}^1 = h_{2b}^2$. Summing up, we have

$$h_{1b}^1 = h_{2a}^1 = h_{1a}^2 = h_{2b}^2 \equiv h. \quad (4.31)$$

Further, we have

$$p_a = p_b + t. \quad (4.32)$$

Substituting Eqs. (4.28)–(4.32) into Eqs. (4.24) and (4.25) results in

$$1 - th = 2(2 - h)p_b, \quad (4.33)$$

and

$$1 - th = 2h(p_b + t). \quad (4.34)$$

Equation (4.33) implies that

$$p_b = \frac{1 - th}{2(2 - h)}.$$

(4.35)

Substituting Eq. (4.35) into Eq. (4.34) results in the quadratic equation

$$2th^2 - (3t + 1)h + 1 = 0,$$

(4.36)

which has real roots. The smaller of these gives equilibrium security holding h.[1]

   Solution values for (h, p_b) are $(1, 0.5)$ when $t = 0$, $(0.990, 0.490)$ when $t = 0.01$, $(0.892, 0.411)$ when $t = 0.1$, $(0.5, 0.25)$ when $t = 0.5$, and $(0.293, 0.207)$ when $t = 1$. Thus, the higher the value of t, the lower the quantity of shares traded, as one would expect.   □

Our analysis of the effects of bid-ask spreads on security prices and volume of trade in the preceding example should be regarded as provisional at best. As already noted, the model does not explain why bid-ask spreads exist. It is seldom possible to obtain a reliable analysis of the effects of any economic institution from a model that does not give an account of why that institution exists.

4.9 Notes

In Section 4.4 we used the term "redundant security," carrying over its meaning from Chapter 1. Strictly, the term is a misnomer in the presence of portfolio restrictions: that the payoff of a security can be duplicated by a portfolio of other securities does not mean that it is redundant because the duplicating portfolio may be infeasible owing to portfolio restrictions. That being the case, the presence of portfolio restrictions implies that deleting a "redundant" security from the model may change the equilibrium.

   A model of an equilibrium with transaction costs and trading constraints has been developed by Hahn [4]. Glosten and Milgrom [3] showed that bid-ask spreads can arise owing to differences in information about security payoffs between specialists and agents. Foley [1], Garman and Ohlson [2], Prisman [7], Luttmer [6], and He and Modest [5] explored implications of transaction costs and trading constraints on security prices.

Bibliography

[1] Foley, D. K. Economic equilibrium with costly marketing. In Ross M. Starr, editor, *General Equilibrium Models of Monetary Economics*. Academic Press, 1989.

---

[1] The larger root implies negative values of p_b, from Eq. (4.35), and negative values of date-0 consumption. The larger root decreases from infinity at $t = 0$ to 1.5 at $t = \infty$.

[2] Garman, M. and Ohlson, J. Valuation of risky assets in arbitrage-free economies with transactions costs. *Journal of Financial Economics*, **9**:271–80, 1981.

[3] Glosten, L. R. and Milgrom, P. R. Bid, ask and transaction prices in a specialist model with heterogeneously informed traders. *Journal of Financial Economics*, **14**:71–100, 1985.

[4] Hahn, F. Equilibrium with transaction costs. *Econometrica*, **39**:417–39, 1971.

[5] He, H. and Modest, D. M. Market frictions and consumption-based asset pricing. *Journal of Political Economy*, **103**:94–117, 1995.

[6] Luttmer, E. Asset pricing in economies with frictions. *Econometrica*, **64**:1439–67, 1996.

[7] Prisman, E. Valuation of risky assets in arbitrage free economies with frictions. *Journal of Finance*, **41**:545–60, 1986.

Part Two

Valuation

5

Valuation

5.1 Introduction

In this chapter and in Chapter 6 we assume again that agents can trade without any portfolio restrictions. As established in Chapter 2, security prices can be characterized by a payoff pricing functional mapping the asset span into the reals. The payoff pricing functional is linear and strictly positive (positive) iff security prices exclude arbitrage (strong arbitrage). A *valuation functional* is an extension of the payoff pricing functional to the entire contingent claim space $\mathcal{R}^S$. Thus, the valuation functional is a linear functional

$$Q : \mathcal{R}^S \to \mathcal{R} \tag{5.1}$$

that coincides with the payoff pricing functional on the asset span $\mathcal{M}$; that is,

$$Q(z) = q(z) \quad \text{for every } z \in \mathcal{M}. \tag{5.2}$$

The valuation functional assigns values to all contingent claims, not just to payoffs. Of special interest is a valuation functional that is strictly positive (positive) because, as shown in Chapter 3 in the case of complete markets, this property is equivalent to the absence of arbitrage (strong arbitrage). A strictly positive (positive) valuation functional will be used in Chapter 6 to derive important representations of security prices.

The following simple example illustrates a positive valuation functional:

Example 5.1.1 Suppose that there are two states and a single security with payoff $x_1 = (1, 2)$ and price $p_1 = 1$. The asset span is $\mathcal{M} = \text{span}\{(1, 2)\} = \{(\alpha, 2\alpha) : \alpha \in \mathcal{R}\}$, and the payoff pricing functional is given by $q(\alpha, 2\alpha) = \alpha$. Each functional $Q : \mathcal{R}^2 \to \mathcal{R}$ defined by $Q(z) = q_1 z_1 + q_2 z_2$, where $q_1, q_2 \geq 0$ and $q_1 + 2q_2 = 1$ is a positive valuation functional. $\square$

5.2 The Fundamental Theorem of Finance

In equilibrium the vector $\partial_1 u / \partial_0 u$ of marginal rates of substitution of an agent whose consumption is interior defines a linear functional that maps each contingent claim $z \in \mathcal{R}^S$ to $(\partial_1 u / \partial_0 u)z$. This functional coincides with the equilibrium payoff pricing functional on the asset span (in particular, $p_j = (\partial_1 u / \partial_0 u)x_j$; see Eq. (1.14)). The functional given by the marginal rates of substitution is strictly positive (positive) if utility functions are strictly increasing (increasing). Of course, unless markets are complete, different agents may have different marginal rates of substitution; these give rise to different valuation functionals.

If we consider an arbitrary vector of security prices, can we be assured that a strictly positive (positive) valuation functional exists? It cannot exist if security prices permit arbitrage (strong arbitrage) because then either the payoff pricing functional does not exist or it is not strictly positive (positive).

We come now to a critical question: If security prices are such as to exclude arbitrage, does a strictly positive valuation functional exist? The answer is provided in the following theorem.

Theorem 5.2.1 (Fundamental Theorem of Finance) *Security prices exclude arbitrage iff there exists a strictly positive valuation functional.*

Suppose now only that security prices exclude strong arbitrage. This weakening of the condition implies a weakening of the conclusion:

Theorem 5.2.2 (Fundamental Theorem of Finance, Weak Form) *Security prices exclude strong arbitrage iff there exists a positive valuation functional.*

For both theorems, sufficiency follows from Theorems 3.4.2 and 3.4.1 because existence of a strictly positive (positive) valuation functional implies existence of a strictly positive (positive) payoff pricing functional, the payoff pricing functional being a restriction of the valuation functional. The proof of necessity will occupy us in the remainder of this chapter.

The extension of the payoff pricing functional q from the asset span to the entire commodity space is achieved by extending q one dimension at a time. In the first step we choose a contingent claim $\hat{z}$ not in the asset span $\mathcal{M}$ and extend q to the subspace spanned by $\mathcal{M}$ and $\hat{z}$. This extended subspace has dimension equal to the dimension of $\mathcal{M}$ plus one. The extension of the payoff pricing functional is achieved by specifying a value π for the contingent claim $\hat{z}$. For the extension to remain strictly positive (positive), the chosen value π must be such that all payoffs in $\mathcal{M}$ (greater than but not equal to $\hat{z}$) have prices that are strictly greater (greater) than π, and all payoffs in $\mathcal{M}$ (less than but not equal to $\hat{z}$) have prices that are strictly less (less) than π. These restrictions define an interval in which π must lie. The extension is the payoff pricing functional for security markets consisting of J securities with payoffs $\{x_1, \ldots, x_J\}$ and prices $\{p_1, \ldots, p_J\}$ and a security with payoff $\hat{z}$ and price π.

In the second step, we choose a contingent claim not in the span of the $J + 1$ securities of step 1 and extend the payoff pricing functional to the subspace spanned by the $J + 1$ securities of step 1 and the new contingent claim. After $S - J$ steps we achieve an extension to the entire commodity space. Because all of the steps in this construction are the same, we present only the first.

5.3 Bounds on the Values of Contingent Claims

We now define the upper and lower bounds on the value of a contingent claim $z \in \mathcal{R}^S$ that can be inferred from the prices of the payoffs in $\mathcal{M}$. The upper bound

$$q_u(z) \equiv \min_h \{ph : hX \geq z\} \tag{5.3}$$

is the lowest price of a portfolio, the payoff of which dominates the contingent claim. The lower bound

$$q_\ell(z) \equiv \max_h \{ph : hX \leq z\} \tag{5.4}$$

is the highest price of a portfolio, the payoff of which is dominated by the contingent claim.[1]

For a payoff in the asset span, the lower and the upper bounds coincide with the value under the payoff pricing functional as long as there exists no strong arbitrage:

Proposition 5.3.1 *If security prices exclude strong arbitrage, then $q_u(z) = q_\ell(z) = q(z)$ for every $z \in \mathcal{M}$.*

Proof: By the definitions of the bounds we have $q_u(z) \leq q(z)$ and $q_\ell(z) \geq q(z)$ for $z \in \mathcal{M}$. Suppose that $q_u(z) < q(z)$ for some $z \in \mathcal{M}$. Then there exists a portfolio h' such that

$$h'X \geq z \tag{5.5}$$

and

$$ph' < q(z). \tag{5.6}$$

---

[1] If $\{h : hX \geq z\}$ is empty, we set $q_u(z) = \infty$. This occurs if, for example, $\mathcal{M} = \text{span}\{(1, 0)\}$ and $z = (1, 1)$. Similarly, if $\{h : hX \leq z\}$ is empty, we set $q_\ell(z) = -\infty$.

Let h be a portfolio such that $hX = z$ and $ph = q(z)$. Then portfolio $h' - h$ is a strong arbitrage. This contradicts the assumption. The proof that $q_\ell(z) = q(z)$ is similar. □

The following two examples illustrate the bounds on the values of contingent claims that are not in the asset span.

Example 5.3.2 In Example 5.1.1, the contingent claim $z = (1, 1)$ is not in the asset span. We have

$$q_u(z) = \min\{h : (h, 2h) \geq (1, 1)\} = 1 \tag{5.7}$$

$$q_\ell(z) = \max\{h : (h, 2h) \leq (1, 1)\} = \frac{1}{2}. \tag{5.8}$$

Thus, the bounds on the value of z are $1/2$ and 1. □

Example 5.3.3 Let there be two securities: security 1, a bond with risk-free payoff $x_1 = (1, 1, 1)$, and security 2, a stock with payoff $x_2 = (1, 2, 4)$. The prices of the bond and stock are, respectively, $p_1 = 1/2$ and $p_2 = 1$. A nontraded call option on the stock with strike price of 3 has the payoff $z = (0, 0, 1)$. That payoff is not in the span of the payoffs on the stock and the bond and hence cannot be priced using the payoff pricing functional.

A lower bound on the value of the call is determined by solving

$$\max_{h_1, h_2}(p_1 h_1 + p_2 h_2) \tag{5.9}$$

subject to

$$h_1 x_1 + h_2 x_2 \leq z. \tag{5.10}$$

The constraint implies that h_1 and h_2 satisfy

$$h_1 + h_2 \leq 0, \tag{5.11}$$
$$h_1 + 2h_2 \leq 0, \tag{5.12}$$
$$h_1 + 4h_2 \leq 1. \tag{5.13}$$

The linear program (5.9) can easily be solved graphically.

One can also argue as follows: because there are two choice variables, it is permissible to assume that at the solution at least two of the constraints are satisfied with equality. Constraints (5.11) and (5.12) are satisfied at equality by $h_1 = h_2 = 0$, at which point constraint (5.13) is satisfied. Constraints (5.11) and (5.13) are satisfied at equality by $h_1 = -1/3, h_2 = 1/3$, at which point constraint (5.12) is violated. Constraints (5.12) and (5.13) are satisfied at equality by $h_1 = -1, h_2 = 1/2$, at which point constraint (5.11) is satisfied.

The two points at which two of the constraints are satisfied as equalities and the third constraint is satisfied both give portfolios with zero price, and thus zero is the lower bound for the value of the call.

The upper bound on the value of the call is determined by solving

$$\min_{h_1, h_2}(p_1 h_1 + p_2 h_2) \tag{5.14}$$

subject to

$$h_1 + h_2 \geq 0, \tag{5.15}$$
$$h_1 + 2h_2 \geq 0, \tag{5.16}$$
$$h_1 + 4h_2 \geq 1. \tag{5.17}$$

As above, the minimum is attained at a point at which at least two of the constraints are satisfied with equality. Because constraints (5.15)–(5.17) are the reverse inequalities to (5.11)–(5.13), the only point that satisfies two of the constraints with equality is $h_1 = -1/3$, $h_2 = 1/3$. The price of this portfolio is $1/6$. Thus, the bounds on the value of the call option are zero and $1/6$. $\quad \frac{1}{2}(-\frac{1}{3}) + 1 \cdot \frac{1}{3} = \frac{1}{6}$ $\qquad\square$

Important properties of the bounds q_ℓ and q_u are given in the following propositions.

Proposition 5.3.4 *If security prices exclude strong arbitrage, then* $q_u(z) \geq q_\ell(z)$ *for every contingent claim* $z \in \mathcal{R}^S$.

Proof: Suppose that $q_u(z) < q_\ell(z)$ for some $z \in \mathcal{R}^S$. By the definitions of the bounds q_u and q_ℓ, there exist portfolios h' and h'' such that

$$h'X \leq z \leq h''X \tag{5.18}$$

and

$$ph' > ph''. \tag{5.19}$$

But then the portfolio $h'' - h'$ satisfies $(h'' - h')X \geq 0$ and $p(h'' - h') < 0$, and thus it is a strong arbitrage. This contradicts the assumption. $\qquad\square$

Also

Proposition 5.3.5 *If security prices exclude arbitrage, then* $q_u(z) > q_\ell(z)$ *for every contingent claim* z *not in the asset span.*

Proof: In view of Proposition 5.3.4, we only have to prove that $q_u(z) \neq q_\ell(z)$ for every $z \notin \mathcal{M}$. Suppose that $q_u(z) = q_\ell(z)$ for some $z \notin \mathcal{M}$. Then there exist portfolios h' and h'' such that

$$h'X \le z \le h''X \tag{5.20}$$

and

$$ph' = ph'' = q_u(z). \tag{5.21}$$

Neither of the weak inequalities in expression (5.20) can be an equality because z is not in the asset span; that is, it cannot be generated by a portfolio. Consequently, $(h'' - h')X > 0$, and $p(h'' - h') = 0$, and thus the portfolio $h'' - h'$ is an arbitrage. This is a contradiction.   □

5.4 The Extension

Having derived upper and lower bounds on the value of any contingent claim, we turn now to how these bounds are used to extend the payoff pricing functional.

Fix a contingent claim $\hat{z} \notin \mathcal{M}$. Define $\mathcal{N}$ by

$$\mathcal{N} = \{z + \lambda\hat{z} : z \in \mathcal{M} \text{ and } \lambda \in \mathcal{R}\}. \tag{5.22}$$

Thus $\mathcal{N}$ is the subspace of $\mathcal{R}^S$ that has dimension equal to the dimension of $\mathcal{M}$ plus one and contains $\mathcal{M}$ and $\hat{z}$. It is the asset span of $J + 1$ securities with payoffs $\{x_1, \ldots, x_J\}$ and $\hat{z}$.

If there is no strong arbitrage – equivalently, if the payoff pricing functional q is positive – then Proposition 5.3.4 implies that a finite value π can be chosen to satisfy [2]

$$q_\ell(\hat{z}) \le \pi \le q_u(\hat{z}). \tag{5.23}$$

We extend q to a linear functional on $\mathcal{N}$ in that we define $Q : \mathcal{N} \to \mathcal{R}$ by

$$Q(z + \lambda\hat{z}) \equiv q(z) + \lambda\pi. \tag{5.24}$$

We now prove that Q, as just defined, is the desired positive extension of q.

Proposition 5.4.1 *If* $q : \mathcal{M} \to \mathcal{R}$ *is positive, so is* $Q : \mathcal{N} \to \mathcal{R}$.

Proof: Let $y \in \mathcal{N}$. Then

$$y = z + \lambda\hat{z} \tag{5.25}$$

---

[2] One can show that the assumption of no strong arbitrage implies that the lower and upper bounds cannot both be equal to $+\infty$ or both equal to $-\infty$.

for some $z \in \mathcal{M}$ and some $\lambda \in \mathcal{R}$. Of the three possibilities for λ, suppose first that $\lambda > 0$. Then $y \geq 0$ implies

$$\hat{z} \geq -\frac{z}{\lambda}. \tag{5.26}$$

If we apply q_ℓ to both sides of inequality (5.26) and use the implication of definition (5.4) that q_ℓ is an increasing function, the result is

$$q_\ell(\hat{z}) \geq q_\ell\left(-\frac{z}{\lambda}\right). \tag{5.27}$$

By Proposition 5.3.1, the functions q and q_ℓ coincide on $\mathcal{M}$. Because $-z/\lambda \in \mathcal{M}$, we have $q_\ell(-z/\lambda) = q(-z/\lambda)$. Therefore, inequality (5.27) becomes

$$q_\ell(\hat{z}) \geq q\left(-\frac{z}{\lambda}\right). \tag{5.28}$$

Because $\pi \geq q_\ell(\hat{z})$, inequality (5.28) implies that

$$\pi \geq q\left(-\frac{z}{\lambda}\right), \tag{5.29}$$

or alternatively that

$$q(z) + \lambda\pi \geq 0. \tag{5.30}$$

Because the left-hand side of inequality (5.30) equals $Q(y)$, we obtain that $Q(y) \geq 0$.

If $\lambda < 0$, a similar argument, but using q_u and the fact that $\pi \leq q_u(\hat{z})$, also gives $Q(y) \geq 0$. Finally, if $\lambda = 0$, then $y = z$ and $Q(y) = q(z)$. The positivity of q implies that if $y \geq 0$, then $Q(y) \geq 0$. □

If there is no arbitrage – equivalently, if q is strictly positive – then Proposition 5.3.5 implies that π can be chosen to satisfy

$$q_\ell(\hat{z}) < \pi < q_u(\hat{z}). \tag{5.31}$$

Then

Proposition 5.4.2 *If $q : \mathcal{M} \to \mathcal{R}$ is strictly positive, so is $Q : \mathcal{N} \to \mathcal{R}$.*

The proof is essentially the same as the proof of Proposition 5.4.1.

For the prices $\{p_1, \ldots, p_J\}$ and π, functional Q, as defined in Eq. (5.24), is the payoff pricing functional on $\mathcal{N}$. Therefore Q is strictly positive (positive) on $\mathcal{N}$ iff the indicated prices exclude arbitrage (strong arbitrage) in $J + 1$ securities markets with payoffs $\{x_1, \ldots, x_J\}$ and $\hat{z}$.

Example 5.4.3 In example 5.3.2, define

$$\mathcal{N} = \{z + \lambda \hat{z} : z \in \mathcal{M}, \lambda \in \mathcal{R}\}, \tag{5.32}$$

where $\mathcal{M} = \text{span}\{(1, 2)\}$, and $\hat{z} = (1, 1)$. Thus $\mathcal{N} = \mathcal{R}^2$. We have the following bounds on the value π of $\hat{z}$ (see Eqs. (5.7) and (5.8)):

$$\frac{1}{2} \le \pi \le 1. \tag{5.33}$$

We choose $\pi = 3/4$ and define $Q : \mathcal{N} \to \mathcal{R}$ by

$$Q(z + \lambda \hat{z}) = q(z) + \frac{3}{4}\lambda \tag{5.34}$$

for $z \in \mathcal{M}$ and $\lambda \in \mathcal{R}$. Recall that $q(z) = \alpha$ for $z = (\alpha, 2\alpha)$. One can easily check that

$$Q(1, 0) = \frac{1}{2} \quad \text{and} \quad Q(0, 1) = \frac{1}{4} \tag{5.35}$$

and hence that

$$Q(y_1, y_2) = \frac{1}{2}y_1 + \frac{1}{4}y_2. \tag{5.36}$$

Thus, Q is strictly positive.   □

5.5 Uniqueness of the Valuation Functional

The construction of Section 5.4 indicates that extending the payoff pricing functional does not result in a unique valuation functional. Indeed, as was proved in Proposition 5.3.5, there is a continuum of values of π that define extensions with the desired properties. An exception is the case of complete markets. Then the asset span $\mathcal{M}$ equals the contingent claim space $\mathcal{R}^S$, and the payoff pricing functional is the valuation functional. It turns out that this is the only case of a unique valuation functional.

Theorem 5.5.1 *Suppose that security prices exclude arbitrage (strong arbitrage). Then security markets are complete iff there exists a unique strictly positive (positive) valuation functional.*

Proof: Necessity is obvious. Sufficiency follows from Proposition 5.3.5 (Proposition 5.3.4). If markets are not complete, so that there exists a contingent claim not in the asset span, then there exists a nondegenerate interval of values of that contingent claim that give rise to different strictly positive (positive) valuation functionals.   □

We pointed out in Section 5.1 that if security prices are equilibrium prices, then the marginal rates of substitution of an agent define a valuation functional. If markets are incomplete, the marginal rates may be different for different agents, and the associated valuation functionals are different. Otherwise, if markets are complete, there is a unique valuation functional. Hence, the marginal rates of substitution of all agents have to be the same.

5.6 Notes

The term *fundamental theorem of finance* was coined by Dybvig and Ross [3]. The first statement and proof of the fundamental theorem of finance appears in Ross [4] and [5]. See also Beja [1].

The derivation of the valuation functional by extending the payoff pricing functional is from Clark [2]. Note, though, that Clark does not restrict himself, as we do, to finite-dimensional contingent claim spaces.

Bibliography

[1] Beja, A. The structure of the cost of capital under uncertainty. *Review of Economic Studies*, **38**:359–69, 1971.

[2] Clark, S. A. The valuation problem in arbitrage price theory. *Journal of Mathematical Economics*, **22**:463–78, 1993.

[3] Dybvig, P. and Ross, S. A. Arbitrage. In M. Milgate, J. Eatwell, and P. Newman, editors, *The New Palgrave: A Dictionary of Economics*. McMillan, 1987.

[4] Ross, S. A. Risk, return and arbitrage. In Irwin Friend and James Bicksler, editors, *Risk and Return in Finance*. Ballinger, Cambridge, MA, 1976.

[5] Ross, S. A. A simple approach to the valuation of risky streams. *Journal of Business*, **51**:453–75, 1978.

6

State Prices and Risk-Neutral Probabilities

6.1 Introduction

By the fundamental theorem of finance, the payoff pricing functional can be extended to a strictly positive (positive) valuation functional iff security prices exclude arbitrage (strong arbitrage). We show in this chapter that each strictly positive (positive) valuation functional can be represented by a vector of strictly positive (positive) state prices. State prices can easily be calculated as a strictly positive (positive) solution to a system of linear equations relating security prices and their payoffs. An implication of the existence of strictly positive (positive) state prices is the absence of arbitrage (strong arbitrage). An implication of the uniqueness of state prices is that markets are complete.

The valuation functional can also be represented by strictly positive (positive) probabilities of the states. These probabilities, commonly known as risk-neutral probabilities, are simple transforms of the state prices and therefore just as useful as those prices. Under the risk-neutral probabilities representation, the price of each security equals its expected payoff discounted by the risk-free return.

6.2 State Prices

In Chapter 3 we derived the state prices associated with given security prices under the assumption of complete markets. If markets are complete, the payoff pricing functional q is defined on the entire contingent claim space $\mathcal{R}^S$, and the state price vector $q = (q_1, \ldots, q_S)$ provides a representation of the functional q as $q(z) = qz$ for every payoff $z \in \mathcal{R}^S$. The derivation of Chapter 3 can now be extended to incomplete markets using the valuation functional rather than the payoff pricing functional.

A valuation functional, being a linear functional on $\mathcal{R}^S$, can be identified by its values on the basis vectors of that space. Let

$$q_s \equiv Q(e_s), \tag{6.1}$$

for every s, where e_s is the state claim for state s. The value q_s is the *state price* of state s. If Q is strictly positive (positive), then each state price q_s is strictly positive (positive).

Because every contingent claim $z \in \mathcal{R}^S$ can be written as $z = \sum_s z_s e_s$, we have

$$Q(z) = \sum_s z_s Q(e_s) = \sum_s z_s q_s, \tag{6.2}$$

or

$$Q(z) = qz. \tag{6.3}$$

Equation (6.3) is the state-price representation of the valuation functional Q. It defines a one-to-one relation between valuation functionals and state-price vectors. Because the valuation functional in incomplete markets is not unique (Theorem 5.5.1), state prices are not unique either.

Equation (6.3) provides a simple method for pricing payoffs without determining a portfolio that generates the payoff under consideration. Once state prices are known, the price of every payoff can be obtained. Equation (6.3) can also be applied to contingent claims not in the asset span, although for any such claim the derived value will depend on the state-price vector used. It follows from the proof of the fundamental theorem of finance, provided in Section 5.4, that the derived value is independent of the state-price vector iff the contingent claim lies in the asset span.

State prices can be characterized as solutions to a system of linear equations just as under complete markets (recall Eq. (2.14)). To see this we apply Eq. (6.3) to the payoff x_j of security j. Because $Q(x_j) = p_j$, we obtain

$$p_j = qx_j, \tag{6.4}$$

or in vector-matrix notation

$$p = Xq. \tag{6.5}$$

State prices are a solution to the system of J equations (6.4) with S unknowns q_s. Strictly positive state prices are a strictly positive solution; positive state prices are a positive solution. If markets are incomplete, then the payoff matrix X has rank less than S, and the independent equations of (6.4) are fewer in number than the number of unknowns. If markets are complete, then state prices are unique. Of course, if markets are incomplete there are also nonpositive solutions to Eqs. (6.4), but they do not qualify as state prices.

We have

Theorem 6.2.1 *There exists a strictly positive valuation functional iff there exists a strictly positive solution to Eq. (6.5). Each strictly positive solution q defines a strictly positive valuation functional Q satisfying $Q(z) = qz$ for every $z \in \mathcal{R}^S$.*

Proof: It was proved in Eqs. (6.1)–(6.5) that state prices associated with a strictly positive valuation functional are a solution to Eq. (6.5). Existence of a valuation functional follows from the fact that, if q is a strictly positive solution to Eq. (6.5), then the functional Q defined by $Q(z) = qz$ is linear and strictly positive. Whenever $z \in \mathcal{M}$, then $z = hX$ for some portfolio h, and $Q(z) = qz = hXq = ph$ (that is, Q coincides with the payoff pricing functional on $\mathcal{M}$). Thus, Q is a strictly positive valuation functional. $\square$

Similarly,

Theorem 6.2.2 *There exists a positive valuation functional iff there exists a positive solution to Eq. (6.5). Each positive solution q defines a positive valuation functional Q satisfying $Q(z) = qz$ for every $z \in \mathcal{R}^S$.*

Theorems 6.2.1 and 6.2.2 say that state-price vectors can be defined either as the values of the state claims under valuation functionals, as in Eq. (6.1), or as a strictly positive (positive) solution to Eq. (6.5). The fundamental theorem of finance can be restated to say that security prices exclude arbitrage (strong arbitrage) iff there exists a strictly positive (positive) state-price vector.

Example 6.2.3 In Example 5.3.3, there were two securities: a risk-free bond with payoff $x_1 = (1, 1, 1)$ and price $p_1 = 1/2$ and a risky stock with payoff $x_2 = (1, 2, 4)$ and price $p_2 = 1$. Positive state prices q_1, q_2, q_3 are a positive solution to the system of two equations

$$q_1 + q_2 + q_3 = \frac{1}{2} \tag{6.6}$$

and

$$q_1 + 2q_2 + 4q_3 = 1. \tag{6.7}$$

Using q_3 as a parameter (we have two equations and three unknowns), the solution is

$$q_1 = 2q_3, \qquad q_2 = \frac{1}{2} - 3q_3. \tag{6.8}$$

For state prices to be positive, we must have $0 \le q_3 \le 1/6$. If $0 < q_3 < 1/6$, then state prices are strictly positive. The existence of a strictly positive solution verifies that security prices $p_1 = 1/2$ and $p_2 = 1$ exclude arbitrage.

It is worth noticing that the value of a call option on the stock with exercise price 3 is q_3 under the valuation functional given by q_1, q_2, and q_3. The condition $0 \le q_3 \le 1/6$ is precisely the condition that the value of the option has to lie between the lower and upper bounds derived in Example 5.3.3. □

6.3 Farkas–Stiemke Lemma

The equivalence of the absence of strong arbitrage and the existence of positive state prices can be derived directly from a well-known mathematical result, Farkas' Lemma. This result is essential in deriving state prices under portfolio restrictions. A derivation will be provided in Chapter 7.

Let y and a be m-dimensional vectors, b an n-dimensional vector, and Y an $m \times n$ matrix for arbitrary m, n.

Theorem 6.3.1 (Farkas' Lemma) *There does not exist $a \in \mathcal{R}^m$ such that*

$$aY \ge 0 \quad \text{and} \quad ay < 0 \tag{6.9}$$

iff there exists $b \in \mathcal{R}^n$ such that

$$y = Yb \quad \text{and} \quad b \ge 0. \tag{6.10}$$

With $Y = X$, $y = p$, $a = h$, and $b = q$, Farkas' Lemma says that no strong arbitrage and the existence of positive state prices are equivalent. That result was proved in Theorems 5.2.2 and 6.2.1.

The equivalence of the absence of arbitrage and the existence of strictly positive state prices can be derived directly from Stiemke's Lemma, a strict version of Farkas' Lemma under which b is strictly positive.

Theorem 6.3.2 (Stiemke's Lemma) *There does not exist $a \in \mathcal{R}^m$ such that*

$$aY \ge 0 \text{ and } ay \le 0, \text{ with at least one strict inequality} \tag{6.11}$$

iff there exists $b \in \mathcal{R}^n$ such that

$$y = Yb \quad \text{and} \quad b \gg 0. \tag{6.12}$$

With $Y = X$, $y = p$, $a = h$, and $b = q$, Stiemke's Lemma says that the no arbitrage is equivalent to the existence of strictly positive state prices. That result was proved in Theorems 5.2.1 and 6.2.2.

6.4 Diagrammatic Representation

In Chapter 3 we presented a diagrammatic analysis of security prices for two securities. It was shown that security prices exclude strong arbitrage whenever the price vector lies in the convex cone generated by the vectors of payoffs of the two securities in each state. Security prices exclude arbitrage whenever the vector of security prices lies in the interior of that cone. That is precisely the diagrammatic interpretation of the existence of strictly positive (positive) state prices. Equation (6.5) with positive state prices q_s means that the vector of security prices p lies in the cone generated by vectors $x_{.s} = (x_{1s}, \ldots, x_{Js})$ in $\mathcal{R}^J$. If the state prices are strictly positive, then vector p lies in the interior of that cone.

6.5 State Prices and Value Bounds

In the proof of the fundamental theorem of finance in Section 5.4 we showed that for any value lying between the lower bound $q_\ell(z)$ and the upper bound $q_u(z)$ of a contingent claim z, it is possible to define a positive valuation functional that maps z onto this assumed value. It follows that the set of values of z under all positive valuation functionals is the interval with $q_\ell(z)$ as the lower limit and $q_u(z)$ as the upper limit. Because each valuation functional has a state-price representation (6.3), the same set of values of z obtains when applying all positive state prices associated with given security prices to z. Using the characterization (6.5) of state prices, we obtain the following expressions for the upper and the lower bounds:

$$q_u(z) = \max_{q \geq 0} \{qz : p = Xq\}, \tag{6.13}$$

and

$$q_\ell(z) = \min_{q \geq 0} \{qz : p = Xq\}. \tag{6.14}$$

The use of these expressions for calculating bounds is illustrated by the following example.

Example 6.5.1 Value bounds for the contingent claim $(1, 1)$ of Example 5.3.2 can be calculated using Eqs. (6.13) and (6.14). We have

$$q_u(1, 1) = \max_{(q_1, q_2) \geq 0} \{q_1 + q_2 : q_1 + 2q_2 = 1\}, \tag{6.15}$$

and

$$q_\ell(1, 1) = \min_{(q_1, q_2) \geq 0} \{q_1 + q_2 : q_1 + 2q_2 = 1\}. \tag{6.16}$$

The maximum equals 1 and is attained at $q = (1, 0)$. The minimum equals $1/2$ and is attained at $q = (0, 1/2)$. □

Example 6.5.2 The value bounds in Example 5.3.3 can be derived using Eqs. (6.13) and (6.14) as

$$q_u(0, 0, 1) = \max_{(q_1,q_2,q_3)\geq 0} \left\{ q_3 : q_1 + q_2 + q_3 = \frac{1}{2}; q_1 + 2q_2 + 4q_3 = 1 \right\}, \quad (6.17)$$

and

$$q_\ell(0, 0, 1) = \min_{(q_1,q_2,q_3)\geq 0} \left\{ q_3 : q_1 + q_2 + q_3 = \frac{1}{2}; q_1 + 2q_2 + 4q_3 = 1 \right\}. \quad (6.18)$$

The maximum equals $1/6$ and is attained at $q = (1/3, 0, 1/6)$. The minimum equals 0 and is attained at $q = (0, 1/2, 0)$. □

6.6 Risk-Free Payoffs

A contingent claim that does not depend on the state is *risk free*. If markets are complete, risk-free claims are necessarily in the asset span. If markets are incomplete, it may or may not be possible to construct a portfolio with a nonzero risk-free payoff.

Given the presence of Treasury debt, which is free of default risk, it might seem that there is no reason to consider the possibility that risk-free claims are not in the asset span. However, the payoff on nominal debt is subject to inflation risk and therefore is random in real terms. Because we are not modeling monetary economies we will not attempt to explain inflation risk, but we do not want to restrict the analysis to the case in which investors are guaranteed to have access to investments that are completely risk free.

If a nonzero risk-free payoff lies in the asset span, then all risk-free payoffs lie in the asset span and, as long as the law of one price holds, they all have the same return. We denote that *risk-free return* by $\bar{r}$. It follows from Eq. (6.2) that $\bar{r}$ satisfies

$$\bar{r} = \frac{1}{\sum_s q_s}. \quad (6.19)$$

6.7 Risk-Neutral Probabilities

Suppose that security prices exclude arbitrage (strong arbitrage) and that a risk-free payoff with strictly positive return $\bar{r}$ lies in the asset span. Let q be a strictly positive (positive) state price vector. Define

$$\pi_s^* \equiv \bar{r}q_s = \frac{q_s}{\sum_s q_s}, \quad (6.20)$$

for every s. So defined, the π_s^*'s are strictly positive (positive) and sum to one. It is natural to interpret them as probabilities. We call them *risk-neutral probabilities*. The motivation for this term will be presented in Chapter 14.

When equipped with risk-neutral probabilities, the set of states S can be regarded as a probability space. Date-1 consumption plans, security payoffs, contingent claims, and others, which we have thus far regarded as vectors with S components, can now be regarded as random variables on the probability space S. Here and throughout this book we make no distinction in notation between a random variable and the vector of values the random variables takes on.

Let E^* denote the expectation with respect to the probabilities π^*. Then $E^*(z) = \sum_s \pi_s^* z_s$ for a contingent claim z. We have

$$qz = \sum_s q_s z_s = \frac{1}{\bar{r}} \sum_s \pi_s^* z_s = \frac{1}{\bar{r}} E^*(z). \tag{6.21}$$

Substituting Eq. (6.21) in Eq. (6.4), we obtain

$$p_j = \frac{1}{\bar{r}} E^*(x_j) \tag{6.22}$$

for every security j.

Equation (6.22) says that the price of each security equals the expectation of its payoff with respect to probabilities π^* discounted by the risk-free return. We emphasize that the expectation is taken with respect to probabilities π^* derived from state prices rather than agents' subjective probabilities.

Equation (6.22) can also be written in terms of returns as

$$\bar{r} = E^*(r_j). \tag{6.23}$$

Substituting Eq. (6.21) in Eq. (6.4), we obtain

$$Q(z) = \frac{1}{\bar{r}} E^*(z) \tag{6.24}$$

for every $z \in \mathcal{R}^S$. Equation (6.24) is the representation of the valuation functional Q by risk-neutral probabilities. The value of each contingent claim equals the discounted expectation of the claim with respect to risk-neutral probabilities.

Because risk-neutral probabilities are rescaled state prices, they have all the properties of those prices. They are characterized as strictly positive (positive) solutions to Eq. (6.22). Their existence and strict positivity (positivity) are equivalent to the absence of arbitrage (strong arbitrage); their uniqueness is equivalent to market completeness.

Using risk-neutral probabilities instead of state prices, we can write the upper and lower bounds on values of a contingent claim Eqs. (6.13) and (6.14) as

$$q_u(z) = \frac{1}{\bar{r}} \max_{\pi^*} E^*(z) \tag{6.25}$$

and

$$q_\ell(z) = \frac{1}{\bar{r}} \min_{\pi^*} E^*(z), \tag{6.26}$$

where the maximum and minimum are taken over all risk-neutral probabilities.

Risk-neutral probabilities play an important role in multidate security markets. A natural extension of the pricing relationship (6.22) is the martingale property of security prices; see Chapter 26.

Example 6.7.1 The risk-neutral probabilities of Example 6.2.3 can be derived by multiplying state prices by the risk-free return $\bar{r}$. Because $\bar{r} = 2$, we have

$$\pi_1^* = 2\pi_3^*, \qquad \pi_2^* = 1 - 3\pi_3^*, \qquad \text{and } 0 \le \pi_3^* \le \frac{1}{3}. \tag{6.27}$$

Because state prices are not unique, neither are risk-neutral probabilities.

Risk-neutral probabilities can also by derived directly from the system of equations (6.22); that is,

$$1 = \pi_1^* + \pi_2^* + \pi_3^*, \tag{6.28}$$

and

$$2 = \pi_1^* + 2\pi_2^* + 4\pi_3^*. \tag{6.29}$$

$\square$

6.8 Notes

State prices and risk-neutral probabilities were first introduced by Ross [4] and [5]. Further discussion of state prices and risk-neutral probabilities can be found in Dybvig and Ross [2] and Varian [6]. Green and Srivastava [3] studied the relation between state prices and agents' optimal consumption plans.

We presented two ways of deriving state prices under the assumption that security prices exclude arbitrage or strong arbitrage. One uses the extension of the payoff pricing functional (Section 5.4); the other applies the Farkas–Stiemke Lemma (Section 6.3). There are two other ways of deriving state prices: the first, by making use of the duality theorem of linear programming; the second, by making use of the separating hyperplane theorem (see Duffie [1]).

The duality theorem of linear programming says that linear programs come in pairs: with every constrained maximization problem that has a solution there is associated a constrained minimization problem that also has a solution, and the optimized values of the objective functions in the two problems are the same. Absence of strong arbitrage implies that a certain primal problem has a solution, and the duality theorem therefore implies the existence of positive state prices as a solution to a dual problem. The result of Section 6.5 that the upper (lower) bound on the value of a contingent claim can be derived either by minimizing (maximizing) over payoffs or maximizing (minimizing) over state prices associated with given security prices is also an implication of duality of linear programming.

A risk-free payoff that equals the expectation of a risky payoff with respect to the risk-neutral probabilities is called the *certainty–equivalent payoff*. By construction, it is a risk-free payoff with the same price as the risky payoff.

The derivation of risk-neutral probabilities in Section 6.7 relies on the assumption that the risk-free payoff is in the asset span. If it is not, then the return on any security or a portfolio, if strictly positive, can be substituted for the risk-free return. Using the return on security k as the deflator, we can write the price of security j as

$$p_j = \sum_s q_s r_{ks} \frac{x_{js}}{r_{ks}} = \sum_s v_s \frac{x_{js}}{r_{ks}}, \tag{6.30}$$

where

$$v_s \equiv q_s r_{ks}. \tag{6.31}$$

Because $\sum_s v_s = 1$, the v_s's can be interpreted as probabilities, and Eq. (6.30) can therefore be rewritten as

$$p_j = E_v \left(\frac{x_j}{r_k} \right). \tag{6.32}$$

The probabilities v depend on the choice of deflator security. If one security is substituted for another, then, unless the returns are the same, v will change.

Bibliography

[1] Duffie, D. *Dynamic Asset Pricing Theory,* Second Edition. Princeton University Press, Princeton, NJ, 1996.

[2] Dybvig, P. and Ross, S. A. Arbitrage. In M. Milgate, J. Eatwell, and P. Newman, editors, *The New Palgrave: A Dictionary of Economics*. McMillan, 1987.

[3] Green, R. C. and Srivastava, S. S. Risk aversion and arbitrage. *Journal of Finance*, **40**:257–68, 1985.

[4] Ross, S. A. Risk, return and arbitrage. In Irwin Friend and James Bicksler, editors, *Risk and Return in Finance*. Ballinger, Cambridge, MA, 1976.

[5] Ross, S. A. A Simple Approach to the Valuation of Risky Streams. *Journal of Business*, **51**:453–475, 1978.

[6] Varian, H. R. The arbitrage principle in financial economics. *Journal of Economic Perspectives*, **1**:55–72, 1987.

7

Valuation under Portfolio Restrictions

7.1 Introduction

The valuation theory of Chapters 5 and 6 relies on linearity of pricing in security markets or, in other words, on the law of one price. We observed in Chapter 4 that the law of one price may fail in an equilibrium in the presence of portfolio restrictions. We show in this chapter that, nevertheless, many of the results of valuation theory in the absence of portfolio restrictions can be extended, although generally in altered form, to security markets with such portfolio restrictions as short sales restrictions or bid-ask spreads. In particular, there exist strictly positive (positive) state prices iff security prices exclude unlimited arbitrage (unlimited strong arbitrage). The existence of strictly positive (positive) state prices therefore provides a simple test of whether there exist unlimited arbitrages (unlimited strong arbitrage).

7.2 Payoff Pricing under Short Sales Restrictions

As in Chapter 4, we consider short sales restrictions of the form

$$h_j \geq -b_j \tag{7.1}$$

for every security $j \in \mathcal{J}_0$, with positive b_j.

The payoff pricing functional, as introduced in Chapter 2, is a single-valued functional if security prices satisfy the law of one price. As noted above, in the presence of short sales restrictions, the law of one price may fail in an equilibrium as long as the implied strong arbitrage is a limited arbitrage (recall Example 4.4.1). It follows that in the presence of short sales restrictions the payoff pricing functional should be defined in a way that does not presume satisfaction of the law of one price. The appropriate definition of the price of a payoff is as the minimal price of a portfolio that generates that payoff. An agent whose utility function is increasing at date 0 will always select a portfolio that generates its payoff at minimum cost.

Let $\tilde{\mathcal{M}}$ be the set of payoffs that can be generated by portfolios satisfying short sales restriction (7.1):

$$\tilde{\mathcal{M}} \equiv \{z \in \mathcal{R}^S : z = hX \text{ for some } h \text{ such that } h_j \geq -b_j, \ \forall j \in \mathcal{J}_0\}. \quad (7.2)$$

The *payoff pricing functional* $\tilde{q} : \tilde{\mathcal{M}} \to \mathcal{R}$ is defined by

$$\tilde{q}(z) \equiv \min_h \{ph : hX = z, \ h_j \geq -b_j, \ \forall j \in \mathcal{J}_0\} \quad (7.3)$$

for $z \in \tilde{\mathcal{M}}$ whenever the minimum exists.

The set $\tilde{\mathcal{M}}$ is convex, but in general it is not a linear subspace. The payoff pricing functional $\tilde{q}$ is a convex function, but it may be nonlinear.

The price of any security is greater than or equal to the value of its payoff under the payoff pricing functional. Inequality can be strict, and thus there may be a portfolio that generates the same payoff as a particular security but at strictly lower cost.

Example 7.2.1 In Example 4.4.1 there were three securities with payoffs $x_1 = (1, 1)$, $x_2 = (1, 0)$, and $x_3 = (0, 1)$. When holdings of securities were restricted by $h_j \geq -1$ for each j, equilibrium prices were $p_1 = 3/4$, $p_2 = p_3 = 1/2$. The payoff pricing functional associated with these prices is defined by the minimization problem

$$\tilde{q}(z_1, z_2) = \min_h \left(\frac{3}{4}h_1 + \frac{1}{2}h_2 + \frac{1}{2}h_3 \right) \quad (7.4)$$

subject to

$$h_1 + h_2 = z_1, \qquad h_1 + h_3 = z_2, \quad (7.5)$$

$$h_1 \geq -1, \qquad h_2 \geq -1, \qquad h_3 \geq -1, \quad (7.6)$$

for any $(z_1, z_2) \in \tilde{\mathcal{M}}$, where $\tilde{\mathcal{M}}$ consists of all payoffs (z_1, z_2) for which there exists a portfolio $h = (h_1, h_2, h_3)$ that satisfies constraints (7.5) and (7.6). Using constraint (7.5) to eliminate h_2 and h_3 in Eq. (7.4), the latter becomes

$$\tilde{q}(z_1, z_2) = \min_h \left(\frac{1}{2}z_1 + \frac{1}{2}z_2 - \frac{1}{4}h_1 \right) \quad (7.7)$$

subject to constraints (7.5) and (7.6). If $z_1 \geq z_2$, then the minimum in Eq. (7.7) is attained at $h_1 = z_2 + 1$, $h_2 = z_1 - z_2 - 1$ and $h_3 = -1$. If $z_1 < z_2$, it is attained at $h_1 = z_1 + 1$, $h_2 = -1$, and $h_3 = z_2 - z_1 - 1$. Summing up, we have

$$\tilde{q}(z_1, z_2) = \frac{1}{2}z_1 + \frac{1}{2}z_2 - \frac{1}{4}\min\{z_1, z_2\} - \frac{1}{4}. \quad (7.8)$$

The functional $\tilde{q}$ is nonlinear.

Note that the price (measured by $\tilde{q}$) of the payoff of each security is strictly less than the security price; for instance, $\tilde{q}(x_1) = 1/2 < 3/4 = p_1$. ☐

If the law of one price holds, then the payoff pricing functional $\tilde{q}$ coincides on $\tilde{\mathcal{M}}$ with the functional q defined in Chapter 2 and is linear. In particular, if there are no redundant securities (that is, if each payoff is generated by a unique portfolio), then $\tilde{q}$ is linear.

Using the payoff pricing functional, we can write an agent's consumption choice problem (4.3)–(4.6) as

$$\max_{c_0, c_1, z} u(c_0, c_1) \tag{7.9}$$

subject to

$$c_0 \leq w_0 - \tilde{q}(z) \tag{7.10}$$
$$c_1 \leq w_1 + z \tag{7.11}$$
$$z \in \tilde{\mathcal{M}}, \tag{7.12}$$

whenever u is increasing in c_0, and thus when making their portfolio and consumption decisions agents evaluate payoffs using the payoff pricing functional. This representation of the agents' consumption-portfolio choice problem coincides with that of Section 2.6 in the absence of portfolio restrictions.

7.3 State Prices under Short Sales Restrictions

Even though the payoff pricing functional may fail to be linear or positive in the presence of short sales restrictions, there exist positive state prices that satisfy a weaker form of Eq. (6.5) whenever security prices exclude unlimited arbitrage opportunities. The existence of positive state prices therefore provides a useful characterization of security prices that exclude unlimited arbitrage.

Theorem 7.3.1 *Security prices p exclude unlimited strong arbitrage under short sales restrictions iff there exists a positive vector $q \in \mathcal{R}^S$ such that*

$$p_j \geq x_j q \quad \forall j \in \mathcal{J}_0, \tag{7.13}$$

and

$$p_j = x_j q \quad \forall j \notin \mathcal{J}_0. \tag{7.14}$$

Proof: Let J_0 be the number of securities in the set $\mathcal{J}_0$. Let Y be a $J \times (S + J_0)$ matrix consisting of the $J \times S$ payoff matrix X augmented by J_0 column vectors corresponding to securities in the set $\mathcal{J}_0$. For each $j \in \mathcal{J}_0$, the $(S + j)$th column of Y is a J-dimensional vector with the jth coordinate equal to one and all other coordinates equal to zero. Denoting the matrix of such J_0 column vectors by K_0, we can write

$$Y = [X \quad K_0]. \tag{7.15}$$

The inequality $hY \geq 0$ is equivalent to

$$hX \geq 0, \tag{7.16}$$

and

$$h_j \geq 0 \quad \text{for every } j \in \mathcal{J}_0. \tag{7.17}$$

Thus, $hY \geq 0$ and $ph < 0$ is equivalent to h's being an unlimited strong arbitrage portfolio. Farkas' Lemma 6.3.1 says that nonexistence of h with $hY \geq 0$ and $ph < 0$ is equivalent to existence of a vector $b \in \mathcal{R}^{S+J_0}$ such that

$$p = Yb \quad \text{and} \quad b \geq 0. \tag{7.18}$$

Let us partition vector b as $b = (q, \epsilon)$ with $q \in \mathcal{R}^S$ and $\epsilon \in \mathcal{R}^{J_0}$. Using Eq. (7.15), we can write Eq. (7.18) as

$$p_j = x_j q \tag{7.19}$$

for $j \notin \mathcal{J}_0$, and

$$p_j = x_j q + \epsilon_j \tag{7.20}$$

for $j \in \mathcal{J}_0$. Because $q \geq 0$ and $\epsilon_j \geq 0$, Eqs. (7.19) and (7.20) are equivalent to inequality (7.13) and equation (7.14).   □

The strict version of Theorem 7.3.1 is the following:

Theorem 7.3.2 *Security prices p exclude unlimited arbitrage under short sales restrictions iff there exists a strictly positive vector $q \in \mathcal{R}^S$ such that*

$$p_j \geq x_j q \quad \forall j \in \mathcal{J}_0, \tag{7.21}$$

and

$$p_j = x_j q \quad \forall j \notin \mathcal{J}_0. \tag{7.22}$$

See the chapter notes for discussion of the proof.

Any positive or strictly positive vector q satisfying conditions (7.21) and (7.22) will be referred to as a vector of *state prices* under short sales restrictions. According to Eq. (7.22) the price of a security that is not subject to a short sales restriction equals the value of its payoff under state prices. For a security that is subject to a short sales restriction, the price exceeds the value of the payoff under state prices.

It follows from the first-order conditions (4.7) under short sales restrictions that the vector of marginal rates of substitution of an agent with strictly increasing utility function and interior optimal consumption is one of the vectors of strictly positive state prices.

If there is a risk-free security and that security is not subject to a short sales restriction, then the risk-free return satisfies $\bar{r} = 1/\sum_s q_s$, and risk-neutral probabilities π^* can be defined by $\pi_s^* = \bar{r}q_s$, as in Section 6.7 in the absence of portfolio restrictions. Using risk-neutral probabilities, we can rewrite conditions (7.21) and (7.22) as

$$p_j \geq \frac{1}{\bar{r}} E^*(x_j) \quad \forall j \in \mathcal{J}_0, \tag{7.23}$$

and

$$p_j = \frac{1}{\bar{r}} E^*(x_j) \quad \forall j \notin \mathcal{J}_0. \tag{7.24}$$

Thus, the price of a security that is subject to a short sales constraint exceeds its expected payoff discounted by the risk-free return, whereas the price of a security that is not subject to a short sales constraint equals its expected payoff discounted by the risk-free return when the expectations are taken with respect to the risk-neutral probabilities.

It is important to note that in the presence of short sales restrictions state prices do not in general have the strong association with the prices of Arrow securities that they have in the absence of portfolio restrictions: Theorem 7.5.5 implies that state prices merely provide lower bounds on the prices of Arrow securities. Further, the positive linear functional that can be defined by a vector of positive state prices via $z \mapsto qz$ on the space $\mathcal{R}^S$ of contingent claims does not in general coincide with the payoff pricing functional $\tilde{q}$ on the set $\tilde{\mathcal{M}}$, and hence it is not a valuation functional in the sense of Chapter 5.

Example 7.3.3 In Example 7.2.1, security prices $p_1 = 3/4$, $p_2 = p_3 = 1/2$ are equilibrium prices under short sales restrictions. Consequently, these prices exclude unlimited arbitrage. Strictly positive state prices are all pairs (q_1, q_2) of numbers satisfying

$$\frac{3}{4} \geq q_1 + q_2, \qquad \frac{1}{2} \geq q_1 > 0, \qquad \text{and} \quad \frac{1}{2} \geq q_2 > 0. \tag{7.25}$$

Note that the Arrow security for state 1 is traded at the price of $1/2$. The range of state prices of state 1 is $1/2 \geq q_1 > 0$. $\qquad\square$

7.4 Diagrammatic Representation

In Chapter 4 we presented a diagrammatic analysis of prices of two securities that are subject to short sales restrictions. With a short sales restriction only on security 2, the set of prices that exclude unlimited arbitrage was seen to be the area within and to the north of the convex cone generated by vectors of payoffs of the securities in each state. This is precisely the diagrammatic interpretation of the existence of positive state prices in this case. Equation (7.14), for the unrestricted security 1, and inequality (7.13), for the restricted security 2, mean that a vector of security prices dominates in its second coordinate some vector in the convex cone generated by payoffs.

If short sales of both securities 1 and 2 are restricted, then any positive vector of security prices excludes unlimited arbitrage. This is also the diagrammatic interpretation of inequalities (7.13) for both securities.

7.5 Bid-Ask Spreads

The foregoing analysis of valuation under short sales restrictions can be applied to security markets with bid and ask prices. As explained in Section 4.7, if one considers each security j with bid price p_{bj} and ask price p_{aj}, as two securities each with a single price (one with payoff x_j and price p_{aj}, the other with payoff $-x_j$ and price $-p_{bj}$, and both with a zero short sales restriction), bid-ask spreads can be viewed as a special case of short sales restrictions. The fact that the implied short sales restrictions involve zero bounds leads to a specialization of the results in the general case analyzed earlier.

The set of payoffs that can be generated by arbitrary portfolios under bid-ask spreads coincides with the asset span $\mathcal{M}$ and is a linear subspace. The payoff pricing functional $\tilde{q}$ is given by

$$\tilde{q}(z) = \min_{h_a, h_b}\{p_a h_a - p_b h_b : (h_a - h_b)X = z, \ h_a \geq 0, \ h_b \geq 0\}, \qquad (7.26)$$

for $z \in \mathcal{M}$. It follows that $\tilde{q}$ satisfies

$$\tilde{q}(z + z') \leq \tilde{q}(z) + \tilde{q}(z') \qquad (7.27)$$

for every $z, z' \in \mathcal{M}$, and

$$\tilde{q}(\lambda z) = \lambda \tilde{q}(z) \qquad (7.28)$$

every $z \in \mathcal{M}$ and $\lambda \geq 0$. Properties (7.27) and (7.28) establish that the payoff pricing functional $\tilde{q}$ is *sublinear* on $\mathcal{M}$.

Example 7.5.1 In Example 4.8.1 there were two securities with payoffs $x_1 = (1, 0)$ and $x_2 = (0, 1)$. Ask prices $p_{a1} = p_{a2} = 0.75$ and bid prices $p_{b1} = p_{b2} = 0.25$ were shown to be equilibrium prices for bid-ask spreads of 0.5.

Because the asset span $\mathcal{M}$ equals $\mathcal{R}^2$, the payoff pricing functional associated with equilibrium security prices is defined for every $z = (z_1, z_2) \in \mathcal{R}^2$ as the value of the minimization problem

$$\min_{h_a, h_b} (0.75 h_{a1} - 0.25 h_{b1} + 0.75 h_{a2} - 0.25 h_{b2}) \tag{7.29}$$

subject to

$$h_{a1} - h_{b1} = z_1, \qquad h_{a2} - h_{b2} = z_2, \tag{7.30}$$

$$h_{a1} \geq 0, \qquad h_{b1} \geq 0, \qquad h_{a2} \geq 0, \qquad h_{b2} \geq 0. \tag{7.31}$$

for $(z_1, z_2) \in \mathcal{R}^2$. It follows that

$$\tilde{q}(z_1, z_2) = 0.75 \max\{z_1, 0\} - 0.25 \min\{z_1, 0\}$$
$$+ 0.75 \max\{z_2, 0\} - 0.25 \min\{z_2, 0\}. \tag{7.32}$$

Because each term $0.75 \max\{z_s, 0\} - 0.25 \min\{z_s, 0\}$ is sublinear (but not linear) in z_s for $s = 1, 2$, the functional $\tilde{q}$ is sublinear. $\qquad\square$

Because the short sales restrictions implied by bid-ask spreads involve zero bounds, bid and ask security prices (p_b, p_a) exclude strong unlimited arbitrage iff the payoff pricing functional $\tilde{q}$ is positive; that is, $\tilde{q}(z) \geq 0$ for every $z \geq 0$. Further, bid and ask prices (p_b, p_a) exclude unlimited arbitrage iff the payoff pricing functional $\tilde{q}$ is strictly positive. Note that the payoff pricing functional in Example 7.5.1 is strictly positive.

Bid and ask prices that exclude strong unlimited arbitrage can be characterized by the existence of positive state prices.

Theorem 7.5.2 *Bid and ask security prices (p_b, p_a) exclude strong unlimited arbitrage iff there exists a positive vector $q \in \mathcal{R}^S$ such that*

$$p_{aj} \geq x_j q \geq p_{bj} \tag{7.33}$$

for each security j.

Proof: As indicated above, bid-ask spreads can be viewed as a special case of short sales restrictions by considering each security as two securities with single price and zero short sales restriction. Applying Theorem 7.3.1, we obtain that the exclusion of strong unlimited arbitrage is equivalent to the existence of a vector $q \in \mathcal{R}^S$, $q \geq 0$ such that

$$p_{aj} \geq x_j q, \tag{7.34}$$

and

$$-p_{bj} \geq -x_j q, \tag{7.35}$$

for each security j. Inequalities (7.34) and (7.35) are equivalent to (7.33). $\qquad\square$

The strict version of Theorem 7.5.2 is the following:

Theorem 7.5.3 *Bid and ask security prices* (p_b, p_a) *exclude unlimited arbitrage iff there exists a strictly positive vector* $q \in \mathcal{R}^S$ *such that*

$$p_{aj} \geq x_j q \geq p_{bj} \tag{7.36}$$

for every security j.

Any positive or strictly positive vector q satisfying inequality (7.33) will be referred to as a vector of *state prices* under bid-ask spreads. If there exists a risk-free security and that security has the same bid and ask price, then the risk-free return satisfies $\bar{r} = 1/\sum_s q_s$ and risk-neutral probabilities π^* can be defined by $\pi_s^* = \bar{r} q_s$. Using risk-neutral probabilities, we can rewrite inequality (7.33) as

$$p_{aj} \geq \frac{1}{\bar{r}} E^*(x_j) \geq p_{bj}, \tag{7.37}$$

for every security j. Thus, the expected payoff of a security discounted by the risk-free return lies between the bid and the ask prices of the security when the expectation is taken with respect to the risk-neutral probabilities.

Example 7.5.4 In Example 7.5.1, ask prices $p_{a1} = p_{a2} = 0.75$ and bid prices $p_{b1} = p_{b2} = 0.25$ exclude arbitrage. Strictly positive state prices are pairs (q_1, q_2) of strictly positive numbers satisfying inequality (7.33); that is,

$$0.75 \geq q_1 \geq 0.25, \quad \text{and} \quad 0.75 \geq q_2 \geq 0.25. \tag{7.38}$$

□

Any vector of strictly positive (positive) state prices q can be used to define a strictly positive (positive) linear functional on the contingent claim space $\mathcal{R}^S$ by $z \mapsto qz$. Again, this functional is not a valuation functional in the sense of Chapter 5. However, it provides a lower bound on the payoff pricing functional $\tilde{q}$ on the asset span $\mathcal{M}$.

Theorem 7.5.5 *For any vector of positive state prices* q *under bid-ask spreads, we have*

$$\tilde{q}(z) \geq qz, \tag{7.39}$$

for every payoff $z \in \mathcal{M}$.

Proof: Let (h_a, h_b) be any portfolio such that $(h_a - h_b)X = z$ with $h_a \geq 0$ and

$h_{\mathrm{b}} \geq 0$. Using inequality (7.33), we obtain

$$(p_{\mathrm{a}}h_{\mathrm{a}} - p_{\mathrm{b}}h_{\mathrm{b}}) \geq h_{\mathrm{a}}Xq - h_{\mathrm{b}}Xq = qz. \qquad (7.40)$$

If we take the minimum over $(h_{\mathrm{a}}, h_{\mathrm{b}})$ on the left-hand side of inequality (7.40), $\tilde{q}(z) \geq qz$ results. $\qquad\qquad\square$

If there is a risk-free security with the same bid and ask price so that the risk-neutral probabilities π^* can be defined by $\pi_s^* = \bar{r}q_s$, then inequality (7.39) can be written as

$$\tilde{q}(z) \geq \frac{1}{\bar{r}}E^*(z), \qquad (7.41)$$

for every $z \in \mathcal{M}$.

7.6 Notes

The proof of Theorem 7.3.2 is similar to that of Theorem 7.3.1. Instead of applying Farkas' Lemma, one has to apply a strict version of it. However, the required strict version is not Stiemke's Lemma (6.3.2), but a slightly different variant of Farkas' Lemma. To see this, observe that an application of Stiemke's Lemma in place of Farkas' Lemma in the proof of Theorem 7.3.1 would give the following equivalence: there exists $q \gg 0$ such that $p_j = x_j q$ for every $j \notin \mathcal{J}_0$ and $p_j > x_j q$ for every $j \in \mathcal{J}_0$, iff there does not exist h satisfying (1) $hX \geq 0$, (2) $ph \leq 0$, and (3) $h_j \geq 0$ for every $j \in \mathcal{J}_0$ with at least one strict inequality in (1), (2), or (3). This is a different equivalence than that of Theorem 7.3.2. Observe that the condition that security prices exclude unlimited arbitrage says that there is no portfolio h satisfying (1), (2), and (3) with at least one strict inequality required to hold in (1) or (2). A version of Farkas' Lemma that can be used to prove Theorem 7.3.2 can be found in Luenberger [4].

The existence of positive state prices in security markets with bid-ask spreads was demonstrated by Garman and Ohlson [1]. The payoff pricing functional, as defined in Section 7.2, was introduced by Prisman [6]. Ross [7] studied implications of the exclusion of arbitrage in securities markets with taxation. General results on valuation and the existence of state prices under so-called cone constraints (that is, when the set of agent's feasible portfolios forms a convex cone, as is the case under zero short sales restrictions or bid-ask spreads) can be found in Luttmer [5] and Jouini and Kallal [3].

Luttmer [5] and He and Modest [2] examined empirical implications of portfolio restrictions in security markets.

Bibliography

[1] Garman, M. and Ohlson, J. Valuation of risky assets in arbitrage-free economies with transactions costs. *Journal of Financial Economics*, **9**:271–80, 1981.

[2] He, H. and Modest, D. M. Market frictions and consumption-based asset pricing. *Journal of Political Economy*, **103**:94–117, 1995.

[3] Jouini, E. and Kallal, H. Martingales and arbitrage in securities markets with transaction costs. *Journal of Economic Theory*, **66**:178–97, 1995.

[4] Luenberger, D. G. *Optimization by Vector Space Methods*. Wiley, New York, 1969.

[5] Luttmer, E. Asset pricing in economies with frictions. *Econometrica*, **64**:1439–67, 1996.

[6] Prisman, E. Valuation of risky assets in arbitrage-free economies with frictions. *Journal of Finance*, **41**:545–60, 1986.

[7] Ross, S. A. Arbitrage and martingales with taxation. *Journal of Political Economy*, **195**:371–93, 1987.

Part Three

Risk

8

Expected Utility

8.1 Introduction

Up to now preferences over uncertain consumption plans have been handled in the most general fashion: we have merely assumed the existence of a utility function on the set of admissible consumption plans. The canonical model of preferences under uncertainty is the expected utility model. Expected utility is based on axiomatic foundations and provides a framework for the analysis of agents' attitudes toward risk. Consequently, expected utility plays a central role in the analysis of portfolio choice.

It is assumed (except in Section 8.8) that date-0 consumption does not enter agents' utility functions. There are no restrictions on admissible state-contingent consumption plans, and thus utility functions are defined on the entire date-1 consumption space. However, the results to be presented remain valid if agents' admissible consumption plans are restricted to being positive.

8.2 Expected Utility

An agent's utility function $u : \mathcal{R}^S \to \mathcal{R}$ on state-contingent consumption plans has a *state-dependent expected utility representation* if there exist functions $v_s : \mathcal{R} \to \mathcal{R}$ (one for each state s) and a probability measure π on S such that

$$u(c_1, \ldots, c_S) \geq u(c'_1, \ldots, c'_S) \text{ iff } \sum_{s=1}^{S} \pi_s v_s(c_s) \geq \sum_{s=1}^{S} \pi_s v_s(c'_s). \quad (8.1)$$

Utility function u has a *state-independent expected utility representation* if the functions v_s can be taken to be the same in all states; that is, if

$$u(c_1, \ldots, c_S) \geq u(c'_1, \ldots, c'_S) \text{ iff } \sum_{s=1}^{S} \pi_s v(c_s) \geq \sum_{s=1}^{S} \pi_s v(c'_s) \quad (8.2)$$

for some probability measure π and some function $v : \mathcal{R} \to \mathcal{R}$. Hereafter "expected utility" will mean "state-independent expected utility." The utility function v in condition (8.2) will be referred to as the *von Neumann–Morgenstern* utility function.

The probability measure in the state-dependent expected utility of condition (8.1) is indeterminate; one can rescale functions v_s to associate u with any probability measure. Condition (8.1) therefore says nothing more than that u has an additively separable representation. In contrast, the probability measure in the state-independent expected utility of condition (8.2) is unique. The von Neumann–Morgenstern utility function v is unique up to a strictly increasing affine transformation. That is, v can be replaced by $a + bv$ for any constants a and $b > 0$ without changing the preference ordering of u.

When equipped with the probability measure π of expected utility representation (8.2), the set of states S can be regarded as a probability space. State-contingent consumption plans can then be regarded as random variables. Expected value of a random variable with respect to the probability measure π is indicated by E_π, or simply by E when there is no ambiguity about the probability measure. Expected utility in condition (8.2) is written as $E[v(c)]$.

Under either conditions (8.1) or (8.2), the marginal rate of substitution between consumption in any two states is independent of consumption in other states. In the context of choice among many goods under certainty, independence of the marginal rate of substitution between two goods from the level of consumption of other goods would be a restrictive assumption, but in the present context it is reasonable because one state can occur only if other states do not occur.

8.3 Von Neumann–Morgenstern

The first derivation of an expected utility representation of preferences under uncertainty was provided by von Neumann and Morgenstern. They assumed that agents choose among lotteries. A lottery is by definition a random variable with specified payoffs and specified probabilities. The critical assumption of the von Neumann–Morgenstern approach is that agents know the relevant probabilities. Thus, the approach is relevant to situations like games of chance in which the existence of objective probabilities can be assumed. In settings characterized by what has become known as "Knightian uncertainty," meaning settings in which agents cannot specify probability distributions, the von Neumann–Morgenstern approach does not apply because agents are not assumed to be able to characterize the available choices as lotteries.

8.4 Savage

Savage's subjective expected utility theory takes as the object of choice state-contingent outcomes rather than lotteries. The difference between Savage and von Neumann–Morgenstern is that under Savage's approach probabilities are derived rather than taken as given. Specifically, Savage proved that if agents' preferences on state-contingent outcomes obey certain axioms, then they have an expected utility representation through which the probabilities as well as the utility function are derived from the assumed ordering on outcomes. Thus, Savage's approach, unlike that of von Neumann–Morgenstern, is immune to the objection that agents may not know the relevant probabilities; if agents are able to choose consistently (and in conformity with the Savage axioms), then they act as if they know the probabilities, which is all that is relevant for economic problems. These probabilities, being subjective, may, of course, differ across agents.

From our point of view, Savage's derivation of expected utility has one shortcoming. It requires that there be an infinite number of states. This conflicts with the assumption here that the number of states is finite. We present an alternative axiomatization that applies to the case of finitely many states.

8.5 Axiomatization of State-Dependent Expected Utility

The principal axiom that implies that an agent's utility function $u : \mathcal{R}^S \to \mathcal{R}$ has a state-dependent expected utility representation is the *independence* axiom. The independence axiom requires that

$$u(c_{-s}y) \geq u(d_{-s}y) \ \text{ iff } \ u(c_{-s}w) \geq u(d_{-s}w) \tag{8.3}$$

for all $c, d \in \mathcal{R}^S$ and $y, w \in \mathcal{R}$. Here, $c_{-s}y$ refers to the consumption plan c with consumption c_s in state s replaced by y.

The independence axiom states that the preference between $c_{-s}y$ and $d_{-s}y$ will be unaffected if y is replaced by w. This must be true for any c, d, y, and w. That is, the independence axiom implies that the level of consumption in state s does not interact with consumption in other states in such a way as to reverse the preference.

Assume that u is strictly increasing and continuous. We have

Theorem 8.5.1 *Assume that there are at least three states, $S \geq 3$. Utility function u has a state-dependent expected utility representation iff it obeys the independence axiom.*

Proof: It can be easily verified that a state-dependent expected utility satisfies the independence axiom. The proof that the independence axiom implies the representation is not presented.   □

An example of a utility function that does not satisfy the independence axiom, and hence does not have a state-dependent expected utility representation, is the following.

Example 8.5.2 Consider the utility function $u : \mathcal{R}_+^3 \to \mathcal{R}$ given by $u(c_1, c_2, c_3) = c_1 + \sqrt{c_2 c_3}$. Because $u(2, 1, 1) > u(0, 1, 4)$, we would have that $u(2, w, 1) > u(0, w, 4)$ for every $w \geq 0$ if the independence axiom held. However, for $w = 25$ we have $u(2, 25, 1) < u(0, 25, 4)$. Thus, u does not have a state-dependent expected utility representation.   □

The sufficiency part of Theorem 8.5.1 does not hold in the case of two states. In that case every strictly increasing utility function u on $\mathcal{R}^2$ satisfies the independence axiom. To see this, note that $u(c_1, y) \geq u(d_1, y)$ iff $c_1 \geq d_1$ regardless of y. However, not every utility function of state-contingent consumption in two states has a state-dependent expected utility representation. An axiomatization of state-dependent expected utility with two states can be found in sources cited in the notes.

8.6 Axiomatization of Expected Utility

A strengthening of the independence axiom implies that preferences have a state-independent expected utility representation. The strengthened version is called the *cardinal coordinate independence* axiom. To understand this axiom, suppose that c and d are consumption plans such that

$$u(c_{-s}y) \leq u(d_{-s}w), \tag{8.4}$$

so that the plan including w is preferred to that including y. Now assume that if y is replaced by y' and w by w', the preference is reversed:

$$u(c_{-s}y') \geq u(d_{-s}w'). \tag{8.5}$$

Further, consider any other pair of consumption plans c' and d' that provide the consumptions y and w, respectively, in state t, and are such that $c'_{-t}y$ is preferred to $d'_{-t}w$:

$$u(c'_{-t}y) \geq u(d'_{-t}w). \tag{8.6}$$

Then the axiom of cardinal coordinate independence states that if y' and w' are substituted for y and w, the preference is preserved:

$$u(c'_{-t}y') \geq u(d'_{-t}w'). \tag{8.7}$$

This must be true for any $s, t, c, d, c', d', w, w', y$, and y'.

Cardinal coordinate independence is a stronger assumption than independence. This is worth proving explicitly.

Proposition 8.6.1 *Cardinal coordinate independence implies independence.*

Proof: Set $c = d$, and replace both by c in inequalities (8.4) and (8.5). Set $y = w$, and replace both by w in inequalities (8.4) and (8.6). Set $y' = w'$ and replace both by w' in inequalities (8.5) and (8.7). Then inequalities (8.4) and (8.5) become trivial. Further, inequalities (8.6) and (8.7) become

$$u(c'_{-t}w) \geq u(d'_{-t}w) \tag{8.8}$$

and

$$u(c'_{-t}w') \geq u(d'_{-t}w'). \tag{8.9}$$

If cardinal coordinate independence holds, then inequality (8.8) implies (8.9). Because w, w', and t are arbitrary, we actually have an equivalence of (8.8) and (8.9). This equivalence coincides with the independence axiom (8.3). □

Again, assume that u is strictly increasing and continuous. We have

Theorem 8.6.2 *Utility function u has a state-independent expected utility representation iff it obeys the cardinal coordinate independence axiom.*

Proof: As with Theorem 8.5.1, it can be easily verified that an expected utility satisfies the cardinal coordinate independence axiom. The proof of the reverse implication is not given here. □

In contrast to Theorem 8.5.1, the assumption of at least three states is not needed in Theorem 8.6.2. Cardinal coordinate independence is not vacuous in the case of two states.

Example 8.6.3 Consider the utility function $u : \mathcal{R}^2_+ \to \mathcal{R}$ given by $u(c_1, c_2) = c_1 + \sqrt{c_2}$. The following three pairs of consumption plans are indifferent under this utility function: $(2, 1)$ and $(1, 4)$, $(2, 4)$ and $(1, 9)$, $(1, 16)$ and $(4, 1)$. If the cardinal coordinate independence axiom held, we would have that $(4, 16)$ and $(9, 1)$ are indifferent. However, $4 + \sqrt{16} < 9 + \sqrt{1}$. Consequently, cardinal coordinate independence fails, implying that u does not have an expected utility representation.   □

8.7 Nonexpected Utility

Despite its simplicity and intuitive appeal, expected utility theory has proven to be a poor description of preferences over uncertain consumption plans. There exists ample evidence of behavior that violates the axioms of expected utility. Much effort has been devoted to developing alternatives. Rather than surveying this work, we present a class of nonexpected utility functions that have strong intuitive appeal.

Agents whose preferences have an expected utility representation know, or act as if they knew, probabilities of all states. One might argue that agents do not know exact probabilities of each state but instead have a vague assessment of the probabilities. This leads us to consider agents' beliefs not as a single probability measure π on S but rather as a set P of probability measures on S. The set P is assumed to be closed and convex. An agent's utility function is then defined as

$$u(c) = \min_{\pi \in P} E_\pi[v(c)], \tag{8.10}$$

for some function $v : \mathcal{R} \rightarrow \mathcal{R}$. The preferences represented by u of Eq. (8.10) exhibit uncertainty aversion in the following sense: a smaller set of probabilities increases the agent's utility. Thus, more precise information about probabilities is utility increasing.

The case of an agent who is completely uninformed about probabilities of the states can be described as using the set $\Delta = \{\pi : \sum_1^S \pi_s = 1\}$ of all probability measures on S. In this case

$$\min_{\pi \in \Delta} E_\pi[v(c)] = \min_s v(c_s) \tag{8.11}$$

and represents "maxmin" behavior with extreme uncertainty aversion. Another simple example is the following.

Example 8.7.1 Suppose that the set P of probability measures is given by $P = \{\pi : \pi_s \geq \eta_s, \sum_1^S \pi_s = 1\}$, where $\eta_s \geq 0$ is a lower bound on the probability of state s, and $\sum_1^S \eta_s \leq 1$. One can easily show that

$$\min_{\pi \in P} E_\pi[v(c)] = (1 - \eta) \min_s v(c_s) + \eta E_{\pi^*}[v(c)], \tag{8.12}$$

where $\eta = \sum_1^S \eta_s$, and the probability measure π^* is given by $\pi_s^* = \eta_s/\eta$.   □

Such nonexpected utility functions are not everywhere differentiable. For instance, u is nondifferentiable when consumption is state independent.

8.8 Expected Utility with Two-Date Consumption

In the case of consumption at both dates 0 and 1 the (state-independent) expected utility function takes the form

$$\sum_{s=1}^{S} \pi_s v(c_0, c_s),\qquad(8.13)$$

for some function $v : \mathcal{R}^2 \to \mathcal{R}$. Specification (8.13), which will be written as $E[v(c_0, c_1)]$, displays separability across states but not over time. A general form of expected utility that is additively separable over time is

$$v_0(c_0) + \sum_{s=1}^{S} \pi_s v_1(c_s),\qquad(8.14)$$

for some functions $v_0 : \mathcal{R} \to \mathcal{R}$ and $v_1 : \mathcal{R} \to \mathcal{R}$. A frequently used form of time-separable expected utility is

$$v(c_0) + \delta \sum_{s=1}^{S} \pi_s v(c_s)\qquad(8.15)$$

with time-invariant period utility function $v : \mathcal{R} \to \mathcal{R}$ and $\delta > 0$.

Variations of the cardinal coordinate independence axiom allow derivation of expected utility representations when consumption occurs at more than one date. If the cardinal coordinate independence axiom holds for a strictly increasing and continuous utility function $u : \mathcal{R}^{S+1} \to \mathcal{R}$ with date-0 consumption treated like any other coordinate of a consumption plan, then u has a time-separable expected utility representation (8.15).

The more general representation (8.14) involves additive separability over time and an expected utility representation for date-1. Axiomatization of additive separability with two dates is similar to that of state-dependent expected utility with two states (neither of which is presented here). Once a time-separable representation is achieved, an expected utility representation of the utility of date-1 consumption results when the cardinal coordinate independence axiom is satisfied.

To obtain the representation (8.13) one assumes that agents' preferences are described by a utility function $u : \mathcal{R}^{2S} \to \mathcal{R}$ on state-contingent consumption plans. Here, both date-0 and date-1 consumption are state dependent. The cardinal coordinate independence axiom with two-date consumption in each of S states implies a representation of u in the form $\sum_{s=1}^{S} \pi_s v(c_{0s}, c_s)$. In this setting, a consumption plan with deterministic date-0 consumption is identified by state-independent date-0 consumption, $c_{0s} = c_0$ for every s. Restricting attention to such consumption plans, we obtain the expected utility representation (8.13).

8.9 Notes

For a general discussion of expected utility theory, see Fishburn [4] and Karni and Schmeidler [9].

The major sources for Sections 8.3 and 8.4 are von Neumann–Morgenstern [17] and Savage [15]. The results of Sections 8.5 and 8.6 and their proofs can be found in Debreu [2] and Wakker [18], [19]. An axiomatization of state-dependent expected utility with two states can also be found in Debreu [2] and Wakker [18], [19]. Leontief [11] proved that a differentiable utility function has a state-dependent expected utility representation iff the marginal rate of substitution between consumption in any two states is independent of consumption in other states. For an alternative axiomatization of expected utility with finitely many states (different from the one given in Section 8.6), see Gul [6].

Questionnaires readily elicit responses that are inconsistent with expected utility theory from the large majority of those surveyed. The best-known of these responses are the "Allais paradox" (Allais [1]) and the "Ellsberg paradox" (Ellsberg [3]). For a collection of articles attempting to account for these paradoxes, mostly from a psychological point of view, see Kahneman, Slovic, and Tversky [8].

For a generalization of expected utility theory, and also a general discussion of expected utility theory, see Machina [13]. Axiomatic foundations of the nonexpected utility theory of Section 8.7 can be found in Schmeidler [16] and Gilboa and Schmeidler [5].

The axioms of expected utility do not imply that probability measure π and function v are the same across agents. Nevertheless, we will almost always assume subsequently that π is common across agents because the characterizations of security prices and portfolios are much weaker when agents are assumed to disagree about state probabilities. Hereafter, π is assumed to be common across agents, except as noted.

On a more methodological level, there is something unsatisfying about simply taking as exogenous state probabilities that differ across agents. Suppose that one agent wants to hold long a security another wants to sell short, where the difference in the desired holdings reflects differing state probabilities. Expected utility theory with agent-specific probabilities implies that the transaction will increase both agents' expected utilities. Agents who are not completely naive will, however, be aware that they are able to complete a desirable trade only because they disagree about state probabilities. They will be led to reassess the reliability of the evidence on which their probabilities are based and perhaps revise these probabilities because differently informed agents are arriving at different probabilities.

This line is pursued by assuming that agents start out with common prior probabilities but have differing "naive" posterior distributions – derived by applying

Bayesian updating to the priors – because they have differing information. These posteriors are naive because rational agents will condition their posterior probabilities not only on their own information but also on the knowledge about the information of others as revealed by security prices. In many settings this sophisticated processing of information results in common state probabilities. This suggests that simply assuming differing state probabilities and an absence of sophisticated learning from prices imputes an element of irrationality to agents. The analysis just summarized was originated by Harsanyi [7] and has been developed considerably in recent years.

The association of the term "Knightian uncertainty" with settings in which agents do not act as if they attach subjective probabilities to outcomes – equivalently, under the axioms of choice, in which agents are unable to choose among nondeterministic outcomes – is all but universal in the economics literature. In fact Knight [10] went to some pains to point out that, in his opinion, nothing was to be learned by modeling agents as unable to act in uncertain settings.

LeRoy and Singell [12] documented that Knight, by distinguishing between risk and uncertainty, wished to focus attention on whether markets fail due to moral hazard and adverse selection, not on whether agents can form subjective probabilities. In fact, in later work Knight substituted the term "noninsurable risk" for "uncertainty" (Netter [14]).

Bibliography

[1] Allais, M. Le comportement de l'homme rationnel devant le risque: Critique des postulats et axiomes de l'ecole Americaine. *Econometrica*, **21**:503–46, 1953.

[2] Debreu, G. Topological methods in cardinal utility theory. In Kenneth J. Arrow, Samuel Karlin, and Patrick Suppes, editors, *Mathematical Methods in Social Sciences*. Stanford University Press, 1959.

[3] Ellsberg, D. Risk, ambiguity, and the Savage axioms. *Quarterly Journal of Economics*, **75**:643–69, 1961.

[4] Fishburn, P. C. *Utility Theory for Decision Making*. Wiley, New York, 1970.

[5] Gilboa, I. and Schmeidler, D. Maximin expected utility with nonunique prior. *Journal of Mathematical Economics*, **18**:141–53, 1989.

[6] Gul, F. Savage's theorem with a finite number of states. *Journal of Economic Theory*, **57**:99–110, 1992.

[7] Harsanyi, J. C. Games with incomplete information played by 'Bayesian' players. *Management Science*, **14**:159–82, 1967.

[8] Kahneman, D. Slovic, P., and Tversky, A. *Judgment Under Uncertainty: Heuristics and Biases*. Cambridge University Press, Cambridge, UK, 1982.

[9] Karni, E. and Schmeidler, D. Utility theory with uncertainty. In Werner Hildenbrand and Hugo Sonnenschein, editors, *Handbook of Mathematical Economics, Vol. 4*. North-Holland, Amsterdam, 1991.

[10] Knight, F. H. *Risk, Uncertainty and Profit*. Houghton Mifflin, Boston, 1921.

[11] Leontief, W. A note on interrelation of subsets of independent variables of a continuous function with continuous first derivatives. *Bulletin of the American Mathematical Society*, **53**:343–50, 1947.

[12] LeRoy, S. F. and Singell, L. D. Knight on risk and uncertainty. *Journal of Political Economy*, **95**:394–406, 1987.

[13] Machina, M. Expected utility without the independence axiom. *Econometrica*, **50**:277–323, 1982.

[14] Netter, M. Radical uncertainty and its economic scope according to Knight and according to Keynes. In Christian Schmidt, editor, *Uncertainty in Economic Thought*. Edward Elgar, 1996.

[15] Savage, L. J. *The Foundations of Statistics*. Wiley, New York, 1954.

[16] Schmeidler, D. Subjective probability and expected utility without additivity. *Econometrica*, **57**:571–87, 1989.

[17] von Neumann, J. and Morgenstern, O. *Theory of Games and Economic Behavior*. Princeton University Press, Princeton, NJ, 1947.

[18] Wakker, P. P. Cardinal coordinate independence for expected utility. *Journal of Mathematical Psychology*, **28**:110–17, 1984.

[19] Wakker, P. P. *Additive Representations of Preferences*. Kluwer, Amsterdam, 1989.

9

Risk Aversion

9.1 Introduction

Expected utility provides a framework for the analysis of agents' attitudes toward risk. In this chapter we present a formal definition of risk aversion and introduce measures of the intensity of risk aversion such as the Arrow–Pratt measures and risk compensation. The main result of this chapter, the Pratt Theorem, establishes the equivalence of these different measures of risk aversion.

Agents' preferences over risky consumption plans are assumed to have an expected utility representation with continuous von Neumann–Morgenstern utility functions. The consumption plans in the domain of an expected utility function may be defined either narrowly or broadly. The axioms of expected utility imply that any consumption plan can be viewed as a random variable on the set S of states equipped with an agent's subjective probability measure. Thus, if the objects of choice are specified as the consumption plans that emerge from the axioms of expected utility, these are appropriately defined narrowly as random variables that can take S values with given probabilities. However, the analysis of this chapter applies equally well if consumption plans are broadly interpreted as arbitrary random variables (that is, as random variables with an arbitrary number of realizations and arbitrary probabilities). The choice between these interpretations is a matter of taste.

Except in Section 9.10, it is assumed that date-0 consumption does not enter the utility functions, and throughout it is assumed that there are at least two states at date 1, $S \geq 2$.

9.2 Risk Aversion and Risk Neutrality

An agent's attitude toward risk is characterized by his or her preference between a risky consumption plan and the deterministic consumption plan equal to the expectation of the risky plan.

An agent with von Neumann–Morgenstern utility function $v : \mathcal{R} \to \mathcal{R}$ is *risk averse* if he or she prefers the expectation of any consumption plan to the consumption plan itself; that is,

$$E[v(c)] \leq v(E(c)) \tag{9.1}$$

for every consumption plan c.

An agent is *risk neutral* if

$$E[v(c)] = v(E(c)) \tag{9.2}$$

for every consumption plan c.

An agent is *strictly risk averse* if

$$E[v(c)] < v(E(c)) \tag{9.3}$$

for every nondeterministic consumption plan c.

Our term *risk aversion* means "weak risk aversion" because only weak preference is required in inequality (9.1). Note that in this usage risk neutrality is a special case of risk aversion.

An agent may be neither risk averse nor risk neutral nor strictly risk averse and may prefer some nondeterministic consumption plans to the expectations of the plans. Also, an agent may be risk averse but neither risk neutral nor strictly risk averse; he or she may strictly prefer the expectation of some nondeterministic consumption plans to the plans themselves but be indifferent for others.

9.3 Risk Aversion and Concavity

Risk aversion, risk neutrality, and strict risk aversion can be characterized by, respectively, concavity, linearity, and strict concavity of the von Neumann–Morgenstern utility function:

Theorem 9.3.1

  (i) *An agent is risk averse iff his or her von Neumann–Morgenstern utility function v is concave.*

 (ii) *An agent is risk neutral iff his or her von Neumann–Morgenstern utility function v is linear.*

(iii) *An agent is strictly risk averse iff his or her von Neumann–Morgenstern utility function v is strictly concave.*

Proof: (i) If v is concave, then inequality (9.1) holds (it is *Jensen's inequality*), and the agent is risk averse. The proof of the converse is straightforward if consumption plans in definition (9.1) are arbitrary random variables. We present a proof that applies when consumption plans take S values with given probabilities. Suppose

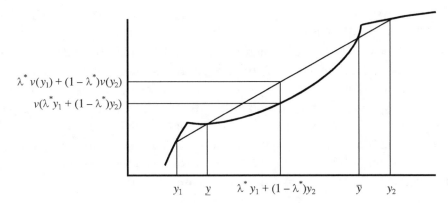

Figure 9.1 Construction of a consumption plan c such that $v(E(c)) < E[v(c)]$ if v is not concave.

that the agent is risk averse but v is not concave. Then there exist y_1, y_2 and λ^* satisfying $0 < \lambda^* < 1$ such that

$$v(\lambda^* y_1 + (1 - \lambda^*)y_2) < \lambda^* v(y_1) + (1 - \lambda^*)v(y_2) \qquad (9.4)$$

(Figure 9.1). Consider the set of λ satisfying $0 \leq \lambda \leq \lambda^*$ and

$$v(\lambda y_1 + (1 - \lambda)y_2) = \lambda v(y_1) + (1 - \lambda)v(y_2). \qquad (9.5)$$

This set is nonempty ($\lambda = 0$ is an element) and closed because v is continuous. Therefore, there exists a supremum denoted by $\underline{\lambda}$. Similarly, there exists an infimum of the set of λ satisfying $\lambda^* \leq \lambda \leq 1$ and Eq. (9.5). Let $\bar{\lambda}$ denote that infimum. We have $\underline{\lambda} < \lambda^* < \bar{\lambda}$ and

$$v(\lambda y_1 + (1 - \lambda)y_2) < \lambda v(y_1) + (1 - \lambda)v(y_2) \qquad (9.6)$$

for every $\underline{\lambda} < \lambda < \bar{\lambda}$.

Let $\underline{y} = \underline{\lambda} y_1 + (1 - \underline{\lambda})y_2$ and $\bar{y} = \bar{\lambda} y_1 + (1 - \bar{\lambda})y_2$. It follows from inequality (9.6) that

$$v(\gamma \underline{y} + (1 - \gamma)\bar{y}) < \gamma v(\underline{y}) + (1 - \gamma)v(\bar{y}) \qquad (9.7)$$

for every $0 < \gamma < 1$.

Consider consumption plan c that takes value $\underline{y}$ in some (but not all) states and value $\bar{y}$ in the remaining states. Note that the deterministic consumption plan $E(c)$ lies in the interval $(\underline{y}, \bar{y})$. Using inequality (9.7), we obtain

$$v[E(c)] < E[v(c)], \qquad (9.8)$$

which contradicts the assumption of risk aversion.

(ii) If v is of the linear form $v(y) = ay + b$, then Eq. (9.2) holds, and the agent is risk neutral. The proof of the converse is very similar to the proof in part (i). The only difference is that the assumption that v is nonlinear implies that either inequality (9.4) holds or the opposite strict inequality holds. Both cases lead to a contradiction of risk neutrality.

(iii) If v is strictly concave, then inequality (9.3) holds (it is *Jensen's strict inequality*), and the agent is strictly risk averse. To show the converse, suppose that the agent is strictly risk averse but v is not strictly concave. If v is linear on some interval $[y_1, y_2]$ with $y_1 < y_2$, then it follows from part (ii) that $v[E(c)] = E[v(c)]$ for any consumption plan that takes values in that interval. This contradicts strict risk aversion. Otherwise, if v is not linear on any nondegenerate interval in its domain, then the strict inequality (9.4) must hold. The proof in part (i) leads to a contradiction with strict risk aversion in this case.   □

9.4 Arrow–Pratt Measures of Absolute Risk Aversion

Risk aversion affects agents' portfolio choices and equilibrium security prices. It is useful to have a measure of the intensity of risk aversion. In light of Theorem 9.3.1, the candidate that comes to mind is the second derivative v'' of the von Neumann–Morgenstern utility function. However, the second derivative is not invariant to affine transformations of v. As noted in Chapter 8, a strictly increasing affine transformation of the von Neumann–Morgenstern utility function does not change preferences. Therefore, such a transformation should not change the measure of risk aversion. The *Arrow–Pratt measure of absolute risk aversion* is defined by

$$A(y) \equiv -\frac{v''(y)}{v'(y)} \tag{9.9}$$

for a scalar variable y such that $v'(y) \neq 0$. It is invariant to strictly increasing affine transformations of the utility function v.

If nonzero, the reciprocal of the Arrow–Pratt measure of absolute risk aversion

$$T(y) \equiv \frac{1}{A(y)} \tag{9.10}$$

can be used as a measure of *risk tolerance*.

9.5 Risk Compensation

Another measure of risk aversion that is closely related to the Arrow–Pratt measure of absolute risk aversion is risk compensation. We define risk compensation as the amount of deterministic consumption one would have to charge an agent in exchange for relieving him or her of a risk (Figure 9.2, where the risk has payoff plus or minus 1 with equal probability). In nonfinance applications of the theory of choice under uncertainty, this variable is almost always referred to as the *risk*

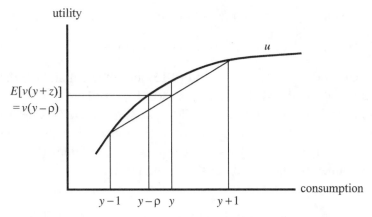

Figure 9.2 Here z takes on values of plus or minus 1 with equal porbability. The expected utility of $y + z$ equals the utility of $y - \rho$, and thus ρ is the compensation for risk z.

premium. Here and in other finance applications, however, the term *risk premium* refers to the expected return on a security less the risk-free return.

The *risk compensation* for the additional consumption plan ("risk") z at deterministic initial consumption y is the value $\rho(y, z)$ that satisfies

$$E[v(y + z)] = v(y - \rho(y, z)), \tag{9.11}$$

and thus the deterministic consumption $y - \rho(y, z)$ is the certainty equivalent of risky consumption $y + z$.

Note that an agent is risk averse iff risk compensation $\rho(y, z)$ is positive (that is, strictly positive or zero) for every y and every risk z with $E(z) = 0$. An agent is risk neutral iff risk compensation is zero for all risks z with $E(z) = 0$.

For small risk z, risk compensation $\rho(y, z)$ equals approximately half the product of the variance σ_z^2 of z and the Arrow–Pratt measure of absolute risk aversion at y.

Theorem 9.5.1 *For small z with $E(z) = 0$,*

$$\rho(y, z) \cong \frac{A(y)\sigma_z^2}{2}. \tag{9.12}$$

Proof: The quadratic approximation of $v(y + z)$ is

$$v(y + z) \cong v(y) + v'(y)z + v''(y)\frac{z^2}{2}. \tag{9.13}$$

Taking expectations, we obtain

$$E[v(y + z)] \cong v(y) + v''(y)\frac{\sigma_z^2}{2}. \tag{9.14}$$

Similarly, a linear expansion of the right-hand side of Eq. (9.11) yields

$$v(y - \rho(y, z)) \cong v(y) - v'(y)\rho(y, z). \tag{9.15}$$

If the left-hand sides of Eqs. (9.14) and (9.15) are set equal and the definition of the measure of absolute risk aversion A is used, Eq. (9.12) results.

The forms of approximation used in Eqs. (9.13) and (9.15) reveal the meaning of "small" in the statement of Theorem 9.5.1. For random variable z, small means that the variance is of first-order significance. Approximations (9.13) and (9.15) take into account only the first-order significant terms.   □

9.6 The Pratt Theorem

The two measures of risk aversion – the Arrow–Pratt measure and risk compensation – can be used to compare the risk aversion of two agents. An important theorem says that comparisons using the Arrow–Pratt measure and risk compensation always give the same result. Further, one agent is more risk averse than another if the von Neumann–Morgenstern utility function of the first is a concave transformation of that of the second.

Let v_1 and v_2 be two von Neumann–Morgenstern utility functions on $\mathcal{R}$, and let ρ_i and A_i denote the risk compensation and the Arrow–Pratt measure of absolute risk aversion, respectively, of v_i for $i = 1, 2$.

We have

Theorem 9.6.1 *Suppose that utility functions v_1 and v_2 are twice differentiable with continuous second derivatives and strictly increasing. Then, the following conditions are equivalent:*

(i) $A_1(y) \geq A_2(y)$ for every y.
(ii) $\rho_1(y, z) \geq \rho_2(y, z)$ for every y and every random variable z.
(iii) v_1 is a concave transformation of v_2; that is, $v_1 = f \circ v_2$ for f concave and strictly increasing.

Proof: We first show that (i) implies (iii). Because v_2 is strictly increasing, the inverse function v_2^{-1} exists, and the function f of (iii) is defined by $f(t) = v_1(v_2^{-1}(t))$.

We have to show now that f is strictly increasing and concave. The derivative of f is

$$f'(t) = \frac{v_1'\left(v_2^{-1}(t)\right)}{v_2'\left(v_2^{-1}(t)\right)} \tag{9.16}$$

and is strictly positive because $v_i' > 0$ for $i = 1, 2$. Calculation of the second derivative of f yields

$$f''(t) = \frac{v_1''(y) - (v_2''(y)v_1'(y))/v_2'(y)}{[v_2'(y)]^2}, \tag{9.17}$$

where $y = v_2^{-1}(t)$. This can be rewritten as

$$f''(t) = (A_2(y) - A_1(y))\frac{v_1'(y)}{[v_2'(y)]^2}. \tag{9.18}$$

Thus $f'' \leq 0$, and hence f is concave.

Next we show that (*iii*) implies (*ii*). By the definition of risk compensation we have

$$E[v_1(y + z)] = v_1(y - \rho_1(y, z)). \tag{9.19}$$

Because $v_1 = f \circ v_2$ and f is concave, application of Jensen's inequality yields

$$E[v_1(y + z)] = E\{f[v_2(y + z)]\} \leq f\{E[v_2(y + z)]\}. \tag{9.20}$$

The right-hand side of inequality (9.20) equals $f[v_2(y - \rho_2(y, z))]$. Combining inequality (9.20) with Eq. (9.19) yields

$$v_1(y - \rho_1(y, z)) \leq v_1(y - \rho_2(y, z)). \tag{9.21}$$

Because v_1 is strictly increasing, inequality (9.21) implies $\rho_1(y, z) \geq \rho_2(y, z)$.

Finally, we show that (*ii*) implies (*i*). Suppose that

$$A_1(y^*) < A_2(y^*) \tag{9.22}$$

for some y^*. Because A_1 and A_2 are continuous, there is an interval around y^* such that $A_1(y) < A_2(y)$ for every y in this interval. Using the arguments of the proofs above with interchanged roles of v_1 and v_2, it can be shown that $\rho_1(y, z) < \rho_2(y, z)$ whenever $y + z$ takes values in that interval. This contradicts (*ii*). □

We emphasize again that the set of random variables z in Theorem 9.6.1 (condition (*ii*)) can be either the set of all random variables on the set of states S with given probabilities or the set of all arbitrary random variables. Note also that no restriction on consumption has been imposed in Theorem 9.6.1. Therefore, the theorem is valid as stated only for utility functions defined on the entire real line. However, the same equivalence holds for utility functions defined only for positive (strictly positive) consumption when risk z in (*ii*) is such that $y + z$ is positive (strictly positive).

There is also a strict version of Theorem 9.6.1. The equivalence of conditions (*i*), (*ii*), and (*iii*) remains valid if the inequalities in (*i*) and (*ii*) are strict, and the transformation f in (*iii*) is strictly concave as well as strictly increasing.

Further, there is an equality version of Theorem 9.6.1: conditions (*i*), (*ii*), and (*iii*) remain equivalent with equalities in (*i*) and (*ii*) and strictly increasing affine transformation f in (*iii*). This version is a simple corollary to 9.6.1. It implies that if two utility functions have equal Arrow–Pratt measures of risk aversion, then each is a strictly increasing affine transformation of the other. For instance, the only constant absolute risk aversion utility function is (up to a strictly increasing affine transformation) the negative exponential function. Because a strictly increasing affine transformation of a utility function describes the same expected utility preferences, the Arrow–Pratt measure completely characterizes preferences.

9.7 Decreasing, Constant, and Increasing Risk Aversion

If absolute risk aversion $A(y)$ of an agent is decreasing in y, then he or she has *decreasing absolute risk aversion*. If $A(y)$ is constant (increasing) in y, the agent has *constant (increasing) absolute risk aversion*.

The Pratt theorem implies that an equivalent expression of decreasing (constant, increasing) absolute risk aversion is that risk compensation $\rho(y, z)$ is decreasing (constant, increasing) in y for every z.

Corollary 9.7.1 *For a strictly increasing and twice-differentiable (with continuous second derivative) utility function v,*

(*i*) $\rho(y, z)$ *is increasing in y for every z iff $A(y)$ is increasing in y.*
(*ii*) $\rho(y, z)$ *is constant in y for every z iff $A(y)$ is constant in y.*
(*iii*) $\rho(y, z)$ *is decreasing in y for every z iff $A(y)$ is decreasing in y.*

Proof: Let us define utility function v_1 by $v_1(y) \equiv v(y + \Delta y)$ for some $\Delta y \geq 0$. The Arrow–Pratt measure of absolute risk aversion and the risk compensation of v_1 are $A_1(y) = A(y + \Delta y)$ and $\rho_1(y, z) = \rho(y + \Delta y, z)$. Applying Pratt's theorem 9.6.1 to v_1 and v yields that $A(y + \Delta y) \geq A(y)$ iff $\rho(y + \Delta y, z) \geq \rho(y, z)$. Because Δy is arbitrary, (*i*) follows.

The proofs of (*ii*) and (*iii*) are similar. $\qquad\qquad\square$

9.8 Relative Risk Aversion

Sometimes it is of interest to measure risk aversion relative to the initial consumption. There are two measures of relative risk aversion the Arrow–Pratt measure of relative risk aversion and relative risk compensation.

The *Arrow–Pratt measure of relative risk aversion* is defined by

$$R(y) \equiv -\frac{v''(y)}{v'(y)} y, \tag{9.23}$$

and thus $R(y) = yA(y)$.

The *relative risk compensation* for the relative risk z at deterministic initial consumption y is the value $\rho_r(y, z)$ that satisfies

$$E[v(y + yz)] = v(y - y\rho_r(y, z)). \tag{9.24}$$

Relative risk compensation ρ_r is related to (absolute) risk compensation ρ via

$$\rho_r(y, z) = \frac{\rho(y, yz)}{y}. \tag{9.25}$$

For small relative risk z with $E(z) = 0$, it follows from Theorem 9.5.1 that

$$\rho_r(y, z) \cong \frac{R(y)\sigma_z^2}{2}. \tag{9.26}$$

The parallel forms of approximations (9.12) and (9.26) provide a motivation for definition (9.23) of the measure R of relative risk aversion.

A version of Pratt's theorem holds for relative risk aversion: comparisons of relative risk aversion of two agents using the Arrow–Pratt measure and the relative risk compensation always give the same result. A reference is given in the notes.

9.9 Utility Functions with Linear Risk Tolerance

The functions most often used as von Neumann–Morgenstern utility functions in applied work and as examples are linear utility and the following utility functions:

- *Negative exponential utility.* The utility function

$$v(y) = -e^{-\alpha y}, \tag{9.27}$$

  for $\alpha > 0$, has absolute risk aversion that is constant and equal to α.
- *Logarithmic utility.* The utility function

$$v(y) = \ln(y + \alpha), \quad -\alpha < y, \tag{9.28}$$

  has absolute risk aversion that is decreasing and equal to $1/(y + \alpha)$. If α equals zero, relative risk aversion equals one.
- *Power utility.* The utility function

$$v(y) = \frac{1}{\gamma - 1}(\alpha + \gamma y)^{1-\frac{1}{\gamma}}, \quad -\alpha < \gamma y, \tag{9.29}$$

for $\gamma \neq 0$ and $\gamma \neq 1$, has absolute risk aversion equal to $1/(\alpha + \gamma y)$. If $\gamma > 0$, absolute risk aversion is decreasing. Otherwise, if $\gamma < 0$, it is increasing. If α equals zero, relative risk aversion equals γ.

A special case of power utility is *quadratic utility*. For $\gamma = -1$

$$v(y) = -\frac{1}{2}(\alpha - y)^2, \quad y < \alpha, \tag{9.30}$$

with absolute risk aversion that is increasing and equal to $1/(\alpha - y)$.

Logarithmic and negative exponential utility can be viewed as limiting cases of power utility when γ approaches 1 or 0. If the power utility function is written as

$$v(y) = \frac{1}{\gamma - 1}\left[(\alpha + \gamma y)^{1-\frac{1}{\gamma}} - 1\right], \tag{9.31}$$

which is an affine transformation of (9.29), then by using l'Hopital's rule it can be shown that $v(y)$ converges to $\ln(y + \alpha)$ as γ approaches one. If a different affine transformation of (9.29) is considered,

$$v(y) = \frac{1}{\gamma - 1}\left(1 + \frac{\gamma y}{\alpha}\right)^{1-\frac{1}{\gamma}}, \tag{9.32}$$

where $\alpha > 0$, then $v(y)$ converges to $-e^{-y/\alpha}$ as γ approaches zero.

All these utility functions are strictly increasing, strictly concave, and have risk tolerance that depends linearly on consumption (strictly, the dependence is affine, not linear). For the negative exponential utility function (9.27), risk tolerance is constant, $T(y) = 1/\alpha$; for the logarithmic utility function (9.28), risk tolerance is $T(y) = y + \alpha$; for the power utility function (9.29), risk tolerance is $T(y) = \alpha + \gamma y$. These utility functions are called *linear risk tolerance* (LRT) utility functions (alternatively, HARA utility functions, where HARA stands for hyperbolic absolute risk aversion because $A(y)$ defines a hyperbola).

The domain of an LRT utility function can be conveniently written as $\{y : T(y) > 0\}$. Note that the parameter γ (with $\gamma = 0$ for the negative exponential utility function and $\gamma = 1$ for the logarithmic utility function) is the slope of the risk tolerance function.

The LRT utility functions have many attractive properties, as will be seen in Chapters 13 and 16.

9.10 Risk Aversion with Two-Date Consumption

The definitions of risk aversion and risk neutrality can easily be adapted to the case in which date-0 consumption enters agents' utility functions.

An agent with von Neumann–Morgenstern utility function $v : \mathcal{R}^2 \rightarrow \mathcal{R}$ is risk averse if

$$E[v(c_0, c_1)] \leq v(c_0, E(c_1)), \tag{9.33}$$

for every c_0 and every c_1, and is risk neutral if

$$E[v(c_0, c_1)] = v(c_0, E(c_1)), \tag{9.34}$$

for every c_0 and every c_1.

By Theorem 9.3.1 an agent is risk averse iff the von Neumann–Morgenstern utility function $v(y_0, y_1)$ is concave in y_1 for every y_0 and risk neutral iff $v(y_0, y_1)$ is linear in y_1 for every y_0. For instance, utility functions $v(y_0, y_1) = y_0 + \delta y_1$ and $v(y_0, y_1) = y_0 y_1$ imply risk neutrality.

When v is not additively separable over time, the measures of date-1 risk aversion of Section 9.4 depend on date-0 consumption. Consequently, an agent can be risk neutral in date-1 consumption for some values of c_0 and strictly risk averse for others, for example. In the case of time-separable expected utility (8.14), an agent's attitude toward date-1 risk depends only on the form of the date-1 utility function v_1; the level of date-0 consumption is irrelevant.

For a time-separable power utility function (with $\alpha = 0$),

$$v(y_0, y_1) = \frac{1}{\gamma - 1} \left[(\gamma y_0)^{1 - \frac{1}{\gamma}} + (\gamma y_1)^{1 - \frac{1}{\gamma}} \right], \tag{9.35}$$

where $\gamma \neq 0, 1$, the measure of absolute (date-1) risk aversion is $1/\gamma y_1$ and depends only on y_1; the measure of relative (date-1) risk aversion is γ. Note that the marginal rate of substitution between date-0 consumption and date-1 consumption under this power utility function is $(y_1/y_0)^{-1/\gamma}$, and the elasticity of substitution is $1/\gamma$. Thus, the elasticity of substitution depends on the coefficient of relative risk aversion. In general, the intertemporal elasticity of substitution and the coefficient of risk aversion are interdependent under the expected utility representation.

9.11 Notes

The equivalences proved in Theorem 9.3.1 between risk aversion (strict risk aversion, risk neutrality) and concavity (strict concavity, linearity) of utility function are also an implication of the Pratt Theorem (take $v_1 = v$ and linear v_2). However, the Pratt Theorem applies only to differentiable utility functions, whereas Theorem 9.3.1 applies to all continuous utility functions.

The Arrow–Pratt measures of absolute and relative risk aversion were proposed in Arrow [1], [2] and Pratt [6]. The Pratt Theorem is found in Pratt [6]. A version of the Pratt Theorem for relative risk aversion can also be found in Pratt [6].

An illuminating discussion of measures of risk aversion can be found in Yaari [8].

Measures of risk aversion introduced in this chapter are based on the assumption that a risk-free payoff is attainable. More general measures that apply when a risk-free payoff is not attainable have been proposed by Ross [7]; see also Machina and Neilsen [5]. Cohen [3] discussed concepts of risk aversion without the expected utility representation of preferences.

Kihlstrom and Mirman [4] addressed problems in extending the Arrow–Pratt theory of risk aversion to multivariate risks (for example, state-contingent consumption plans with multiple goods).

Bibliography

[1] Arrow, K. J. Comment. *Review of Economics and Statistics*, **45**, Supplement:24–7, 1963.

[2] Arrow, K. J. *Aspects of the Theory of Risk Bearing*. Yrjo Jahnssonin Saatio, Helsinki, 1965.

[3] Cohen, M. D. Risk-aversion concepts in expected- and non-expected utility models. *The Geneva Papers on Risk and Insurance Theory*, **20**:73–91, 1995.

[4] Kihlstrom, R. E. and Mirman, L. J. Risk aversion with many commodities. *Journal of Economic Theory*, **8**:361–88, 1974.

[5] Machina, M. J. and Neilsen, W. S. The Ross characterization of risk aversion: Strengthening and extension. *Econometrica*, **55**:1139–49, 1987.

[6] Pratt, J. W. Risk aversion in the small and in the large. *Econometrica*, **32**:122–36, 1964.

[7] Ross, S. A. Some stronger measures of risk aversion in the small and in the large with applications. *Econometrica*, **49**:621–38, 1981.

[8] Yaari, M. Some remarks on measures of risk aversion and on their uses. *Journal of Economic Theory*, **55**:95–115, 1969.

10

Risk

10.1 Introduction

In Chapter 9 we defined an agent as risk averse if he or she prefers the expectation of a consumption plan to the consumption plan itself. The consumption plan is obviously riskier than its expectation, and a risk-averse agent prefers the latter.

A natural extension of this discussion is to consider a risk-averse agent who compares two consumption plans, neither of which is deterministic. In general, without more information about an agent's preferences, two risky consumption plans cannot be ranked: some risk-averse agents prefer one and some the other. However, in the spirit of the discussion of Chapter 9, it is appropriate to ask whether there is some condition on the distribution of two consumption plans such that if the two consumption plans have the same expectation, then all risk-averse agents do prefer one to the other. In Section 10.2 an ordering on consumption plans is defined which, as will be seen in Section 10.5, has the desired property.

In this chapter, we assume that date-0 consumption does not enter the utility functions.

10.2 Greater Risk

Let y and z be two (date-1) consumption plans. As in Chapter 9, these consumption plans can be viewed narrowly as random variables on the set of states S with given probabilities or broadly as arbitrary random variables (with finite expectations).

Consumption plan y is *riskier* than consumption plan z if there exists a random variable ϵ such that

$$y - E(y) =^d z - E(z) + \epsilon \quad \text{and} \quad E(\epsilon|z) = E(\epsilon) = 0. \tag{10.1}$$

If Eq. (10.1) holds, and in addition ϵ is not the zero random variable, then y is *strictly riskier* than z.

The symbol $=^d$ means that the left-hand side equals the right-hand side in distribution; that is, the left-hand side is a random variable that takes the same values with the same probabilities as the random variable defined by the right-hand side. The condition $E(\epsilon|z) = E(\epsilon)$ states that ϵ is *mean independent* of z. That is, the expectation of ϵ conditional on (any realization of) z does not depend on z.

Equality in distribution is a much weaker condition than equality: two random variables are equal if they take on the same value in every state, which is sufficient, but not necessary, for equality in distribution. For example, a payoff consisting of 0 in state 1 and 1 in state 2 is equal in distribution to a payoff of 1 in state 1 and 0 in state 2 if the two states are equally probable. These payoffs are not equal because they do not coincide in every state.

Example 10.2.1 Let z take on values of plus or minus 1 with equal probabilities and ϵ take on values of 1 and -3 with probabilities $3/4$ and $1/4$ when $z = 1$, and values of 3 and -1 with probabilities $1/4$ and $3/4$ when $z = -1$. Then $2z$ and $z + \epsilon$ have the same distributions. Because ϵ is mean independent of z, Eq. (10.1) is satisfied with y equal to $2z$. Therefore, $2z$ is strictly riskier than z. Obviously $2z$ and $z + \epsilon$ are not equal as random variables, for then z would equal ϵ, which is not the case.   □

Our definition of one consumption plan being riskier than another is a condition on the deviations of those plans from the respective expectations. Therefore, it is not necessary that the consumption plans have the same expectation. Note that y is riskier than z iff $y - E(y)$ is riskier than $z - E(z)$ or, equivalently, iff y is riskier than $z - E(z) + E(y)$. Any consumption plan is riskier than its expectation, and any nondeterministic consumption plan is strictly riskier than its expectation.

10.3 Uncorrelatedness, Mean Independence, and Independence

The condition of mean-independence defined in Section 10.1 is a stronger restriction than uncorrelatedness. However, it is less strong than independence. Independence implies mean independence, but the converse is not true. In Example 10.2.1, ϵ is mean independent of z but not independent of z. This is so because the distribution of ϵ conditional on z depends on the realization of z even though the conditional expectation of ϵ is zero for both values of z. Similarly, mean independence implies uncorrelatedness, but again the converse is not true. For example, suppose that the pair (z, ϵ) takes on values $(1, 1)$, $(2, 0)$, and $(3, 1)$ with equal probabilities. Here ϵ is uncorrelated with z but not mean independent of z.

Uncorrelatedness and independence are symmetric. If z is uncorrelated with (independent of) ϵ, then ϵ is uncorrelated with (independent of) z. Mean independence, however, is not symmetric. The fact that z is mean independent of ϵ does not imply that ϵ is mean independent of z.

When the joint distribution of z and ϵ is bivariate normal, then uncorrelatedness, mean independence, and independence are all equivalent.

10.4 A Property of Mean Independence

A useful property of mean independence is the following:

Proposition 10.4.1 *If ϵ is mean independent of z, then*

$$E[f(z)\epsilon] = E[f(z)]E(\epsilon). \tag{10.2}$$

for any function f.

Proof: The expectation of $f(z)\epsilon$ over the joint distribution of z and ϵ can be taken first over the distribution of ϵ conditional on z and then over the marginal distribution of z:

$$E[f(z)\epsilon] = E[E(f(z)\epsilon|z)]. \tag{10.3}$$

Here $f(z)$ can be passed out of the inner expectation, resulting in

$$E[f(z)\epsilon] = E[f(z)E(\epsilon|z)]. \tag{10.4}$$

The rightmost term equals $E[f(z)]E(\epsilon)$ by mean independence.   □

If ϵ is uncorrelated with z, then Eq. (10.2) holds for any linear function f. The stronger assumption of mean independence is needed to ensure that Eq. (10.2) is valid even when f is nonlinear. It is worth pointing out that if ϵ is mean independent of z, then it is also mean independent of $f(z)$.

10.5 Risk and Risk Aversion

The motivation for our definition of risk is that every risk-averse agent prefers a less risky consumption plan to a more risky one if the two have the same expectation:

Theorem 10.5.1 *For consumption plans y and z that have the same expectation, y is riskier than z iff every risk-averse agent prefers z to y.*

Proof: If y is riskier than z and they have the same expectation, Eq. (10.1) becomes $y =^d z + \epsilon$, where $E(\epsilon|z) = 0$. For utility function v (the domain of which includes the values that y and z take on) we have

$$E[v(y)] = E[v(z + \epsilon)] = E\{E[v(z + \epsilon)|z]\}. \tag{10.5}$$

If v is concave so that the agent is risk averse, Jensen's inequality implies that

$$E[v(z + \epsilon|z)] \leq v(E(z + \epsilon|z)) = v(z). \tag{10.6}$$

Taking expectations, we obtain

$$E[v(y)] \leq E[v(z)]. \tag{10.7}$$

The proof of the converse, that if every risk-averse agent prefers z to y, where $E(y) = E(z)$, then y is riskier than z, is much more difficult. The proof can be found in the sources cited in the notes at the end of this chapter. $\square$

Note that risk-averse agents' utility functions in Theorem 10.5.1 are not assumed to be increasing. However, the result remains true if one takes only risk-averse agents with increasing utility functions. For a discussion of this point see the notes.

There is a strict version of Theorem 10.5.1.

Theorem 10.5.2 *For consumption plans z and y that have the same expectation, y is strictly riskier than z iff every strictly risk-averse agent strictly prefers z to y.*

Both parts of the equivalence of Theorem 10.5.2 are useful: sometimes one knows that y is strictly riskier than z and uses the necessity part of Theorem 10.5.2 to infer that all strictly risk-averse agents strictly prefer z to y, whereas sometimes one knows that all strictly risk-averse agents strictly prefer z to y, and therefore the sufficiency part of the theorem is used to infer that y is strictly riskier than z.

The following two examples illustrate the use of Theorem 10.5.2.

Example 10.5.3 Let y and z be two nondeterministic consumption plans with independent and identical distributions. We show here that every strictly risk-averse agent strictly prefers the equally weighted average $(y + z)/2$ to any other weighted average of y and z (and also, therefore, to y and z themselves).

Let $ay + (1 - a)z$ denote an arbitrary weighted average of y and z (which equals y when $a = 1$ and z when $a = 0$). We can write

$$ay + (1 - a)z = \frac{y + z}{2} + \left(a - \frac{1}{2}\right)(y - z). \tag{10.8}$$

We have

$$E(y - z|y + z) = E(y|y + z) - E(z|y + z), \tag{10.9}$$

and

$$E(y|y + z) = E(z|y + z), \tag{10.10}$$

because y and z are independent and have identical distributions. Therefore $(a - \frac{1}{2})(y - z)$ is mean independent of $(y + z)/2$ and has zero expectation. By Eq. (10.1), if $a \neq 1/2$, then $ay + (1 - a)z$ is strictly riskier than $(y + z)/2$. By the necessity part of Theorem 10.5.2, every strictly risk-averse agent strictly prefers the equally weighted average. □

Example 10.5.4 For any nondeterministic consumption plan z, $2z$ is strictly riskier than z. To see this, observe first that

$$v(z + E(z)) > \frac{1}{2}v(2z) + \frac{1}{2}v(2E(z)), \tag{10.11}$$

for every strictly concave v, for $z + E(z)$ is an (equally weighted) average of $2z$ and $2E(z)$. Here inequality (10.11) is to be interpreted as a vector inequality rather than state-by-state (strict inequality holds only in states s for which $z_s \neq E(z)$). Taking expectations on both sides of inequality (10.11), we obtain

$$E[v(z + E(z))] > \frac{1}{2}E[v(2z)] + \frac{1}{2}v(2E(z)). \tag{10.12}$$

Jensen's inequality implies that

$$v(2E(z)) > E[v(2z)]. \tag{10.13}$$

Substituting inequality (10.13) in (10.12) results in

$$E[v(z + E(z))] > E[v(2z)]. \tag{10.14}$$

The sufficiency part of Theorem 10.5.2 implies that $2z$ is strictly riskier than $z + E(z)$. Because expectations do not matter, it follows that $2z$ is strictly riskier than z. □

An argument similar to that of Example 10.5.4 can be used to prove a result that will be used later.

Proposition 10.5.5 *For any consumption plan z, if $\epsilon \neq 0$ is mean independent of z and $E(\epsilon) = 0$, then $z + \lambda\epsilon$ is strictly riskier than $z + \gamma\epsilon$ for every $\lambda > \gamma \geq 0$.*

Proof: Let $a = \gamma/\lambda$. Then

$$z + \gamma\epsilon = a(z + \lambda\epsilon) + (1 - a)z. \tag{10.15}$$

Because $0 \leq a < 1$, for every strictly concave utility function v we have

$$v(z + \gamma\epsilon) > av(z + \lambda\epsilon) + (1 - a)v(z) \tag{10.16}$$

(again, this inequality is to be interpreted as a vector inequality). Taking expectations on both sides of inequality (10.16), we obtain

$$E[v(z + \gamma\epsilon)] > aE[v(z + \lambda\epsilon)] + (1 - a)E[v(z)]. \qquad (10.17)$$

Because $z + \lambda\epsilon$ is strictly riskier than z, we have $E[v(z)] > E[v(z + \lambda\epsilon)]$. Using this inequality in (10.17), we obtain

$$E[v(z + \gamma\epsilon)] > E[v(z + \lambda\epsilon)]. \qquad (10.18)$$

Theorem 10.5.2 implies that $z + \lambda\epsilon$ is strictly riskier than $z + \gamma\epsilon$.   □

Note that, because expectations do not matter in orderings by riskiness, Proposition 10.5.5 remains true for any $\epsilon \neq 0$ that is mean independent of z even if $E(\epsilon) \neq 0$. A corollary to Proposition 10.5.5 provides an extension of Example 10.5.4.

Corollary 10.5.6 *For any nondeterministic consumption plan z, λz is strictly riskier than z for every $\lambda > 1$.*

Proof: Proposition 10.5.5 implies that $0 + \lambda[z - E(z)]$ is strictly riskier than $0 + [z - E(z)]$ for every $\lambda > 1$ and nondeterministic z. Because expectations do not matter, λz is strictly riskier than z.   □

10.6 Greater Risk and Variance

A simple and frequently used measure of risk is variance. It follows from the definition of greater risk (Eq. (10.1)) that if one consumption plan is riskier than another, then it also has higher variance. The converse is not true: a consumption plan that has higher variance than another consumption plan need not be riskier. We present an example of two consumption plans that have the same expectation such that there exists a risk-averse agent who prefers the consumption plan with higher variance. In view of Theorem 10.5.1, this implies that the consumption plan with higher variance is not riskier than the one with lower variance.

Example 10.6.1 Let z take on the values 1, 3, 4, 6 with equal probabilities, and let y take value 2 with probability $1/2$ and values 3 and 7, each with probability $1/4$. We have

$$E(z) = E(y) = 3.5, \quad \text{and} \quad \text{var}(y) = 4.25 > \text{var}(z) = 3.25. \qquad (10.19)$$

Consider the logarithmic utility function $v(c) = \ln(c)$. The expected utilities of z and y are

$$E[v(z)] = \frac{1}{4}[\ln(1) + \ln(3) + \ln(4) + \ln(6)] = \frac{1}{4}\ln(72), \quad (10.20)$$

and

$$E[v(y)] = \frac{1}{2}\ln(2) + \frac{1}{4}[\ln(3) + \ln(7)] = \frac{1}{4}\ln(84). \quad (10.21)$$

Thus,

$$E[v(z)] < E[v(y)], \quad (10.22)$$

which implies that y is not riskier than z. $\qquad\square$

Example 10.6.1 also illustrates that y need not be riskier than z if $y = z + \epsilon$ for some ϵ that is uncorrelated with z and has zero expectation. To see this, note that ϵ, which takes on value 1 if z equals 1 or 6 and value -1 if z equals 3 or 4, is uncorrelated with z. Also, $y = z + \epsilon$. We have seen that there exists a risk-averse agent – the agent with logarithmic utility – who prefers z to y.

According to Theorem 10.5.1, greater risk is an ordering of consumption plans with equal expectation generated by all concave utility functions. Similarly, one can think of the ranking according to variance as one generated by all quadratic utility functions. To see this, recall that a quadratic von Neumann–Morgenstern utility function takes the form

$$v(c) = -(c - \alpha)^2, \quad \text{for} \quad c \le \alpha, \quad (10.23)$$

for some α. The expected utility of consumption plan z is

$$E[v(z)] = -\{\text{var}(z) + [E(z) - \alpha]^2\}, \quad (10.24)$$

and depends only on the expectation and variance of z. For two consumption plans y and z that have the same expectation, y has higher variance than z iff every agent with quadratic utility function prefers z to y. Because the class of quadratic utility functions is much smaller than the class of all concave utility functions, the ranking according to variance is stronger than that according to risk. In fact, the former is a complete ordering, whereas the latter is a partial ordering.

The two rankings coincide for normally distributed consumption plans. We have

Proposition 10.6.2 *Let y and z be two normally distributed consumption plans with variances σ_y^2 and σ_z^2, respectively. Then y is strictly riskier than z iff $\sigma_y^2 > \sigma_z^2$.*

Proof: Define $\lambda = \sigma_y/\sigma_z$, and note that $\lambda > 1$. The random variable $\lambda[z - E(z)]$ is normally distributed with zero mean and variance equal to $\lambda^2\sigma_z^2 = \sigma_y^2$. Therefore,

$\lambda[z - E(z)]$ has the same distribution as $y - E(y)$. It follows from Corollary 10.5.6 that $\lambda[z - E(z)]$, and therefore also $y - E(y)$, is strictly riskier than $z - E(z)$. Because expectations do not matter, y is strictly riskier than z.   □

10.7 A Characterization of Greater Risk

A useful condition characterizing two consumption plans, one of which is riskier than the other, involves their cumulative distribution functions. Let F_z and F_y be the cumulative distribution functions of consumption plans z and y (that is, $F_z(w) = \text{prob}(z \leq w)$, and $F_y(w) = \text{prob}(y \leq w)$).

We have

Proposition 10.7.1 *For consumption plans y and z that have the same expectations, y is riskier than z iff*

$$\int_{-\infty}^{w} F_z(t)\,dt \leq \int_{-\infty}^{w} F_y(t)\,dt \tag{10.25}$$

for every w.

Proof: For simplicity, we assume that there exist a and b such that $F_y(a) = F_z(a) = 0$ and $F_y(b) = F_z(b) = 1$. The more general case is treated in sources cited in the notes.

We will prove that the integral condition (10.25) is equivalent to

$$\int_{a}^{b} v(t)\,dF_z(t) \geq \int_{a}^{b} v(t)\,dF_y(t) \tag{10.26}$$

for every concave function v on the interval $[a, b]$. Because $\int_a^b v(t)dF_z(t) = E[v(z)]$, the conclusion follows from Theorem 10.5.1.

We first prove that condition (10.25) implies inequality (10.26) for every concave v. For a twice differentiable function v, we can use integration by parts (twice) as follows:

$$\int_{a}^{b} v(t)\,dF_y(t) = v(b) - \int_{a}^{b} F_y(w)v'(w)\,dw \tag{10.27}$$

$$= v(b) - v'(b)\int_{a}^{b} F_y(w)\,dw + \int_{a}^{b} v''(w)\left[\int_{a}^{w} F_y(t)\,dt\right]dw. \tag{10.28}$$

Because $\int_a^b F_y(w)\,dw = b - E(y)$ (as can be verified by integrating by parts) and $E(y) = E(z)$, the first two terms of Eq. (10.28) are the same for F_y and F_z. Because $v'' \leq 0$, condition (10.25) implies that the last term in Eq. (10.28) is greater for F_z than for F_y, and hence that inequality (10.26) holds. This argument can be extended to nondifferentiable concave utility functions by approximation.

We now assume that inequality (10.26) is true for any concave function v and prove condition (10.25). In particular, for the concave function

$$v_w(t) = \begin{cases} t, & t \le w \\ w, & w \le t \end{cases} \tag{10.29}$$

we have

$$\int_a^b v_w(t)\,dF_z(t) \ge \int_a^b v_w(t)\,dF_y(t). \tag{10.30}$$

We can use integration by parts again to obtain

$$\int_a^b v_w(t)\,dF_y(t) = \int_a^w t\,dF_y(t) + w[1 - F_y(w)] = w - \int_a^w F_y(t)\,dt. \tag{10.31}$$

Inequality (10.25) follows from inequality (10.30) and Eq. (10.31) for every w. $\square$

The following example illustrates Proposition 10.7.1.

Example 10.7.2 Let z take on values -1 and 1, each with probability π, and value 0 with probability $1 - 2\pi$ where $0 < \pi < 1/2$, which is a symmetric three-point distribution. The cumulative distribution function of z is given by

$$F_z(w) = \begin{cases} 0, & w < -1 \\ \pi, & -1 \le w < 0 \\ 1 - \pi, & 0 \le w < 1 \\ 1, & 1 \le w. \end{cases} \tag{10.32}$$

The integral of the distribution function of z is

$$\int_{-\infty}^w F_z(t)\,dt = \begin{cases} 0, & w < -1 \\ \pi w + \pi, & -1 \le w < 0 \\ (1 - \pi)w + \pi, & 0 \le w < 1 \\ w, & 1 \le w. \end{cases} \tag{10.33}$$

If y takes values -1 and 1 with equal probability ϕ and value 0 with probability $1 - 2\phi$ for $\phi > \pi$, then the integral of F_y is everywhere greater than or equal to that of F_z. Thus y is riskier than z. The distribution of y puts more (probability) weight at the tails than does the distribution of z. $\square$

For two consumption plans y and z that may have different expectations, y is riskier than z iff the deviation of y from its expectation is riskier than the deviation of z from its expectation. Because the deviations from the expectations have zero expectations, Proposition 10.7.1 can be applied. Consequently, the characterization of greater risk by the integral condition (10.25) holds for consumption plans that have different expectations provided that the cumulative distribution functions of y and z in condition (10.25) are replaced by those of the deviations of y and z from their respective expectations.

10.8 Notes

The risk of a security or portfolio can be defined as the the risk of its payoff. In the proof of Proposition 10.7.1 we demonstrated that the integral condition (10.25) is equivalent to z being preferred to y by every risk-averse agent. An inspection of this proof shows that this holds true independently of whether agents' von Neumann–Morgenstern utility functions are increasing. Therefore, z is preferred to y for every risk-averse agent iff the same holds for every risk-averse agent with an increasing utility function. Consequently, Theorems 10.5.1 and 10.5.2 remain true if one takes a risk-averse agent to mean an agent with an increasing and concave (strictly concave) utility function.

The concept of greater risk is that of Rothschild and Stiglitz [4] generalized to apply to random variables with unequal expectations. It is closely related to the concept of second-order stochastic dominance: if z and y have the same expectations, then z second-order stochastically dominates y iff y is riskier than z. On stochastic dominance (of the first and second order), see Hadar and Russell [2] and Bawa [1]. The proof of Theorem 10.5.1 can be found in Rothschild and Stiglitz [4]. A proof of Proposition 10.7.1 without the assumption of a bounded set of values of the two random variables can be found in Tesfatsion [5]. See also Hanoch and Levy [3].

Bibliography

[1] Bawa, V. S. Optimal rules for ordering uncertain prospects. *Journal of Financial Economics*, **2**:95–121, 1975.
[2] Hadar, J. and Russell, W. R. Rules of ordering uncertain prospects. *American Economic Review*, **59**:25–34, 1969.
[3] Hanoch, G. and Levy, H. Efficiency analysis of choices involving risk. *Review of Economic Studies*, **36**:335–46, 1969.
[4] Rothschild, M. and Stiglitz, J. Increasing risk I: A definition. *Journal of Economic Theory*, **2**:225–43, 1970.
[5] Tesfatsion, L. Stochastic dominance and the maximization of expected utility. *Review of Economic Studies*, **XLIII**:301–15, 1976.

Part Four

Optimal Portfolios

11

Optimal Portfolios with One Risky Security

11.1 Introduction

An agent's willingness to invest in a risky security depends on, among other things, the expected return of that security. In this chapter we analyze agents' optimal portfolios in a simple setting of two securities: a single risky security and a risk-free security.

Agents' utility functions are assumed to have an expected utility representation with strictly increasing and twice differentiable von Neumann–Morgenstern utility functions. It is also assumed that date-0 consumption does not enter agents' utility functions. Furthermore, their endowments at date 1 are assumed to lie in the asset span (securities market economy).

11.2 Portfolio Choice and Wealth

The consumption-portfolio choice problem of an agent with strictly increasing expected utility function that depends only on date-1 consumption can be written as

$$\max_{c_1,h} E[v(c_1)] \tag{11.1}$$

subject to

$$ph = w_0 \tag{11.2}$$

and

$$c_1 = w_1 + \sum_{j=1}^{J} x_j h_j, \tag{11.3}$$

with an additional restriction on consumption if such is imposed. Date-1 consumption plan c_1, date-1 endowment w_1, and security payoff x_j in problem (11.1)–(11.3) are understood as random variables on the set of states S with probability measure

111

π. If, as assumed, the agent's date-1 endowment lies in the asset span so that $w_1 = \sum_j x_j \hat{h}_j$ for some portfolio $\hat{h}$, then we can substitute the agent's total portfolio holding $\tilde{h}$ for the net trade portfolio h plus the portfolio $\hat{h}$ and rewrite problem (11.1)–(11.3) as

[handwritten: $\tilde{h}$ - total holding]

$$\max_{c_1, \tilde{h}} E[v(c_1)] \qquad (11.4)$$

subject to

[handwritten: $ph = w_0 \Rightarrow p\tilde{h} - p\hat{h} = w_0^- \Rightarrow$]

$$p\tilde{h} = w_0 + p\hat{h} \qquad (11.5)$$

$$c_1 = \sum_{j=1}^{J} x_j \tilde{h}_j. \qquad (11.6)$$

An agent's *wealth* is defined as the sum of his or her date-0 endowment plus the price of the portfolio generating his or her date-1 endowment:

$$w \equiv w_0 + p\hat{h}. \qquad (11.7)$$

Note that the price of portfolio $\hat{h}$ equals the value of the date-1 endowment w_1 under the payoff pricing funtional; that is, $p\hat{h} = q(w_1)$. Unless the agent's date-1 endowment is zero, his or her wealth w depends on security prices.

Using wealth w and substituting Eq. (11.6) in the expected utility function, we obtain the portfolio choice problem

$$\max_{h} E\left[v\left(\sum_j x_j h_j\right)\right] \qquad (11.8)$$

subject to

$$ph = w, \qquad (11.9)$$

where portfolio $\tilde{h}$ has been relabeled h.

If the agent is strictly risk averse, then the optimal consumption plan $c_1 = \sum_j x_j h_j$ is unique. Two consumption plans cannot both be optimal, since any strictly convex combination of the two would also be budget-feasible and would yield strictly higher expected utility. If, in addition, there are no redundant securities, then his or her optimal portfolio is also unique.

11.3 Optimal Portfolios with One Risky Security

Let there be two securities: a risky security with return denoted by r and a risk-free security with return $\bar{r}$. The difference $r - \bar{r}$, which is assumed to be nonzero, is the *excess return* on the risky security.

It is convenient to describe a budget-feasible portfolio of two securities in terms of wealth invested in each security instead of in terms of security holdings. For a portfolio (h_1, h_2) such that $p_1 h_1 + p_2 h_2 = w$, let $a = p_2 h_2$ denote the amount invested in the risky security. The amount invested in the risk-free security is $w - a = p_1 h_1$, and the payoff of investment $(w - a, a)$ is $w\bar{r} + (r - \bar{r})a$.

The agent's optimal investment,[1] denoted by a^*, is a solution to the problem

$$\max_a E[v(w\bar{r} + (r - \bar{r})a)], \tag{11.10}$$

which, as noted, may involve an additional restriction that consumption be positive: $w\bar{r} + (r - \bar{r})a \geq 0$. The agent's wealth w is assumed to be strictly positive.

If security prices exclude arbitrage and if consumption is restricted to be positive, then Theorem 3.6.5 implies that maximization problem (11.10) has a solution. In the present context of two securities, one of which is risk free, the condition that there be no arbitrage has a simple characterization in terms of securities' returns. The risky return r must be lower than the risk-free return $\bar{r}$ in some states and higher in other states. Otherwise, if r is uniformly above $\bar{r}$, for example, then $r - \bar{r}$ is an arbitrage.

If the agent is strictly risk averse, the optimal investment is unique because in the present setting neither security is redundant. The optimal investment a^* is then a function of the agent's wealth w, the risk-free return $\bar{r}$, and the (distribution of the) risky return r. Further, because utility function v is twice differentiable, a^* is a differentiable function of its arguments whenever the consumption plan generated by a^* is interior.

The interior optimal investment a^* satisfies the first-order condition

$$E[v'(w\bar{r} + a^*(r - \bar{r}))(r - \bar{r})] = 0. \tag{11.11}$$

Example 11.3.1 One of the attractive features of quadratic utility is a closed-form expression for the optimal investment. For

$$v(y) = -(\alpha - y)^2, \qquad y < \alpha \tag{11.12}$$

the first-order condition (11.11) is

$$E\{[\alpha - w\bar{r} - a^*(r - \bar{r})](r - \bar{r})\} = 0. \tag{11.13}$$

Evaluating the expectation and solving for a^* results in

$$a^* = \frac{(\alpha - w\bar{r})(\mu - \bar{r})}{\sigma^2 + (\mu - \bar{r})^2}, \tag{11.14}$$

where $\mu = E(r)$ and $\sigma^2 = \text{var}(r)$. Note that, if $\mu > \bar{r}$, then the optimal investment a^* is a decreasing function of variance σ^2 and of wealth w. □

---

[1] Up to now we have not found it necessary to adopt a separate notation to distinguish optimum values of variables from nonoptimum values. Here, however, we discuss both optimum and nonoptimum portfolios, and thus the distinction must be made.

11.4 Risk Premium and Optimal Portfolios

The *risk premium* on a security is defined as its expected excess return; that is, its expected return less the risk-free return. If the risk premium is zero, then the security is priced *fairly*, meaning that the excess return on the security is a fair game (that is, a random variable with zero expectation). Of course, there is no suggestion that anything is unfair about nonzero risk premia.

A risk-neutral agent is indifferent among all investments if the risk premium on the risky security is zero. If the risk premium is nonzero and there are no restrictions on consumption, then his or her optimal investment does not exist. If his or her consumption is restricted to be positive, then the agent will hold long the security with high expected return and sell short the security with low expected return until the positivity restriction becomes binding.

Whether a strictly risk-averse agent chooses a positive or a negative investment in the risky security depends on the risk premium on the risky security.

Theorem 11.4.1 *If an agent is strictly risk averse, then the optimal investment in the risky security is strictly positive, zero, or strictly negative iff the risk premium on the risky security is strictly positive, zero, or strictly negative.*

Proof: Because w is strictly positive, zero investment in the risky security results in a strictly positive risk-free consumption. Therefore $a = 0$ is an interior point of the interval of the investment choices whether or not consumption is restricted to be positive. The derivative of expected utility in maximization problem (11.10) with respect to a at $a = 0$ is $v'(w\bar{r})(\mu - \bar{r})$, where $\mu \equiv E(r)$. Because $v'(w\bar{r})$ is strictly positive, the derivative is strictly positive, zero, or strictly negative iff $\mu - \bar{r}$ is strictly positive, zero, or strictly negative. Because expected utility is strictly concave in a, the sign of the derivative at zero investment determines whether the optimal investment is positive, zero, or negative (see Figure 11.1). □

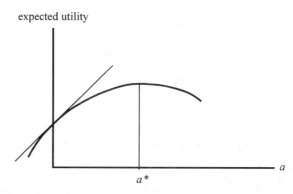

Figure 11.1 The derivative of expected utility with respect to a at $a = 0$ is positive; a^* is positive.

It is important to keep in mind that the optimal investment a^* characterized in Theorem 11.4.1 is the part of total wealth w invested in the risky security. Since w consists of date-0 endowment and the price of the portfolio the agent is endowed with (see Eq. (11.7)), zero investment a^* means that the agent sells all of the shares of the risky security that he is endowed with and invests the proceeds in the risk-free security.

If the risk premium is zero, then any nonzero investment in the risky security has a strictly riskier return than the risk-free return and the same expected return. It follows from Theorem 10.5.1 that the optimal investment must be the risk-free investment. Thus, this part of Theorem 11.4.1 holds even in the absence of the maintained assumption that the agent's utility function is differentiable. This is not the case for other parts of Theorem 11.4.1. For instance, the optimal investment in the risky security may be zero when the risk premium is strictly positive.

Example 11.4.2 There are two states with equal probabilities. The risk-free return is $\bar{r} = 1$, and the return on the risky security is $r = (1.3, 0.8)$, and thus the risk premium is strictly positive. The agent's von Neumann–Morgenstern utility function v, given by

$$v(y) = \begin{cases} 2y, & y \leq 5 \\ y + 5, & y \geq 5 \end{cases} \tag{11.15}$$

is strictly increasing and concave. The expected utility

$$E[v(c)] = \frac{1}{2}v(c_1) + \frac{1}{2}v(c_2) \tag{11.16}$$

is nondifferentiable whenever $c_1 = 5$ or $c_2 = 5$. If the agent's wealth is $w = 5$, then the optimal choice is to invest his or her entire wealth in the risk-free security (Figure 11.2). □

Theorem 11.4.1 implies that the return on the optimal portfolio of a strictly risk-averse agent (with differentiable utility function) is risk free iff the risky security is priced fairly: $E(r) = \bar{r}$. Otherwise, if the risk premium is nonzero, the return on the optimal portfolio is risky. The expected return on the optimal portfolio equals

$$\bar{r} + \frac{a^*}{w}[E(r) - \bar{r}] \tag{11.17}$$

and is strictly higher than the risk-free return. Thus, the risk of the optimal return is compensated by a relatively high expected return.

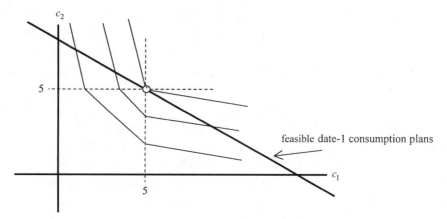

Figure 11.2 With nondifferentiable utility the optimal portfolio may be risk free even in the absence of fair pricing.

11.5 Optimal Portfolios When the Risk Premium Is Small

It follows from Theorem 11.4.1 and continuity of the optimal portfolio as a function of the risk premium that if the risk premium is small, then the amount invested in the risky security is small. Much more can be said. If the risk premium is small (that is, if the risky security is priced approximately fairly), then the optimal investment a^* is approximately proportional to the risk premium $E(r) - \bar{r}$, inversely proportional to the Arrow–Pratt measure of absolute risk aversion, and inversely proportional to the variance σ^2 of the risky return.

Theorem 11.5.1 *If the risk premium $E(r) - \bar{r}$ is small, then the optimal investment in the risky security of a strictly risk-averse agent with zero date-1 endowment is*

$$a^* \cong \frac{E(r) - \bar{r}}{\sigma^2 A(w\bar{r})}. \tag{11.18}$$

Proof: If the risk premium is zero so that $\bar{r} = \mu$ where $\mu \equiv E(r)$, then, by Theorem 11.4.1, the optimal investment a^* equals zero. For small risk premium, the linear approximation of a^* is

$$a^* \cong (\bar{r} - \mu)\partial_{\bar{r}}a^*, \tag{11.19}$$

where $\partial_{\bar{r}}a^*$ is the partial derivative of a^* with respect to $\bar{r}$ at $\bar{r} = \mu$.

To find the partial derivative $\partial_{\bar{r}}a^*$ at $\bar{r} = \mu$, we differentiate condition (11.11) with respect to $\bar{r}$. Since the agent has zero date-1 endowment, wealth w does not depend on $\bar{r}$, and we obtain

$$E[v''(w\bar{r} + a^*(r - \bar{r}))(r - \bar{r})(w + (r - \bar{r})\partial_{\bar{r}}a^* - a^*) - v'(w\bar{r} + a^*(r - \bar{r}))] = 0. \tag{11.20}$$

Setting $\bar{r} = \mu$ and using the fact that a^* is zero when $\bar{r} = \mu$, we can solve Eq. (11.20) for

$$\partial_{\bar{r}} a^* = -\frac{1}{A(w\bar{r})\sigma^2}. \tag{11.21}$$

Substituting the right-hand side of Eq. (11.21) in Eq. (11.19), we get Eq. (11.18). □

The form of approximation used in Eq. (11.19) reveals the meaning of "small" risk premium. "Small" means that the terms of second and higher order of Taylor's expansion of a^* as a function of $\bar{r}$ around $\bar{r} = \mu$ are negligible. Further, the positivity constraint on consumption, which is nonbinding when the risk premium is zero, remains nonbinding at a "small" risk premium.

Example 11.5.2 For the quadratic utility function of Example 11.3.1, the Arrow–Pratt measure of absolute risk aversion is

$$A(w\bar{r}) = \frac{1}{\alpha - w\bar{r}}. \tag{11.22}$$

Expression (11.14) for the optimal investment can be written as

$$a^* = \frac{\mu - \bar{r}}{[\sigma^2 + (\mu - \bar{r})^2]A(w\bar{r})}. \tag{11.23}$$

The approximate expression (11.18) differs from the exact solution (11.23) in that the former neglects the second-order term $(\mu - \bar{r})^2$ in the denominator.

11.6 Notes

The portfolio choice problem with single risky security was first analyzed in Tobin [10], Arrow [1] and Pratt [2].

Extending a result by Pratt [2], Wang and Werner [4] showed that the optimal investment in a single risky security provides a measure of risk aversion equivalent to the Arrow–Pratt measure. One risk-averse agent is less risk-averse than another iff the investment in the risky security of the first is higher than that of the second for all levels of wealth and all risky returns with strictly positive risk premium.

Bibliography

[1] Arrow, K. J. *Aspects of the Theory of Risk Bearing*. Yrjo Jahnssonin Saatio, Helsinki, 1965.
[2] Pratt, J. W. Risk aversion in the small and in the large. *Econometrica*, **32**:122–36, 1964.
[3] Tobin, J. Liquidity preference as behaviour towards risk. *Review of Economic Studies*, **25**:65–86, 1958.
[4] Wang, Z. and Werner J. Portfolio characterization of risk aversion. *Economics Letters*, **45**:259–65, 1994.

12

Comparative Statics of Optimal Portfolios

12.1 Introduction

In this chapter we investigate how optimal portfolios depend on agents' wealth, on the risk-free return, and on the expected return and the riskiness of the risky return. As in Chapter 11, our analysis is restricted to the simple setting of two securities: a single risky security and a risk-free security.

We assume that agents' wealth consists only of date-0 endowment; date-1 endowments are assumed zero. This implies that the wealth does not depend on security prices or returns, and allows us to abstract from the effects of price or return changes on wealth. For most of this chapter it is assumed that date-0 consumption does not enter agents' utility functions. An exception is Section 12.5 in which we analyze optimal portfolios with intertemporal consumption.

Our analysis of optimal portfolios in this chapter draws on methods and results of comparative statics in consumer theory.

12.2 Wealth

We recall that the optimal investment a^* in the risky security is a solution to the problem

$$\max_a E[v(w\bar{r} + (r - \bar{r})a)], \tag{12.1}$$

where utility function v is strictly increasing and twice-differentiable. The first-order condition for an interior optimal investment is

$$E[v'(w\bar{r} + a^*(r - \bar{r}))(r - \bar{r})] = 0. \tag{12.2}$$

Our concern in this section is with the response of optimal investment a^* to changes in wealth. Whether a^* increases, decreases, or remains unchanged when wealth increases depends on how the absolute risk aversion changes as a function of wealth.

Theorem 12.2.1 *If an agent is strictly risk averse, if his or her absolute risk aversion is decreasing, and if the risk premium on the risky security is positive, then the optimal investment a^* in the risky security is increasing in wealth.*

Proof: Differentiating the first-order condition (12.2) with respect to w results in

$$E[v''(w\bar{r} + a^*(r - \bar{r}))(r - \bar{r})(\bar{r} + (r - \bar{r})\partial_w a^*)] = 0, \quad (12.3)$$

or

$$\partial_w a^* = -\frac{\bar{r}E[v''(w\bar{r} + a^*(r - \bar{r}))(r - \bar{r})]}{E[v''(w\bar{r} + a^*(r - \bar{r}))(r - \bar{r})^2]}. \quad (12.4)$$

The denominator in expression (12.4) is strictly negative. We will prove that the numerator is positive. Because the measure of absolute risk aversion A is decreasing, we have

$$A[w\bar{r} + a^*(r_s - \bar{r})] \leq A(w\bar{r}) \quad (12.5)$$

for all states s such that $r_s > \bar{r}$. Note that $a^* \geq 0$ follows from Theorem 11.5.1. Substituting the definition of A in the left-hand side of inequality (12.5) and multiplying both sides by $r_s - \bar{r}$, we obtain

$$v''(w\bar{r} + a^*(r_s - \bar{r}))(r_s - \bar{r}) \geq -A(w\bar{r})v'(w\bar{r} + a^*(r_s - \bar{r}))(r_s - \bar{r}). \quad (12.6)$$

In those states in which $r_s \leq \bar{r}$, we have

$$A[w\bar{r} + a^*(r_s - \bar{r})] \geq A(w\bar{r}). \quad (12.7)$$

Performing the same calculations as above (and noting that multiplying by $r_s - \bar{r}$ now reverses the sign of the inequality), we obtain inequality (12.6), which is therefore true for all values of r_s. Taking the expectation of inequality (12.6) and using first-order condition (12.2) results in

$$E[v''(w\bar{r} + a^*(r - \bar{r}))(r - \bar{r})] \geq 0. \quad (12.8)$$

Thus, the numerator on the right-hand side of Eq. (12.4) is positive, implying that

$$\partial_w a^* \geq 0. \quad (12.9)$$

□

Therefore, under the conditions of the theorem, the risky security is a normal good. Results analogous to Theorem 12.2.1 hold under increasing and constant absolute risk aversion. If an agent is strictly risk averse and his or her absolute risk aversion is increasing, then the optimal investment in a risky security with strictly positive risk premium is decreasing in wealth, and thus the risky security is an inferior good. This is the case for the quadratic utility function (see Eq. (11.14)). If an agent's absolute risk aversion is constant (negative exponential utility), his or her optimal investment is independent of wealth.

We also have

Theorem 12.2.2 *If an agent is strictly risk averse, if his or her relative risk aversion is decreasing, and if the risk premium on the risky security is positive, then the fraction of wealth a^*/w invested in the risky security is increasing in wealth.*

Proof: The first-order condition (12.2) can be written as

$$E\left[v'\left(w\bar{r} + w\left(\frac{a^*}{w}\right)(r - \bar{r})\right)(r - \bar{r})\right] = 0. \qquad (12.10)$$

Evaluation of $\partial_w(a^*/w)$ is precisely analogous to evaluation of $\partial_w a^*$ in the proof of Theorem 12.2.1. Here the measure of relative risk aversion replaces the measure of absolute risk aversion used in Theorem 12.2.1.   □

Analogous results hold under increasing and constant relative risk aversion. Thus, under constant relative risk aversion (power and logarithmic utilities with $\alpha = 0$) the fraction of wealth invested in the risky security is invariant to wealth.

12.3 Expected Return

Our concern in this section is with changes of optimal portfolios in response to changes in the risk-free return or the expected return of the risky security. We begin with the risk-free return.

Theorem 12.3.1 *If an agent is strictly risk averse, if his or her absolute risk aversion is increasing, if his or her optimal investment in the risk-free security is positive and if the risk premium on the risky security is positive, then the optimal investment a^* in the risky security is strictly decreasing in the risk-free return.*

Proof: Differentiating the first-order condition (12.2) with respect to $\bar{r}$ (see Eq. (11.20)) results in

$$\partial_{\bar{r}} a^* = \frac{E[v'(w\bar{r} + a^*(r - \bar{r}))] - E[v''(w\bar{r} + a^*(r - \bar{r}))(r - \bar{r})](w - a^*)}{E[v''(w\bar{r} + a^*(r - \bar{r}))(r - \bar{r})^2]}.$$

$$(12.11)$$

Using Eq. (12.4), we obtain

$$\partial_{\bar{r}} a^* = \frac{E[v'(w\bar{r} + a^*(r - \bar{r}))]}{E[v''(w\bar{r} + a^*(r - \bar{r}))(r - \bar{r})^2]} + \frac{w - a^*}{\bar{r}} \partial_w a^*. \tag{12.12}$$

The numerator of the first term on the right-hand side of Eq. (12.12) is strictly positive, whereas the denominator is strictly negative. Therefore, the first term is strictly negative. The counterpart of Theorem 12.2.1 for increasing absolute risk aversion implies that under the assumed conditions $\partial_w a^*$ is negative. Because $w - a^*$ is positive by assumption, it follows that $\partial_{\bar{r}} a^* < 0$. □

The effect of a change in the risk-free return on the investment in the risky security can be decomposed into a substitution effect and an income effect. The first term on the right-hand side of Eq. (12.12) expresses the substitution effect. As shown, the substitution effect is always negative. If the risk-free return increases, the risk-free security becomes more attractive and the risky security less attractive, leading to a decrease in the investment in the risky security.

The second term on the right-hand side of Eq. (12.12) expresses the income effect. A marginal unit increase in the risk-free return generates a date-1 consumption increase that equals the investment in the risk-free security $w - a^*$. This date-1 consumption increase is equivalent to date-0 wealth increase of $(w - a^*)/\bar{r}$. The effect of this wealth increase on the optimal investment in the risky security is $[(w - a^*)/\bar{r}]\partial_w a^*$ and is the income effect.

In general, the income effect may be positive or negative. Under the assumptions of Theorem 12.3.1 it is negative and reinforces the substitution effect. In the following theorem, alternative assumptions are imposed under which the income effect may be positive but it is always dominated by the negative substitution effect.

Theorem 12.3.2 *If an agent is strictly risk averse, if his or her relative risk aversion is less than or equal to one, and if the risky return is positive, then the optimal investment a^* in the risky security is strictly decreasing in the risk-free return.*

Proof: Let c_1^* denote the optimal date-1 consumption

$$c_1^* = w\bar{r} + a^*(r - \bar{r}). \tag{12.13}$$

The numerator in expression (12.11) for $\partial_{\bar{r}} a^*$ can be written using the measure of absolute risk aversion A as

$$E\{v'(c_1^*)[1 + A(c_1^*)(r - \bar{r})(w - a^*)]\}. \tag{12.14}$$

Using Eq. (12.13), we can rewrite expression (12.14) as

$$E\{v'(c_1^*)[1 - A(c_1^*)c_1^* + A(c_1^*)wr]\}. \tag{12.15}$$

Substituting the measure of relative risk aversion $R(c_1^*)$ for $A(c_1^*)c_1^*$ in expression (12.15), we obtain

$$E\{v'(c_1^*)[1 - R(c_1^*) + A(c_1^*)wr]\}. \tag{12.16}$$

Because the agent is strictly risk averse and the risky return r is positive and nonzero, the term $A(c_1^*)wr$ is positive and nonzero. If, as assumed, R is less than or equal to one, then expression (12.16) is strictly positive. Thus, the numerator in (12.11) is strictly positive. Because the denominator is strictly negative, it follows that $\partial_{\bar{r}}a^* < 0$. □

Examples of utility functions with relative risk aversion less than or equal to 1 include power utility functions with $\gamma > 1$ and $\alpha \geq 0$ and logarithmic utility functions with $\alpha \geq 0$.

The dependence of the optimal portfolio on the expected return of the risky security is the opposite of its dependence on the risk-free return. To determine the effect of changes in the expected return, we write $r = \mu + \Delta r$, where $\mu = E(r)$, and we consider variations in μ, keeping the distribution of Δr unchanged. Using the same arguments as in the proof of Theorem 12.3.1, one can show that if an agent is strictly risk averse, if his or her absolute risk aversion A is decreasing, and if the risk premium on the risky security is positive, then the optimal investment a^* is strictly increasing in the expected return of the risky security. If the agent's absolute risk aversion is increasing (as for quadratic utilities), then nothing can be said in general as to whether the investment in the risky security will increase or decrease.

The counterpart to Theorem 12.3.2 when the expected return on the risky security changes is similar.

12.4 Risk

One might expect that the investment in the risky security would decrease if its return became more risky (in the sense of Chapter 10), but its expected return remains unchanged. This is the case for a quadratic utility function: increased risk with no change in the expected return implies that the variance of the return increases, and the investment in the risky security decreases, as indicated by Eq. (11.14). However, this need not be the case in general for a strictly risk-averse utility function.

To investigate the effect on the optimal investment in the risky security of an increase in its riskiness, we consider the first-order condition (12.2) and introduce a function g of two scalar variables a and y given by

$$g(a, y) \equiv v'(w\bar{r} + a(y - \bar{r}))(y - \bar{r}). \qquad (12.17)$$

If the agent is strictly risk averse, then g is a strictly decreasing function of investment a for any y. Equation (12.2) can now be written as

$$E[g(a^*, r)] = 0. \qquad (12.18)$$

Suppose that the risky return r is replaced by the more risky return $\tilde{r}$ with the same expectation. Suppose also (pending discussion below) that $g(a^*, y)$ is a concave function of y. Theorem 10.5.1 can be applied to function $g(a^*, \cdot)$ in place of a utility function, and we obtain

$$E[g(a^*, \tilde{r})] \leq E[g(a^*, r)] = 0. \qquad (12.19)$$

If inequality in expression (12.19) is strict, so that a^* is not the optimal investment with the return $\tilde{r}$, then the investment a has to be decreased to restore the first-order condition. The opposite holds if g is a convex function of y.

One can show (see the sources cited in the notes) that a sufficient condition for function g of Eq. (12.17) to be concave in y is that the relative risk aversion be increasing and less than or equal to one and the absolute risk aversion be decreasing. If the risk premium on the risky security is strictly positive, then this condition implies that the investment in the risky security decreases when the risky return becomes more risky. Power utility functions with $\gamma > 1$ and $\alpha \geq 0$ and logarithmic utility functions with $\alpha \geq 0$ satisfy all these conditions on risk aversion.

12.5 Optimal Portfolios with Two-Date Consumption

So far the analysis of optimal portfolios has proceeded under the assumption that date-0 consumption does not enter the agent's utility function. If it does, then the agent has to choose the division of wealth between securities and date-0 consumption in addition to choosing optimal investments in each security.

The portfolio choice problem with two-date consumption can be written as

$$\max_{a_1, a_2} E[v(w - a_1 - a_2, \bar{r}a_1 + ra_2)], \qquad (12.20)$$

where a_1 and a_2 are the amounts of wealth invested in the risk-free and the risky security, respectively. The optimal investments are denoted by a_1^* and a_2^*.

The result of Theorem 11.4.1 is that the optimal investment in the risky security is strictly positive, zero or strictly negative as the risk premium on the risky security is strictly positive, zero or strictly negative if the agent is strictly risk averse extends to the setting of two-date consumption. To see this, let $c_0^* = w - a_1^* - a_2^*$ denote the optimal date-0 consumption and let $\bar{w} = w - c_0^*$ and $\bar{v}(c_s) = v(c_0^*, c_s)$. Then a_2^* is the optimal investment in the risky security for the single-date utility function $\bar{v}$ with wealth $\bar{w}$. Because $\bar{v}$ is strictly concave, Theorem 11.4.1 implies the conclusion.

Optimal portfolios can easily be characterized when the agent is risk neutral. For instance, if the utility function takes the form

$$v(c_0, c_s) = c_0 + \delta c_s \qquad (12.21)$$

for some $\delta > 0$, and if the risk-free return equals δ^{-1} and the risk premium on the risky security is zero, then this risk-neutral agent is indifferent among all portfolios. If one or both securities have expected return not equal to δ^{-1} and there are no restrictions on consumption, then his or her optimal portfolio does not exist. If the agent's consumption is restricted to be positive, then there exists an optimal portfolio. This portfolio is a solution to a linear programming problem. For instance, if the risk-free return equals δ^{-1} and there is a strictly positive risk premium, then the risk-neutral agent will sell short the risk-free security and invest his or her entire wealth in the risky security. Because the risk-free return has to be higher than the risky return in at least one state (otherwise there is an arbitrage opportunity), the restriction that consumption be positive implies a limit on the short position in the risk-free security. This limiting short position determines the agent's optimal portfolio.

We present comparative statics analysis of optimal portfolios with two-date consumption under an additional restriction that there is only one security. Suppose first that the security has a risk-free payoff. Then the agent faces no uncertainty in his portfolio-consumption choice and his optimal investment a^* is a solution to the problem

$$\max_a v(w - a, \bar{r}a). \qquad (12.22)$$

The maximization problem (12.22) is the standard saving problem under certainty.

The first-order condition for an interior solution to (12.22) is

$$\partial_0 v(w - a^*, \bar{r}a^*) = \bar{r}\partial_1 v(w - a^*, \bar{r}a^*). \qquad (12.23)$$

To investigate the effect of an increase in the agent's wealth on the optimal saving a^* we differentiate the first-order condition (12.23) to find that

$$\partial_w a^* = \frac{\partial_{00} v - \bar{r}\partial_{01} v}{D}, \qquad (12.24)$$

where $\partial_{t\tau} v$ denotes the second-order partial derivative of v at $(w - a^*, \bar{r}a^*)$ for $t, \tau = 0, 1$, and $D = (\bar{r})^2 \partial_{11} v - 2\bar{r}\partial_{01} v + \partial_{00} v$. If the agent is strictly risk averse so that v is strictly concave, then, by the second-order condition, D is strictly negative. However, the sign of the numerator in Eq. (12.24), and hence the sign of the derivative $\partial_w a^*$ cannot be determined without further assumptions on the utility function. If the utility function is time separable, then $\partial_{01} v = 0$, and consequently $\partial_w a^* > 0$; that is, the agent's optimal savings increase when wealth increases.

Differentiating the first-order condition (12.23) with respect to the risk-free return $\bar{r}$ results in

$$\partial_{\bar{r}} a^* = -\frac{\partial_1 v}{D} + \frac{a^*(\partial_{01} v - \bar{r}\partial_{11} v)}{D}. \tag{12.25}$$

If the utility function is time-separable so that $\partial_{01} v = 0$, and if $a^* \geq 0$, then $\partial_{\bar{r}} a^* > 0$; that is, the agent's optimal saving increases when the risk-free return increases.

The effect of a change in the risk-free return on the optimal savings can be decomposed into an income effect and a substitution effect. Substituting $\partial_{01} v - \bar{r}\partial_{11} v = (1/\bar{r})(\partial_{00} v - \bar{r}\partial_{01} v - D)$ in Eq. (12.25) and using Eq. (12.24), we obtain

$$\partial_{\bar{r}} a^* = -\frac{\partial_1 v}{D} - \frac{a^*}{\bar{r}} + \frac{a^*}{\bar{r}}\partial_w a^*. \tag{12.26}$$

The first two terms on the right-hand side of Eq. (12.26) add up to the substitution effect, and the third term is the income effect. The sign of the substitution effect is ambiguous.

For a time-separable utility function, the optimal investment in a single security increases with wealth not only when the payoff of the security is risk free but also when the payoff is risky. The optimal investment in a single risky security with return r for an agent with utility function $v(y_0, y_1) = v_0(y_0) + v_1(y_1)$ is a solution to

$$\max_a v_0(w - a) + E[v_1(ra)]. \tag{12.27}$$

The first-order condition for an interior solution to Eq. (12.27) is

$$v_0'(w - a^*) = E[rv_1'(ra^*)]. \tag{12.28}$$

Differentiating Eq. (12.28) with respect to w results in

$$\partial_w a^* = \frac{v_0''}{v_0'' + E(r^2 v_1'')} > 0. \tag{12.29}$$

We investigate now the effect on the optimal investment in the risky security of an increase in its riskiness. We use the method of Section 12.4. Define function g by

$$g(a, y) \equiv y v_1'(ya) - v_0'(w - a). \tag{12.30}$$

The first-order condition (12.28) can now be written

$$E[g(a^*, r)] = 0. \tag{12.31}$$

If both period utility functions v_0 and v_1 are strictly concave, then g is a strictly decreasing function of a. If we assume (pending subsequent discussion) that $g(a^*, y)$ is a concave function of y, then we can conclude that replacing risky return r by a more risky return with the same expectation will lead to a decrease in the optimal investment a^*.

One can show that a sufficient condition for function $g(a^*, y)$ to be concave in y is that the third derivative v_1''' be strictly negative and $a^* > 0$. A strictly negative third derivative implies strictly increasing absolute risk aversion.

12.6 Notes

The literature on comparative statics of the portfolio choice problem with single-date consumption is rich. A few of the relevant references are Tobin [10], Fishburn and Porter [3], Cheng, Magill, and Shafer [1]. A detailed analysis of the dependence of an optimal portfolio on the riskiness of the risky return can be found in Rothschild and Stiglitz [8]. Gollier [4], [5] derived necessary and sufficient conditions for a change in the return of the risky security to induce a decrease of the investment in the risky security for every risk-averse agent.

The literature on saving decisions and portfolio choice with intertemporal consumption is equally large. Main references include Leland [7], Dreze and Modigliani [2], and Sandmo [9]. Kimball [6] derived a characterization of the negative third-order derivative of utility function (see Section 12.5) in terms of prudence.

Bibliography

[1] Cheng, H., Magill, M., and Shafer, W. Some results on comparative statics under uncertainty. *International Economic Review*, **28**:493–509, 1987.

[2] Dreze, J. H., and Modigliani, F. Consumption decisions under uncertainty. *Journal of Economic Theory*, **5**:308–35, 1972.

[3] Fishburn, P. C., and Porter, R. B. Optimal portfolios with one safe and one risky asset: Effects of changes in rate of return and risk. *Management Science*, **22**:1064–72, 1976.

[4] Gollier, C. The comparative statics of changes in risk revisited. *Journal of Economic Theory*, **66**:522-535, 1995.

[5] Gollier, C. A note on portfolio dominance. *Review of Economic Studies*, **64**:147–50, 1997.

[6] Kimball, M. Precautionary saving in the small and in the large. *Econometrica*, **58**:53–73, 1990.

[7] Leland, H. E. Saving and uncertainty: The precautionary demand for saving. *Quarterly Journal of Economics*, **82**:465–73, 1968.

[8] Rothschild, M. and Stiglitz, J. Increasing risk II: Its economic consequences. *Journal of Economic Theory*, **3**:66–84, 1971.

[9] Sandmo, A. Capital risk, consumption, and portfolio choice. *Econometrica*, **37**:586–99, 1969.

[10] Tobin, J. Liquidity preference as behavior towards risk. *Review of Economic Studies*, **25**:65–86, 1958.

13

Optimal Portfolios with Several Risky Securities

.

13.1 Introduction

In this chapter we characterize optimal portfolios in a setting with several risky securities. For the most part, the comparative statics results of the preceding chapter cannot be extended when there are several risky securities. We present the few results that can be extended and derive some further results under additional restrictions on either securities returns or on agents' utility functions.

The assumptions of Chapter 11 are maintained in this chapter: agents' utility functions have expected utility representations, are strictly increasing and differentiable and, with the exception of Section 13.7, depend only on date-1 consumption. Endowments lie in the asset span (securities market economy). It is also assumed that there are no redundant securities.

13.2 Optimal Portfolios

As in Chapters 11 and 12, it is convenient to describe the portfolio choice problem in terms of wealth invested in each security. Let $a_j = p_j h_j$ denote the amount of wealth invested in security j and let $a = (a_1, \ldots, a_J)$. The portfolio choice problem (11.8) of an agent with a strictly increasing utility function can be restated as

$$\max_a E\left[v\left(\sum_{j=1}^{J} a_j r_j\right)\right] \tag{13.1}$$

subject to

$$\sum_{j=1}^{J} a_j = w \tag{13.2}$$

and possibly the additional constraint of positivity of the resulting consumption.

128

The agent's optimal investment will be denoted by $a^* = (a_1^*, \ldots, a_J^*)$ and its return by r^*. Thus,

$$r^* = \frac{\sum_{j=1}^{J} a_j^* r_j}{w}. \tag{13.3}$$

If one of the securities, say security 1, is risk free with return $\bar{r}$, then the portfolio choice problem (13.1) can be written as

$$\max_{a_2, \ldots, a_J} E\left[v\left(w\bar{r} + \sum_{j=2}^{J} a_j(r_j - \bar{r}) \right) \right]. \tag{13.4}$$

The optimal investment a^* is given by a solution $(a_2^*, \ldots, a_J^*)$ to expression (13.4), and the investment in the risk-free security is given by $a_1^* = w - \sum_{j=2}^{J} a_j^*$.

13.3 Risk–Return Trade-Off

It was shown in Chapter 11 that, with one risky security, an optimal portfolio of a strictly risk-averse agent is risky iff its expected return is strictly higher than the risk-free return. The portfolio risk is compensated for by a relatively high expected return. This trade-off between risk and expected return holds in the more general setting of many risky securities:

Theorem 13.3.1 *If r^* is the return on an optimal portfolio of a risk-averse agent and if r^* is riskier than the return r, then $E(r^*) \geq E(r)$.*

Proof: Let v be the agent's von Neumann–Morgenstern utility function. Optimality of the return r^* implies that

$$E[v(wr^*)] \geq E[v(wr)]. \tag{13.5}$$

If r^* is riskier than r, then so is $r^* - E(r^*) + E(r)$. Because $r^* - E(r^*) + E(r)$ and r have the same expectations and the agent is risk averse, we can apply Theorem 10.5.2 to obtain

$$E[v(wr)] \geq E[v(wr^* - wE(r^*) + wE(r))]. \tag{13.6}$$

Inequalities (13.5) and (13.6) imply that $E(r^*) \geq E(r)$ because v is strictly increasing. $\square$

Note that Theorem 13.3.1 holds true even in the absence of the maintained assumption of the differentiability of the utility function.

As usual, there is also a strict version:

Theorem 13.3.2 *If r^* is the return on an optimal portfolio of a strictly risk-averse agent and if r^* is strictly riskier than a return r, then $E(r^*) > E(r)$.*

Theorems 13.3.1 and 13.3.2 give an expression of the risk–return trade-off: the greater the expected return on an optimal portfolio, the greater the risk of that portfolio. What is interesting about this result is that the "return" in the "risk–return trade-off" is identified with the first moment of the return distribution (the expectation), but "risk" is measured by the ordering introduced in Chapter 10 and not by the second moment of the return distribution (variance).

13.4 Optimal Portfolios under Fair Pricing

If all securities are priced fairly, then a risk-neutral agent is indifferent among all (budget-feasible) portfolios, and a strictly risk-averse agent chooses a portfolio with a risk-free payoff (see Theorem 13.3.2) if one is available. Under the assumption of differentiability of the utility function, the converse is also true: only under fair pricing is the payoff of an optimal portfolio of a strictly risk-averse agent risk free.

Theorem 13.4.1 *Suppose that security 1 is risk free with return $\bar{r}$. Then the payoff of an optimal portfolio of a strictly risk-averse agent is risk free iff all securities are priced fairly; that is, iff*

$$E(r_j) = \bar{r} \quad \forall \; j. \tag{13.7}$$

Proof: The first-order condition for optimal investment a^* is

$$E\left[v'\left(w\bar{r} + \sum_{j=2}^{J} a_j^*(r_j - \bar{r}) \right) (r_k - \bar{r}) \right] = 0 \quad \forall \, k \geq 2 \tag{13.8}$$

whenever the resulting consumption is interior.

If the payoff of optimal investment a^* is risk free, then (because there are no redundant securities) $a_j^* = 0$ for each $j \geq 2$ and $a_1^* = w$. The resulting consumption plan $w\bar{r}$ is strictly positive. The first-order condition (13.8) with $a_j^* = 0$ for each $j \geq 2$ implies fair pricing (13.7).

Conversely, because v is differentiable and Eq. (13.7) holds, then $a_j^* = 0$ for each $j \geq 2$ satisfies the first-order conditions (13.8). These conditions are sufficient for optimality, and, if v is strictly concave, the optimal portfolio is unique.   □

13.5 Risk Premia and Optimal Portfolios

When there is only one risky security, the optimal holding of the risky security is strictly positive, zero, or strictly negative according to whether the risk premium on that security is strictly positive, zero, or strictly negative (Theorem 11.4.1). One might expect that this relation continues to hold when there are several risky securities. It does not. For instance, an optimal portfolio can involve a long position in a security with strictly negative risk premium if the payoff on that security covaries strongly and negatively with the payoff on another security with a strictly positive risk premium. In the Capital Asset Pricing Model of Chapter 19, this is exactly the case for a negative-beta security.

As this reasoning suggests, the arguments of the proof of Theorem 11.4.1 do not extend to the case of several risky securities. As before, the sign of the risk premium $E(r_j) - \bar{r}$ determines the sign of the partial derivative of expected utility with respect to investment in that security at zero. Without further knowledge of the agent's utility function, security returns, or both, the signs of the partial derivatives at zero are not enough to determine the location of the optimal investment in the case of many risky securities.

Of course, if the risk premium is zero on every security, then, as seen in Theorem 13.4.1, the optimal investment of a strictly risk-averse agent in every risky security is zero.

If the return of a security can be written as the return on some portfolio of other securities plus a mean-independent term, then the sign of a strictly risk-averse agent's optimal investment in that security is the same as that of the expectation of the mean-independent term.

Theorem 13.5.1 *Suppose that the return on security k satisfies*

$$r_k = \sum_{j \neq k} \eta_j r_j + \epsilon_k, \tag{13.9}$$

where $\sum_{j \neq k} \eta_j = 1$ and ϵ_k is mean-independent of the returns on securities other than security k, that is,

$$E(\epsilon_k | r_1, \ldots, r_{k-1}, r_{k+1}, \ldots, r_J) = E(\epsilon_k). \tag{13.10}$$

Then the optimal investment in security k for a strictly risk-averse agent is strictly positive, zero, or strictly negative as $E(\epsilon_k)$ is strictly positive, zero, or strictly negative.

Proof: Consider the maximization problem

$$\max_{\lambda} E \left[v \left(\sum_{j \neq k} a_j^* r_j + \lambda r_k + (a_k^* - \lambda) \sum_{j \neq k} \eta_j r_j \right) \right]. \tag{13.11}$$

The value of expected utility in problem (13.11) cannot exceed $E[v(\sum_j a_j^* r_j)]$, and the latter value is achieved at $\lambda = a_k^*$. Thus $\lambda = a_k^*$ is the solution to the maximization problem (13.11). Whether a_k^* is strictly positive, zero, or strictly negative depends on the sign of the derivative of the (strictly concave) expected utility in problem (13.11) with respect to λ evaluated at $\lambda = 0$.

The derivative of the expected utility in problem (13.11) with respect to λ evaluated at zero is

$$E\left[v'\left(\sum_{j \neq k}(a_j^* + a_k^* \eta_j)r_j\right)\left(r_k - \sum_{j \neq k}\eta_j r_j\right)\right]. \tag{13.12}$$

Assumptions (13.9) and (13.10) and Proposition 10.4.1 imply that the expression (13.12) is equal to

$$E\left[v'\left(\sum_{j \neq k}\left(a_j^* + a_k^* \eta_j\right)r_j\right)\right]E(\epsilon_k). \tag{13.13}$$

From expression (13.13) we can see that the sign of the derivative of the expected utility in problem (13.11) at $\lambda = 0$ is determined by the sign of $E(\epsilon_k)$. Consequently, the sign of the optimal investment a_k^* is determined by the sign of $E(\epsilon_k)$.   □

A simple but useful corollary to Theorem 13.5.1 relates the risk premium on a security to the optimal investment if the return on that security is mean independent of the returns on other securities.

Corollary 13.5.2 *Suppose that security 1 is risk free with return $\bar{r}$ and that the return on security k is mean independent of the returns on other securities; that is,*

$$E(r_k | r_1, \ldots, r_{k-1}, r_{k+1}, \ldots, r_J) = E(r_k). \tag{13.14}$$

Then the optimal investment in security k for a strictly risk-averse agent is strictly positive, zero, or strictly negative as the risk premium $E(r_k) - \bar{r}$ is strictly positive, zero, or strictly negative.

Proof: We can write the return on security k as

$$r_k = \bar{r} + \epsilon_k. \tag{13.15}$$

If Eq. (13.14) holds, then ϵ_k is mean independent of returns on securities other than security k. Theorem 13.5.1 implies that the optimal investment in security k is strictly positive, zero, or strictly negative as $E(\epsilon_k)$ is strictly positive, zero, or strictly negative. Because $E(\epsilon_k)$ equals the risk premium $E(r_k) - \bar{r}$, the conclusion follows.   □

The intuitive explanation for Corollary 13.5.2 is simple. If the return on a security is mean independent of other returns and the risk premium is zero, then every portfolio with a nonzero holding of that security is strictly riskier than a portfolio in which the investment in that security has been replaced by an investment (of equal value) in the risk-free security. A strictly positive risk premium is required to induce a strictly risk-averse agent to invest a strictly positive amount of wealth in that security.

Corollary 13.5.2 can be viewed as an extension of Theorem 11.4.1. If there is a single risky security, then condition (13.14) is trivially satisfied.

The following example illustrates the results of this section.

Example 13.5.3 There are three states with probabilities $1/2$, $1/4$, and $1/4$ and three securities with returns

$$r_1 = \bar{r} = (1, 1, 1), \qquad r_2 = (0, 3, 3), \qquad \text{and } r_3 = \left(1, \frac{3}{2}, \frac{1}{2}\right). \qquad (13.16)$$

The risk premium on security 3 is zero. Further, the return on security 3 is mean independent of the returns on securities 1 and 2. To see this, note that the expected returns on security 3 conditional on each of the two possible realizations $(1, 0)$ and $(1, 3)$ of the returns on securities 1 and 2 are the same and equal to the expected return $E(r_3) = 1$. Corollary 13.5.2 implies that every strictly risk averse agent will invest zero in security 3.

If the return on security 3 were

$$r_3 = \left(\frac{5}{4}, 2, \frac{1}{2}\right) \qquad (13.17)$$

instead of the return specified in Eq. (13.16), then the risk premium on security 3 would be strictly positive. Mean independence would still hold, and an optimal investment in security 3 would be strictly positive for a strictly risk-averse agent. □

13.6 Optimal Portfolios under Linear Risk Tolerance

Optimal portfolios have a particularly simple form for the linear risk tolerance utility functions introduced in Section 9.9. For the negative exponential utility function, the optimal investment in a single risky security is independent of wealth (see Theorem 12.2.1). We have already shown that for the quadratic utility function, the optimal investment in a single risky security is linear in wealth (see Eq. (11.14)). For other LRT utility functions and when there are many risky securities, the optimal investment in each security is linear in wealth.

Theorem 13.6.1 *If an agent's risk tolerance is linear*

$$T(y) = \alpha + \gamma y, \qquad (13.18)$$

then the optimal investment in each risky security is given by

$$a_j^*(w) = (\alpha + \gamma w\bar{r})b_j, \qquad \text{for } j = 2, \ldots, J, \qquad (13.19)$$

for some b_j that is independent of wealth and of parameter α. Hence, the optimal investment in each security is a linear function of wealth.

Proof: Let v be the agent's von Neumann–Morgenstern utility function with linear risk tolerance given by Eq. (13.18). Fix wealth $\hat{w}$, and let $\hat{a} = a^*(\hat{w})$ be the associated optimal investment. We show that the optimal investment $a^*(w)$ for arbitrary wealth w satisfies

$$a_j^*(w) = \frac{\alpha + \gamma w\bar{r}}{\alpha + \gamma \hat{w}\bar{r}}\hat{a}_j \qquad (13.20)$$

for $j \geq 2$, and thus b_j in Eq. (13.19) is given by

$$b_j = \frac{\hat{a}_j}{\alpha + \gamma \hat{w}\bar{r}}. \qquad (13.21)$$

The first-order condition for $\hat{a}$ is

$$E\left[v'\left(\hat{w}\bar{r} + \sum_{j=2}^{J}\hat{a}_j(r_j - \bar{r})\right)(r_k - \bar{r})\right] = 0 \quad \forall k \geq 2. \qquad (13.22)$$

We consider first the case when $\gamma \neq 0$. If we differentiate Eq. (9.29), marginal utility v' is given by

$$v'(y) = (\alpha + \gamma y)^{-\frac{1}{\gamma}}. \qquad (13.23)$$

Substituting Eq. (13.23) in Eq. (13.22), we obtain

$$E\left\{\left[\alpha + \gamma\hat{w}\bar{r} + \gamma\sum_{j=2}^{J}\hat{a}_j(r_j - \bar{r})\right]^{-\frac{1}{\gamma}}(r_k - \bar{r})\right\} = 0 \quad \forall k \geq 2. \qquad (13.24)$$

Dividing both sides of Eq. (13.24) by $(\alpha + \gamma\hat{w}\bar{r})^{-\frac{1}{\gamma}}$, we obtain

$$E\left\{\left[1 + \gamma\sum_{j=2}^{J}\frac{\hat{a}_j}{\alpha + \gamma\hat{w}\bar{r}}(r_j - \bar{r})\right]^{-\frac{1}{\gamma}}(r_k - \bar{r})\right\} = 0 \quad \forall k \geq 2. \qquad (13.25)$$

Multiplying both sides of Eq. (13.25) by $(\alpha + \gamma w\bar{r})^{-\frac{1}{\gamma}}$ gives

$$E\left\{\left[\alpha + \gamma w\bar{r} + \gamma \sum_{j=2}^{J} \hat{a}_j\left(\frac{\alpha + \gamma w\bar{r}}{\alpha + \gamma \hat{w}\bar{r}}\right)(r_j - \bar{r})\right]^{-\frac{1}{\gamma}} (r_k - \bar{r})\right\} = 0 \quad \forall\, k \geq 2.$$

(13.26)

Thus $a^*(w)$, as given by Eq. (13.20), satisfies the first-order condition when the wealth is w, and hence it is an optimal portfolio.

In the case when $\gamma = 0$, marginal utility is $v'(y) = \alpha e^{-\alpha y}$. The first-order condition (13.22) becomes

$$E\left[\left(\alpha e^{-\alpha[\hat{w}\bar{r}+\sum_j \hat{a}_j(r_j-\bar{r})]}\right)(r_k - \bar{r})\right] = 0 \quad \forall\, k \geq 2.$$

(13.27)

Multiplying both sides of Eq. (13.27) by $e^{-\alpha\bar{r}(w-\hat{w})}$, we obtain

$$E\left[\left(\alpha e^{-\alpha[w\bar{r}+\sum_j \hat{a}_j(r_j-\bar{r})]}\right)(r_k - \bar{r})\right] = 0, \quad \forall\, k \geq 2,$$

(13.28)

which indicates that $\hat{a}$ is also the optimal investment at wealth w, in accordance with Eq. (13.20), when $\gamma = 0$.

Clearly, b_j given by Eq. (13.21) does not depend on wealth w. Further, if we substitute Eq. (13.21) in Eq. (13.25), when $\gamma \neq 0$, or Eq. (13.28), when $\gamma = 0$, it can be seen that b_j does not depend on α. □

Theorem 13.6.1 implies that the ratio of optimal investments in risky securities is independent of wealth for an agent with linear risk tolerance. That is,

$$\frac{a_j^*(w)}{a_k^*(w)} = \frac{b_j}{b_k},$$

(13.29)

for each $j, k \geq 2$ and every w. Consequently, optimal investments at different levels of wealth differ only by the amounts of wealth invested in risky securities and not by the compositions of the portfolios of risky securities. In other words, the optimal investment $a^*(w)$ can be written as

$$a^*(w) = [a_1^*(w), (\alpha + \gamma w\bar{r})b],$$

(13.30)

where $b = (b_2, \ldots, b_J)$ is the wealth-independent portfolio of risky securities, and

$$a_1^*(w) = w - (\alpha + w\gamma\bar{r}) \sum_{j=2}^{J} b_j.$$

(13.31)

Theorem 13.6.1 also implies that portfolios b of risky securities in Eq. (13.30) are the same for all agents with linear risk tolerance with common slope γ. This remark will be useful in the analysis of equilibrium allocations when agents have linear risk tolerance in Chapters 15 and 16.

13.7 Optimal Portfolios with Two-Date Consumption

Theorems 13.3.1 and 13.4.1 continue to hold when the agent's utility function depends on date-0 consumption.

If the agent is risk-neutral with utility function

$$v(c_0, c_s) = c_0 + \delta c_s, \quad \delta > 0, \tag{13.32}$$

the risk-free return equals $1/\delta$, and all securities are priced fairly, then the agent is indifferent among all portfolios. If the risk premium is nonzero on at least one security, or if the risk-free return is different from $1/\delta$ and there are no restrictions on consumption, then no optimal portfolio exists for the risk-neutral agent. But if his or her consumption is restricted to be positive and there is no arbitrage, then for that agent an optimal portfolio does exist (Theorem 3.6.5) and can be obtained by solving a linear programming problem.

13.8 Notes

Further results on optimal portfolios with many risky securities can be found in Merton [4]; see also Cass and Stiglitz [2]. Theorem 13.5.1 is closely related to separation theorems of Ross [8]. If the expectation $E(\epsilon_k)$ is zero in Theorem 13.5.1, then security returns exhibit $(J - 1)$-fund separation.

The results on portfolio demand under linear risk tolerance originated with Rubinstein [9] with a partial anticipation by Pye [7] and Cass and Stiglitz [1]. Milne [5] showed that linear risk tolerance is a necessary condition for linear portfolio demand for arbitrary security returns. Linear portfolio demand implies linear consumption demand. Linear consumption demands for the class of LRT utility functions have been known in consumer theory since Gorman [3] and Pollak [6] as linear Engel curves.

Bibliography

[1] Cass, D. and Stiglitz, J.E. The structure of investor preferences and asset returns and separability in portfolio allocation: A contribution to the pure theory of mutual funds. *Journal of Financial Economics*, **2**:122–60, 1970.
[2] Cass, D. and Stiglitz, J.E. Risk aversion and wealth effects on portfolios with many assets. *Review of Economic Studies*, **2**:331–54, 1973.
[3] Gorman, W.M. Community preference fields. *Econometrica*, **21**:63–80, 1953.
[4] Merton, R.C. Capital market theory and the pricing of financial securities. In Frank H. Hahn and Benjamin M. Friedman, editors, *Handbook of Monetary Economics*. North-Holland, Amsterdam, 1990.
[5] Milne, F. Consumer preferences, linear demand functions and aggregation in competitive asset markets. *Review of Economic Studies*, **46**:407–17, 1979.

[6] Pollak, R.A. Additive utility functions and linear Engel curves. *Review of Economic Studies*, **38**:401–14, 1971.

[7] Pye, G. Portfolio selection and security prices. *Review of Economics and Statistics*, **49**:111–15, 1967.

[8] Ross, S.A. Mutual fund separation in financial theory – the separating distributions. *Journal of Economic Theory*, **17**:254–86, 1978.

[9] Rubinstein, M. An aggregation theorem for securities markets. *Journal of Financial Economics*, **1**:225–44, 1974.

Part Five

Equilibrium Prices and Allocations

14

Consumption-Based Security Pricing

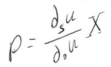

14.1 Introduction

The first-order conditions (1.13) for the consumption-portfolio choice problem relate prices of securities to their payoffs and to the marginal rates of substitution between the agent's consumption at date 0 and in each state at date 1. In equilibrium this relation holds for every agent. Consumption-based security pricing is derived from this relation when agents' utility functions are differentiable and have an expected utility representation.

14.2 Risk-Free Return in Equilibrium

For an agent whose utility function has an expected utility representation $E[v(c_0, c_1)]$, the marginal utility of consumption at date 0 is $\sum_{s=1}^{S} \pi_s \partial_0 v(c_0, c_s)$, and the marginal utility of consumption at date 1 in state s is $\pi_s \partial_1 v(c_0, c_s)$, where $\partial_0 v(c_0, c_s)$ and $\partial_1 v(c_0, c_s)$ denote partial derivatives of the von Neumann–Morgenstern utility function v. The marginal utility of date-0 consumption will be denoted $E(\partial_0 v)$. Further, $\partial_1 v$ will be understood to be a random variable with realizations $\partial_1 v(c_0, c_s)$. If the von Neumann–Morgenstern utility function v is time separable; that is, $v(c_0, c_s) = v_0(c_0) + v_1(c_s)$, then the marginal utility of date-0 consumption is $v_0'(c_0)$ or v_0' for short.

If optimal consumption is assumed to be interior, the first-order condition for the consumption-portfolio choice problem is

$$p_j E(\partial_0 v) = E(\partial_1 v \, x_j).$$

interior optimal consumption (14.1)

for each security j. Equation 14.1 corresponds to first-order conditions (1.13) specialized to expected utility.

In terms of returns, Eq. (14.1) takes the form

$$E(\partial_0 v) = E(\partial_1 v \, r_j).$$ (14.2)

141

If it is assumed that a risk-free security (or portfolio) is traded, Eq. (14.2) implies that the return $\bar{r}$ on this security satisfies

$$\bar{r} = \frac{E(\partial_0 v)}{E(\partial_1 v)}. \tag{14.3}$$

If an agent is risk neutral with von Neumann–Morgenstern utility function $v(c_0, c_s) = c_0 + \delta c_s$, then (if interior consumption is assumed) $\bar{r} = \delta^{-1}$, as was shown in Section 12.5.

14.3 Expected Returns in Equilibrium

The expectation of the product of any two random variables y and z can be written as their covariance plus the product of their expectations:

$$E(yz) = \text{cov}(y, z) + E(y)E(z). \tag{14.4}$$

Using this result, Eq. (14.2) becomes

$$\text{cov}(\partial_1 v, r_j) + E(\partial_1 v)E(r_j) = E(\partial_0 v). \tag{14.5}$$

Solving for the expected return $E(r_j)$ and using Eq. (14.3), we obtain

$$E(r_j) = \bar{r} - \frac{\text{cov}(\partial_1 v, r_j)}{E(\partial_1 v)} = \bar{r} - \bar{r}\frac{\text{cov}(\partial_1 v, r_j)}{E(\partial_0 v)}. \tag{14.6}$$

Equation (14.6) is the equation of *consumption-based security pricing*. It says that the risk premium (that is, the expected excess return) on any security is proportional to the covariance of its return with the marginal rate of substitution between consumption at date 0 and at date 1 (with a negative constant of proportionality). Strictly, the expression $\partial_1 v / E(\partial_0 v)$ seen in Eq. (14.6) is not the marginal rate of substitution between state-contingent consumption at date 1 and consumption at date 0 because of the absence of probabilities. Similarly, we will refer later to the term $\partial_1 v$ as the marginal utility of consumption despite the absence of probabilities. There is no reason to take issue with this imprecision in the terminology, but one should be aware of it.

For a strictly risk-averse agent $\partial_1 v(c_0, c_s)$ is a decreasing function of consumption at date 1. Thus, a security that has a high payoff when consumption is high and a low payoff when consumption is low will have an expected return that is greater than the risk-free return. On the other hand, a security that has high payoff when consumption is low and low payoff when consumption is high will have an expected return that is less than the risk-free return. Such a security could be used to decrease the risk of the agent's consumption. Its relatively low return reflects a relatively high price. A security the return on which has zero covariance with the marginal rate of substitution will have an expected return equal to the risk-free return.

According to Eq. (14.6) the risk premium for a security depends solely on the covariance of its return with the marginal rate of substitution between consumption at dates 0 and 1. This covariance may be considered as a measure of the risk of a security. This measure of risk differs in several respects from that of Chapter 10. First, it applies to returns of securities in an equilibrium. In contrast, the analysis of Chapter 10 applies to contingent claims that are not necessarily in the asset span and does not require that there be an equilibrium. Second, the covariance measure gives a complete ordering of the riskiness of returns, not just a partial ordering.

If the marginal rate of substitution is deterministic, then consumption-based security pricing (Eq. (14.6)) implies fair pricing. There are two cases in which the marginal rate of substitution is deterministic: when the agent's consumption is deterministic and when the agent is risk neutral.

The equation of consumption-based security pricing holds for any portfolio return r:

$$E(r) = \bar{r} - \bar{r} \frac{\mathrm{cov}(\partial_1 v, r)}{E(\partial_0 v)}. \tag{14.7}$$

The following example illustrates the dependence of the expected return on a security on the covariance of its return with the marginal rate of substitution.

Example 14.3.1 Consider a representative-agent economy with two equally probable states at date 1. The agent's endowment is 1 at date 0 and $(2, 1)$ at date 1. His or her expected utility is

$$E[v(c_0, c_1)] = \ln(c_0) + \frac{1}{2} \ln(c_1) + \frac{1}{2} \ln(c_2). \tag{14.8}$$

The two Arrow securities, $x_1 = (1, 0)$, $x_2 = (0, 1)$ and the risk-free security $x_3 = (1, 1)$ are traded. The agent's marginal utility of date-0 consumption evaluated at the endowment is $E(\partial_0 v) = 1$. The values of $\partial_1 v$ are $1/2$ in state 1 and 1 in state 2. The prices of the securities, calculated using Eq. (14.1), are

$$p_1 = \frac{1}{4}, \qquad p_2 = \frac{1}{2}, \qquad p_3 = \frac{3}{4}. \tag{14.9}$$

Security returns are

$$r_1 = \frac{x_1}{p_1} = (4, 0), \qquad r_2 = \frac{x_2}{p_2} = (0, 2), \qquad r_3 = \frac{x_3}{p_3} = \left(\frac{4}{3}, \frac{4}{3}\right), \tag{14.10}$$

and expected returns are

$$E(r_1) = 2, \qquad E(r_2) = 1, \qquad E(r_3) \equiv \bar{r} = \frac{4}{3}. \tag{14.11}$$

Security 1 has an expected return that is greater than the risk-free return because its payoff occurs when consumption is least valued. Security 2 has an expected return that is less than the risk-free return because otherwise its holder would use it to insure against low consumption at date 1. $\qquad\square$

14.4 Volatility of Marginal Rates of Substitution

Consumption-based security pricing provides a link between observable equilibrium security prices and unobservable marginal rates of substitution between consumption at date 0 and at date 1. Several inferences about marginal rates of substitution can be drawn from the characteristics of observed equilibrium prices. An obvious inference is that if risk premia are strictly positive, agents cannot be risk neutral. More interesting is the inference that a lower bound on the standard deviation of agents' marginal rates of substitution can be derived from expected returns and standard deviations of returns on portfolios of securities.

Equations (14.2) and (14.3) imply

$$E[\partial_1 v\,(r_j - \bar{r})] = 0. \tag{14.12}$$

Let ρ be the correlation between $\partial_1 v$ and $r_j - \bar{r}$, given by

$$\rho = \frac{E[\partial_1 v\,(r_j - \bar{r})] - E(\partial_1 v)E(r_j - \bar{r})}{\sigma(\partial_1 v)\sigma(r_j)}, \tag{14.13}$$

where $\sigma(\cdot)$ denotes the standard deviation. Substituting from Eq. (14.12) and using $|\rho| \leq 1$, we obtain

$$\sigma(\partial_1 v) \geq \frac{E(\partial_1 v)|E(r_j) - \bar{r}|}{\sigma(r_j)}. \tag{14.14}$$

Dividing both sides of inequality (14.14) by $E(\partial_0 v)$ and using Eq. (14.3) for the risk-free return, we obtain

$$\sigma\left[\frac{\partial_1 v}{E(\partial_0 v)}\right] \geq \frac{|E(r_j) - \bar{r}|}{\bar{r}\sigma(r_j)}. \tag{14.15}$$

The ratio of the risk premium to the standard deviation of return is called the *Sharpe ratio*. Inequality (14.15) says that the volatility of the marginal rate of substitution between consumption at date 0 and date 1 in equilibrium is greater than the (absolute value of the) Sharpe ratio of each security divided by the risk-free return. Again, because of missing probabilities the expression $\partial_1 v/E(\partial_0 v)$ is not exactly the marginal rate of substitution.

Equation (14.12) – and consequently also inequality (14.15) – holds for any portfolio return r, not just for security returns. Taking the supremum over all returns (other than the risk-free return), we obtain the following lower bound on the volatility of the marginal rate of substitution:

$$\sigma\left(\frac{\partial_1 v}{E(\partial_0 v)}\right) \geq \sup_r \frac{|E(r) - \bar{r}|}{\bar{r}\sigma(r)}. \tag{14.16}$$

Inequality (14.16) produces surprising results when confronted with aggregate stock market data. On the one hand, it has been observed that the risk premium on a broad stock market index is high relative to the volatility of the index returns.

Consequently, the Sharpe ratio on that index is high, and the bound on the volatility of the marginal rate of substitution is high. On the other hand, observed consumption volatility is low. Low volatility of consumption can be reconciled with high volatility of the marginal rate of substitution only if agents are extremely risk averse. To see this, recall that risk aversion is identified with curvature of the utility function, and thus high risk aversion means that the marginal utility of consumption undergoes wide variations even when consumption has little variation. Correspondingly, low risk aversion implies that the marginal utility of consumption differs very little for different levels of consumption. The conclusion that agents are highly risk averse is widely regarded as puzzling because it contradicts much empirical evidence, and also common sense, both of which appear to imply moderate risk aversion. This anomaly is the *equity premium puzzle*.

14.5 A First Pass at the CAPM

Consumption-based security pricing can be used to derive the Capital Asset Pricing Model (CAPM). For an agent whose von Neumann–Morgenstern utility function is quadratic in date-1 consumption,

$$v(c_0, c_s) = v_0(c_0) - (c_s - \alpha)^2, \quad c_s < \alpha, \tag{14.17}$$

where v_0 is some utility function of date-0 consumption, the marginal utility $\partial_1 v$ is

$$\partial_1 v = 2(\alpha - c_1). \tag{14.18}$$

Equation (14.6) becomes

$$E(r_j) = \bar{r} + \frac{\text{cov}(c_1, r_j)}{\alpha - E(c_1)}. \tag{14.19}$$

In a securities market economy, the aggregate endowment is in the asset span, meaning that it is a payoff of some portfolio of securities. This portfolio is termed the *market portfolio*, and its return is denoted by r_m. Equation (14.19) holds for returns on portfolios (see Eq. (14.7)). In particular, it holds for the market return so that

$$E(r_m) = \bar{r} + \frac{\text{cov}(c_1, r_m)}{\alpha - E(c_1)}. \tag{14.20}$$

Moving $\bar{r}$ to the left-hand side of Eqs. (14.19) and (14.20) and dividing the former by the latter, we obtain

$$\frac{E(r_j) - \bar{r}}{E(r_m) - \bar{r}} = \frac{\text{cov}(c_1, r_j)}{\text{cov}(c_1, r_m)}, \tag{14.21}$$

where, as we assume, the market risk premium is nonzero.

In a securities market economy, an agent's equilibrium date-1 consumption is in the asset span. If, in addition, the agent's equilibrium consumption is in the span of the market return and the risk-free return, then the agent's date-1 consumption and the market return are perfectly correlated. Accordingly, c_1 can be replaced by r_m in Eq. (14.21), resulting in

$$\frac{E(r_j) - \bar{r}}{E(r_m) - \bar{r}} = \frac{\text{cov}(r_m, r_j)}{\text{var}(r_m)}. \tag{14.22}$$

Using β_j to denote $\text{cov}(r_m, r_j)/\text{var}(r_m)$, we obtain the equation of the *security market line* of the CAPM:

$$E(r_j) = \bar{r} + \beta_j[E(r_m) - \bar{r}]. \tag{14.23}$$

The assumption that equilibrium consumption is in the span of the market payoff and the risk-free payoff holds trivially in a representative-agent economy, for in that case the equilibrium consumption of each agent equals the payoff of the per capita market portfolio. In the general discussion of CAPM in Chapter 19, we dispense with the assumption of a representative agent economy.

14.6 Notes

The bound on volatility of the marginal rate of substitution of consumption originated with Hansen and Jagannathan [1]. The Sharpe ratio was first proposed in Sharpe [4]. For the equity premium puzzle, see Mehra and Prescott [3] and Kocherlakota [2].

The treatment of risk premia outlined here appears to be very general, yet it conflicts with much informal discussion of risk premia. For example, it is often recommended that the government do all of its financing at short maturity to eliminate the risk premium paid on long-maturity debt relative to short-maturity debt. Under consumption-based security pricing, the risk premium on long-term debt can exceed that on short-term debt only insofar as the one-period return on long-term bonds has smaller covariance with the marginal rate of substitution than does the return on short-term debt. Therefore, if debt payments are weighted by marginal utilities, as is appropriate, shortening the maturity of the debt will not diminish taxpayers' cost.

Bibliography

[1] Hansen, L. P. and Jagannathan, R. Implications of security market data for models of dynamic economies. *Journal of Political Economy*, **99**:225–62, 1991.

[2] Kocherlakota, N. R. The equity premium: It's still a puzzle. *Journal of Economic Literature*, **XXXIV**:42–71, 1996.

[3] Mehra, R. and Prescott, E. C. The equity premium: A puzzle. *Journal of Monetary Economics*, **15**:145–61, 1985.

[4] Sharpe, W. F. Mutual fund performance. *Journal of Business*, **39**:119–38, 1966.

15

Complete Markets and Pareto-Optimal
Allocations of Risk

15.1 Introduction

A basic criterion of efficiency of a consumption allocation is Pareto optimality. A consumption allocation is Pareto optimal if it is impossible to reallocate the aggregate endowment so as to make any agent better off without making some other agent worse off. In an economy under uncertainty, the aggregate endowment represents the economy's aggregate consumption risk. Whether or not a consumption allocation is optimal depends on how the aggregate consumption risk is shared among agents.

The classical welfare theorems state that a competitive equilibrium allocation in complete markets is Pareto optimal and that each Pareto-optimal allocation is an equilibrium allocation under an appropriate distribution of the aggregate endowment.

In this chapter we provide characterizations of Pareto-optimal allocations of risk and prove the first welfare theorem.

15.2 Pareto-Optimal Allocations

Consumption allocation $\{\tilde{c}^i\}$ *weakly Pareto dominates* another allocation $\{c^i\}$ if every agent i weakly prefers consumption plan $\tilde{c}^i$ to c^i, that is,

$$u^i(\tilde{c}^i) \geq u^i(c^i). \tag{15.1}$$

If $\{\tilde{c}^i\}$ weakly Pareto dominates $\{c^i\}$ and, in addition, at least one agent i strictly prefers $\tilde{c}^i$ to c^i (so that (15.1) holds with strict inequality for at least one i), then allocation $\{\tilde{c}^i\}$ *Pareto dominates* allocation $\{c^i\}$. A feasible consumption allocation $\{c^i\}$ is *Pareto optimal* if there does not exist an alternative feasible allocation $\{\tilde{c}^i\}$ that Pareto dominates $\{c^i\}$. Feasibility of an allocation $\{c^i\}$ means that

$$\sum_{i=1}^{I} c^i \leq \bar{w}, \tag{15.2}$$

where $\bar{w} = \sum_{i=1}^{I} w^i$ denotes the aggregate endowment.

An important representation of a Pareto-optimal allocation is as the solution to the optimization problem of a social planner, where the social welfare function being maximized is a weighted sum of the agents' utilities. The planner's problem is

$$\max_{\{c^i\}} \sum_{i=1}^{I} \mu^i u^i(c^i) \tag{15.3}$$

subject to the feasibility constraint

$$\sum_{i=1}^{I} c^i \leq \bar{w}, \tag{15.4}$$

for some positive weights $\{\mu^i\}$.

Every consumption allocation that solves the planner's problem for strictly positive weights is Pareto optimal. Conversely, if agents' utility functions are concave, then every Pareto-optimal allocation is a solution to the planner's problem for some weights μ^i that are all positive with at least one nonzero. Further, if the Pareto-optimal allocation is interior and utility functions are strictly increasing, then the weights are all strictly positive.

The planner's problem has a solution if the set of feasible allocations is compact and under the assumed continuity of utility functions. A sufficient condition for the compactness of the set of feasible allocations is that agents' consumption sets be closed and bounded below.

If consumption sets are unbounded, then there may not exist a solution to the planner's problem for any positive weights; consequently, there may not exist a Pareto-optimal allocation.

Example 15.2.1 Suppose that there is no uncertainty and that two agents have utility functions $u^1(c_0, c_1) = c_0 + \delta^1 c_1$ and $u^2(c_0, c_1) = c_0 + \delta^2 c_1$. If $\delta^1 \neq \delta^2$ and consumption sets are unrestricted, Pareto-optimal allocations do not exist for any specification of endowments.   □

Sufficient conditions for the existence of Pareto-optimal allocations with unbounded consumptions sets can be found in sources cited in the notes.

The first-order conditions for an interior solution to the planner's problem (15.3) are

$$\mu^i \partial_s u^i = \nu_s, \quad \forall s, \quad \forall i, \tag{15.5}$$

where ν_s is the Lagrange multiplier associated with the feasibility constraint on consumption at date 1 in state s or at date 0 when $s = 0$. Equation (15.5) states that at a Pareto-optimal allocation the marginal contribution to social welfare of an increase in agent i's consumption in state s is the same for all agents and equals the Lagrange multiplier associated with consumption in state s.

The first-order conditions (15.5) imply that the marginal rates of substitution

$$\frac{\partial_s u^i}{\partial_0 u^i} \tag{15.6}$$

at an interior Pareto-optimal allocation are the same for all agents.

15.3 Pareto-Optimal Equilibria in Complete Markets

The first welfare theorem holds when security markets are complete.

Theorem 15.3.1 *If security markets are complete and agents' utility functions are strictly increasing, then every equilibrium consumption allocation is Pareto optimal.*

Proof: Let p be a vector of equilibrium security prices and $\{c^i\}$ an equilibrium consumption allocation in complete security markets. Using the framework of Section 2.6, the consumption plan $c^i = (c_0^i, c_1^i)$ maximizes utility $u^i(c_0, c_1)$ subject to the budget constraints

$$c_0 \leq w_0^i - qz \tag{15.7}$$

and

$$c_1 \leq w_1^i + z, \quad z \in \mathcal{R}^S, \tag{15.8}$$

where q is the (unique) vector of state prices associated with p. Note that q is strictly positive.

Suppose that the consumption plan $c = (c_0, c_1)$ satisfies budget constraints (15.7) and (15.8). Multiplying inequality (15.8) by q and adding the result to inequality (15.7), we obtain

$$c_0 + qc_1 \leq w_0^i + qw_1^i. \tag{15.9}$$

Conversely, suppose that c satisfies the budget constraint (15.9). Then c also satisfies budget constraints (15.7) and (15.8) with $z = c_1 - w_1^i$. Thus, budget constraints

(15.7) and (15.8) are equivalent to inequality (15.9). Consequently, the optimal consumption plan c^i maximizes utility u^i subject to inequality (15.9).

Suppose that allocation $\{c^i\}$ is not Pareto optimal, and let $\{\tilde{c}^i\}$ be a feasible allocation that Pareto dominates $\{c^i\}$. Because the utility function u^i is strictly increasing and c^i maximizes utility u^i subject to inequality (15.9), we have

$$\tilde{c}^i_0 + q\tilde{c}^i_1 \geq w^i_0 + qw^i_1 \tag{15.10}$$

for every agent i with strict inequality for agents who are strictly better off with $\tilde{c}^i$ than with c^i. Summing over all agents, we obtain

$$\sum_{i=1}^{I} \tilde{c}^i_0 + \sum_{i=1}^{I} q\tilde{c}^i_1 > \bar{w}_0 + q\bar{w}_1, \tag{15.11}$$

which contradicts the assumption that allocation $\{\tilde{c}^i\}$ is feasible.   □

The second welfare theorem also holds: if every agent's utility function is quasi-concave and strictly increasing, and if security markets are complete, then every interior Pareto-optimal allocation is an equilibrium allocation under an appropriate distribution of the aggregate endowment.

We observed in Section 2.6 that if markets are complete, then the first-order conditions at an (interior) equilibrium consumption allocation are

$$q_s = \frac{\partial_s u^i}{\partial_0 u^i} \tag{15.12}$$

for all agents i and all states s. Equation (15.12) says that marginal rates of substitution are equal to state prices. Consequently, marginal rates of substitution must be the same for all agents in all states. This is the requirement for a Pareto-optimal allocation.

15.4 Complete Markets and Options

The only example of securities that generate complete markets we have thus far is the set of state claims. State claims cannot be regarded as real-world securities, but there is a close connection between state claims and real-world options. The suggestion is that options can do what state claims can do.

Suppose that there exists a payoff z that takes on different values in different states; that is, $z_s \neq z_{s'}$ for every pair of states s, s'. Payoff z can be the payoff of a security or a portfolio of securities. Suppose further that call options on payoff z with arbitrary strike prices can be traded. A call option with strike price k matures out-of-the-money (has zero payoff) in all states in which the payoff of z is less than or equal to k and matures in-the-money (has strictly positive payoff) in all other states. As can easily be shown, if the payoff z and $S - 1$ options with strike prices z_s for all values of z_s (other than the greatest) are traded, then markets are complete. All securities other than that with payoff z and the $S - 1$ options are redundant.

If payoff z takes on the same value in two states, then all options have equal payoffs in these states. It follows that markets will not be complete even if options with arbitrary strike prices can be traded. Options on payoff z do, however, span all payoffs that are state independent in any subset of states in which payoff z is state independent.

That options can imply completeness of markets is illustrated by the following example.

Example 15.4.1 Let there be three states and let the payoff z be $(1, 3, 6)$. The payoff of a call with strike price 3 is $(0, 0, 3)$, and the payoff of a call with strike price 1 is $(0, 2, 5)$. With trading in z and these two calls, markets are clearly complete.

Now let there be four states and let the payoff z be $(1, 3, 3, 6)$. The payoffs of z in states 2 and 3 are the same. Options must therefore have the same payoffs in those states. The same is true of a portfolio made up of z and options on z. Thus, markets are incomplete even if all options with arbitrary strike prices are traded. □

15.5 Pareto-Optimal Allocations under Expected Utility

We provide now a characterization of Pareto-optimal allocations of risk when agents' utility functions have expected utility representations with, as assumed throughout, common probabilities.

Suppose that each agent's von Neumann–Morgenstern utility function v^i is strictly concave, strictly increasing, and differentiable. Thus, agents are strictly risk averse. As noted in Section 15.2, an interior Pareto-optimal allocation $\{c^i\}$ is a solution to the optimization problem (15.3) with strictly positive weights $\{\mu_i\}$. The first-order conditions (15.5) imply that

$$\mu^i \partial_1 v^i (c_0^i, c_s^i) = \mu^k \partial_1 v^k (c_0^k, c_s^k) \tag{15.13}$$

for any two agents i and k and any state s.

For any two states s and t such that consumption of agent i is greater in state s than in state t,

$$c_s^i > c_t^i, \tag{15.14}$$

we have that

$$\partial_1 v^i (c_0^i, c_s^i) < \partial_1 v^i (c_0^i, c_t^i) \tag{15.15}$$

because the marginal utility $\partial_1 v^i$ is strictly decreasing in date-1 consumption. It follows from Eq. (15.13) and inequality (15.15) that the same relation holds for agent k:

$$\partial_1 v^k(c_0^k, c_s^k) < \partial_1 v^k(c_0^k, c_t^k), \tag{15.16}$$

and hence that the consumption of agent k is higher in state s than in state t,

$$c_s^k > c_t^k. \tag{15.17}$$

Thus, if one agent consumes more in state s than state t, all other agents do so as well.

We have demonstrated that agents' date-1 consumption plans at an interior Pareto-optimal allocation are *strictly co-monotone*, that is, $c_s^i > c_t^i$ iff $c_s^k > c_t^k$ for all agents i and k and all states s and t. Because the aggregate consumption equals the aggregate endowment, each agent's date-1 consumption plan is strictly co-monotone with the aggregate endowment.

The argument above required the assumption that utility functions be differentiable and it applied only to interior Pareto-optimal allocations. We now prove that a weaker form of co-monotonicity holds for all Pareto-optimal allocations and without the assumption of differentiability of utility functions. This proof draws on the concept of greater risk, as defined in Chapter 10.

We say that agents' date-1 consumption plans $\{c_1^i\}$ are *co-monotone* if $c_s^i \geq c_t^i$ iff $c_s^k \geq c_t^k$ for all agents i and k, and all states s and t.

Theorem 15.5.1 *If all agents are strictly risk averse, then at every Pareto-optimal allocation their date-1 consumption plans are co-monotone.*

Proof: To simplify notation, we assume that no agent values date-0 consumption. Suppose by contradiction that the consumption plans at a Pareto-optimal allocation $\{c^i\}$ are not co-monotone. Then there exist states s and t and agents i and k such that

$$c_s^i < c_t^i \quad \text{and} \quad c_s^k > c_t^k. \tag{15.18}$$

Define the consumption plan $\tilde{c}^i$ by

$$\tilde{c}_s^i = \tilde{c}_t^i = E(c^i|\{s, t\}), \tag{15.19}$$

and $\tilde{c}_{s'}^i = c_{s'}^i$ for every $s' \neq s, t$. Consumption plan $\tilde{c}^i$ differs from c^i in that the consumptions in states s and t are replaced by their conditional expectation. Define the consumption plan $\tilde{c}^k$ for agent k just as for agent i in Eq. (15.19). Let

$$\epsilon^i = c^i - \tilde{c}^i \quad \text{and} \quad \epsilon^k = c^k - \tilde{c}^k. \tag{15.20}$$

Because ϵ^k and ϵ^i are nonzero only in two states and have zero expectation, they must be collinear; that is,

$$\epsilon^k = -\lambda \epsilon^i, \tag{15.21}$$

where, as follows from inequalities (15.18), $\lambda > 0$.

Suppose first that $\lambda \geq 1$. We show that transferring ϵ^i from agent i to agent k makes both better off. By construction, ϵ^i is mean independent of $\tilde{c}^i$. Similarly, ϵ^k, and hence $-\epsilon^i$, is mean independent of $\tilde{c}^k$. Taking ϵ^i away from agent i leaves him or her with consumption plan $\tilde{c}^i$. Because $c^i = \tilde{c}^i + \epsilon^i$, consumption plan c^i is more risky than $\tilde{c}^i$, and agent i is better off after the transfer. Giving ϵ^i to agent k leaves him or her with consumption plan $c^k + \epsilon^i = \tilde{c}^k + (\lambda - 1)(-\epsilon^i)$. Because $0 \leq \lambda - 1 < \lambda$ and $\tilde{c}^k + \lambda(-\epsilon^i) = c^k$, consumption plan c^k is more risky than $c^k + \epsilon^i$ (see Proposition 10.5.5), and agent k is also better off after the transfer.

If $\lambda < 1$, then, instead of transferring ϵ^i from agent i to agent k, we transfer ϵ^k from agent k to agent i, thereby making both better off. That these transfers are possible contradicts Pareto-optimality of the allocation $\{c^i\}$. □

It follows from Theorem 15.5.1 that if the aggregate date-1 endowment is constant for a subset of states, then at each Pareto-optimal allocation every agent's date-1 consumption is state independent for that subset of states.

Corollary 15.5.2 *If agents are strictly risk averse and the aggregate date-1 endowment is state independent for a subset of states, then each agent's date-1 consumption at every Pareto-optimal allocation is state independent for that subset of states.*

If the aggregate date-1 endowment is state-independent for all states (risk-free), then we say that there is *no aggregate risk* in the economy. Individual endowments, of course, may be risky, but their risky components are offsetting in the aggregate. It follows from Corollary 15.5.2 that, in a no-aggregate-risk economy, if agents are strictly risk averse, then their date-1 consumption plans at any Pareto-optimal allocation are risk free.

15.6 Pareto-Optimal Allocations under Linear Risk Tolerance

A simple characterization of Pareto-optimal allocations emerges under the assumption that all agents have linear risk tolerance (LRT utilities) with the same slope. Agents' date-1 consumption plans at a Pareto-optimal allocation lie in the span of two payoffs: the risk-free payoff and the aggregate endowment.

Agents with LRT utilities are assumed to consume only at date 1, although the result also holds when agents consume at both date 0 and date 1 and have time-separable utility functions. Each agent's risk tolerance is

$$T^i(y) = \alpha^i + \gamma y, \tag{15.22}$$

where γ is the common slope. The consumption set of agent i is given by $\{c \in \mathcal{R}^S : T^i(c_s) > 0 \text{ for every } s\}$.

The assumption of the common slope γ implies that all agents either have negative exponential utility ($\gamma = 0$), all have logarithmic utility ($\gamma = 1$), or all have power utility with the same exponent ($\gamma \neq 0, 1$). This specification is restrictive, but note that agents can have different degrees of risk aversion within the restriction, and their endowments can differ.

Theorem 15.6.1 *If every agent's risk tolerance is linear with common slope γ, then date-1 consumption plans at any Pareto-optimal allocation lie in the span of the risk-free payoff and the aggregate endowment.*

Proof: Let $\{c^i\}$ be a Pareto-optimal allocation. Then, as follows from Eq. (15.5),

$$\mu^i v'^i(c_s^i) = \mu^k v'^k(c_s^k) \tag{15.23}$$

for any two agents i and k. Because every agent's consumption set is open, the allocation $\{c^i\}$ is interior, and therefore the weights μ^i and μ^k are strictly positive. Taking logarithms of both sides of Eq. (15.23) results in

$$\ln(\mu^i) + \ln[v'^i(c_s^i)] = \ln(\mu^k) + \ln[v'^k(c_s^k)]. \tag{15.24}$$

But

$$\ln[v'^i(c_s^i)] = \ln[v'^i(\bar{y}^i)] - \int_{\bar{y}^i}^{c_s^i} A^i(y)\, dy \tag{15.25}$$

for an arbitrary $\bar{y}^i$ in the domain of v^i, where $A^i(y) = 1/T^i(y)$, is the Arrow–Pratt measure of absolute risk aversion. Thus, if use is made of Eqs. (15.22) and (15.25), Eq. (15.24) can be rewritten as

$$\ln(\mu^i) - \int_{\bar{y}^i}^{c_s^i} \frac{1}{(\alpha^i + \gamma y)}\, dy + \ln[v'^i(\bar{y}^i)]$$

$$= \ln(\mu^k) - \int_{\bar{y}^k}^{c_s^k} \frac{1}{(\alpha^k + \gamma y)}\, dy + \ln[v'^k(\bar{y}^k)]. \tag{15.26}$$

Solving for the integrals in Eq. (15.26) when $\gamma \neq 0$ and simplifying, we obtain

$$\ln[\mu^i v'^i(\bar{y}^i)] - \frac{1}{\gamma} \ln(\alpha^i + \gamma c_s^i) + \frac{1}{\gamma} \ln(\alpha^i + \gamma \bar{y}^i)$$

$$= \ln[\mu^k v'^k(\bar{y}^k)] - \frac{1}{\gamma} \ln(\alpha^k + \gamma c_s^k) + \frac{1}{\gamma} \ln(\alpha^k + \gamma \bar{y}^k). \quad (15.27)$$

Multiplying Eq. (15.27) by $-\gamma$, exponentiating both sides, and using $D^i \equiv [\mu^i v'^i(\bar{y}^i)]^\gamma (\alpha^i + \gamma \bar{y}^i)$ where $D^i \neq 0$, we obtain

$$\frac{1}{D^i}(\alpha^i + \gamma c_s^i) = \frac{1}{D^k}(\alpha^k + \gamma c_s^k). \quad (15.28)$$

Then, multiplying both sides of Eq. (15.28) by D^k, summing over k, and using $\sum_i c_s^i = \bar{w}_s$, we obtain

$$\frac{\sum_k D^k}{D^i}(\alpha^i + \gamma c_s^i) = \sum_k \alpha^k + \gamma \bar{w}_s. \quad (15.29)$$

Equation (15.29) can be solved for

$$c_s^i = F^i \bar{w}_s + G^i \quad (15.30)$$

where $F^i > 0$ and G^i are constants.

For $\gamma = 0$ (negative exponential utility), Eq. (15.27) is replaced by

$$\ln[\mu^i v'^i(\bar{y}^i)] - \frac{1}{\alpha^i} c_s^i + \frac{1}{\alpha^i} \bar{y}^i = \ln[\mu^k v'^k(\bar{y}^k)] - \frac{1}{\alpha^k} c_s^k + \frac{1}{\alpha^k} \bar{y}^k. \quad (15.31)$$

Like Eq. (15.27), Eq. (15.31) leads to the conclusion (Eq. (15.30)) that the date-1 consumption plan of every agent i lies in the span of the aggregate endowment and the risk-free payoff. $\quad\square$

If all Pareto-optimal consumption plans lie in the span of the risk-free payoff and the aggregate endowment, then we say that *two-fund spanning* holds. The social planner's problem (15.3) can be simplified to the planner's assigning to agents claims on two mutual funds: one consists of the risk-free payoff and the other is a claim on the aggregate endowment.

15.7 Notes

The first welfare theorem 15.3.1 for complete security markets originated with Arrow [1]. The assumption of strict monotonicity is stronger than necessary; all that is needed is nonsatiation. We used strict monotonicity because we have not introduced nonsatiation. A modern statement of the welfare theorems with no uncertainty can be found in Debreu [3].

The characterization of Pareto-optimal allocations as solutions to the optimization problem (15.3) of a social planner can be found in Mas-Colell, Whinston, and Green [4]. Sufficient conditions for the existence of Pareto-optimal allocations with unbounded consumptions sets can be found in Page and Wooders [5].

The analysis of Section 15.4 is based on Ross [7]. The discussion of Pareto-optimal allocations when agents have LRT utilities follows Pye [6], Rubinstein [8], Borch [2], and Wilson [9].

Bibliography

[1] Arrow, K. J. The role of securities in the optimal allocation of risk bearing. *Review of Economic Studies*, **31**:91–6, 1964.

[2] Borch, K. General equilibrium in the economics of uncertainty. In Karl Borch and Jan Mossin, editors, *Proceedings of a Conference Held by the International Economic Association*. MacMillan and St. Martin's Press, 1968.

[3] Debreu, G. *Theory of Value*. Wiley, New York, 1959.

[4] Mas-Colell, A., Whinston, M. D., and Green, J. *Microeconomic Theory*. Oxford University Press, New York, 1995.

[5] Page, F. H. and Wooders, M. H. A necessary and sufficient condition for the compactness of individually rational and feasible outcomes and the existence of an equilibrium. *Economic Letters*, **52**:153–62, 1996.

[6] Pye, G. Portfolio selection and security prices. *Review of Economics and Statistics*, **49**:111–15, 1967.

[7] Ross, S. A. Options and efficiency. *Quarterly Journal of Economics*, **90**:75–89, 1976.

[8] Rubinstein, M. An aggregation theorem for securities markets. *Journal of Financial Economics*, **1**:225–44, 1974.

[9] Wilson, R. The theory of syndicates. *Econometrica*, **36**:119–31, 1968.

16

Optimality in Incomplete Security Markets

16.1 Introduction

If security markets are incomplete, equilibrium consumption allocations are in general not Pareto optimal. Agents generally cannot implement the trades required to attain a Pareto-optimal allocation. Equilibrium consumption allocations are, however, optimal in a restricted sense. If reallocations are constrained to those that are attainable through security markets, then it is impossible to reallocate the aggregate endowment so as to make any agent better off without making some other agent worse off. We introduce and discuss the concept of constrained optimality in this chapter.

There are particular preferences, endowments, and security payoffs for which equilibrium consumption allocations are Pareto optimal despite markets being incomplete. Those preferences, endowments, and payoffs are also discussed in this chapter.

16.2 Constrained Optimality

A consumption allocation $\{c^i\}$ is *attainable through security markets* if the net trade $c_1^i - w_1^i$ lies in the asset span $\mathcal{M}$ for every agent i. A feasible consumption allocation $\{c^i\}$ is *constrained optimal* if it is attainable through security markets and if there does not exist an alternative feasible allocation $\{\tilde{c}^i\}$, also attainable through security markets, that Pareto dominates the allocation $\{c^i\}$.

Theorem 16.2.1 *If agents' utility functions are strictly increasing, then every security market's equilibrium consumption allocation is constrained optimal.*

Proof: The proof is very similar to that of Theorem 15.3.1. Let p be a vector of equilibrium security prices and $\{c^i\}$ be an equilibrium consumption allocation. It follows that consumption plan c^i of agent i maximizes utility u^i subject to the

157

constraints

$$c_0 \le w_0^i - qz, \tag{16.1}$$

$$c_1 \le w_1^i + z, \quad z \in \mathcal{M}, \tag{16.2}$$

where q is any of the vectors of strictly positive state prices associated with security prices p. Because u^i is strictly increasing, the optimal consumption plan c^i satisfies the budget constraints with equality. Therefore $c_1^i - w_1^i \in \mathcal{M}$.

Suppose now that $\{c^i\}$ is not constrained optimal. Then there exists a feasible allocation $\{\tilde{c}^i\}$ that Pareto dominates $\{c^i\}$ and that is attainable through security markets; that is, $\tilde{c}_1^i - w_1^i \in \mathcal{M}$ for every i. Setting $z^i = \tilde{c}_1^i - w_1^i$, consumption plan $\tilde{c}_1^i$ satisfies date-1 budget constraint (16.2). Because $u^i(\tilde{c}^i) \ge u^i(c^i)$ and u^i is strictly increasing, we have

$$\tilde{c}_0^i \ge w_0^i - q(\tilde{c}_1^i - w_1^i) \tag{16.3}$$

for every agent i, with strict inequality for at least one agent. Summing inequality (16.3) over all i, we obtain a contradiction to the assumption that $\{\tilde{c}^i\}$ is a feasible allocation.   □

16.3 Effectively Complete Markets

If security markets are complete, then every allocation is attainable through security markets. Clearly then, constrained optimal allocations are Pareto optimal. In particular, security markets equilibrium allocations are Pareto optimal. We show in this section that a weaker sufficient condition for constrained optimal allocations to be Pareto optimal is that Pareto-optimal allocations be attainable through security markets.

Security markets are *effectively complete* if every Pareto-optimal allocation is attainable through security markets.

Theorem 16.3.1 *If security markets are effectively complete and if for every feasible allocation there exists a Pareto-optimal allocation that weakly Pareto dominates that allocation, then every constrained optimal allocation is Pareto optimal.*

Proof: Let $\{c^i\}$ be a constrained optimal allocation. By assumption, there exists a Pareto-optimal allocation $\{\tilde{c}^i\}$ that weakly Pareto dominates allocation $\{c^i\}$. Because markets are effectively complete, the allocation $\{\tilde{c}^i\}$ can be obtained through security markets. If $\{c^i\}$ is not Pareto optimal, then $\{\tilde{c}^i\}$ (strictly) Pareto dominates $\{c^i\}$. This contradicts the constrained Pareto optimality of $\{c^i\}$.   □

A sufficient condition for the existence of a Pareto-optimal allocation that weakly dominates an arbitrary feasible allocation is that consumption sets be bounded below and closed (an alternative sufficient condition will be given in Section 16.7).

Proposition 16.3.2 *If agents' consumption sets are bounded below and closed, then, for every feasible allocation there exists a Pareto-optimal allocation that weakly Pareto dominates that allocation.*

Proof: Let $\{c^i\}$ be a feasible allocation and suppose that it is not Pareto optimal. Because utility functions are continuous, the set of feasible allocations that weakly Pareto dominate $\{c^i\}$ is a closed subset of the set of all feasible allocations. The latter set is compact because consumption sets are bounded below and closed (Section 15.2). Therefore, the set of feasible allocations that weakly Pareto dominate $\{c^i\}$ is compact. Maximizing the social welfare function (15.3) with strictly positive weights over this set generates the required Pareto-optimal allocation.   □

The most important instances of effectively complete markets are to be found in security markets economies (that is, when agents' endowments lie in the asset span). Markets are effectively complete in a security markets economy iff agents' date-1 consumption plans at any Pareto-optimal allocation lie in the asset span. Thus, if markets are effectively complete for one allocation of endowments that lies in the asset span, then they are effectively complete for all endowment allocations in the asset span.

16.4 Equilibria in Effectively Complete Markets

Combining Theorems 16.2.1 and 16.3.1, we obtain the first welfare theorem for effectively complete security markets.

Theorem 16.4.1 *If agents' utility functions are strictly increasing and if the assumption of Theorem 16.3.1 is satisfied, then every equilibrium consumption allocation in effectively complete security markets is Pareto optimal.*

It is natural to inquire whether equilibrium consumption allocations in effectively complete markets are the same as the equilibrium allocations that would result if security markets were complete.

Even though there are many distinct sets of security payoffs that generate complete markets, equilibria under complete security markets can be identified by a consumption allocation and a vector of state prices without any reference to a particular set of securities. Equilibrium prices of a particular set of securities can be obtained using the usual relation between state prices and security prices. The existence of the corresponding equilibrium portfolio allocation follows from the feasibility of the equilibrium consumption allocation, as noted in Section 1.7. When comparing equilibrium allocations in effectively complete security markets and complete security markets we will not specify a particular set of securities generating complete markets but rather specify an equilibrium in complete markets by state prices and a consumption allocation. An equilibrium in effectively complete security markets will be specified by security prices and a consumption allocation.

Theorem 16.4.2 *Suppose that security markets are effectively complete. If a vector of state prices q and a consumption allocation $\{c^i\}$ are a complete markets equilibrium, then security prices given by*

$$p_j = qx_j, \quad \forall j, \tag{16.4}$$

and allocation $\{c^i\}$ are a security markets equilibrium.

Proof: The vector q is a vector of state prices associated with security prices defined by Eq. (16.4). It follows from the representation (16.1) and (16.2) of the budget constraints in security markets that the set of budget-feasible consumption plans in security markets at prices p is a subset of the budget set in complete markets at state prices q.

By the first welfare theorem 15.3.1, consumption allocation $\{c^i\}$ is Pareto optimal. Because security markets are effectively complete, allocation $\{c^i\}$ is attainable through security markets; that is, the net trade $c_1^i - w_1^i$ lies in the asset span of security markets for every agent i. Therefore, the consumption plan c^i lies in the set of budget-feasible consumption plans in security markets, and hence it remains optimal. Consequently, allocation $\{c^i\}$ is an equilibrium allocation in security markets. □

A partial converse to Theorem 16.4.2 holds if agents' utility functions are differentiable.

Theorem 16.4.3 *Suppose that security markets are effectively complete, agents' utility functions are strictly increasing and quasi-concave, and the assumption of Theorem 16.3.1 is satisfied. If a vector of security prices p and a consumption allocation $\{c^i\}$ are a security markets equilibrium such that $\{c^i\}$ is interior, then state prices given by*

$$q_s = \frac{\partial_s u^i}{\partial_0 u^i}, \quad \forall s, \tag{16.5}$$

and the allocation $\{c^i\}$ are a complete markets equilibrium.

Proof: It follows from Theorems 16.2.1 and 16.3.1 that the security markets equilibrium allocation $\{c^i\}$ is Pareto optimal. Because it is interior, the marginal rates of substitution in Eq. (16.5) are the same for all agents. Setting the state prices equal to the marginal rates of substitution implies that the first-order conditions for the consumption choice in complete markets are satisfied for each agent at the allocation $\{c^i\}$. Because utility functions are quasi-concave, the first-order conditions are sufficient, and the allocation $\{c^i\}$ and state-price vector q are a complete markets equilibrium. □

The need for interiority of the equilibrium allocation in Theorem 16.4.3 is illustrated by the following example.

Example 16.4.4 Suppose that there are two states and a single security with payoff $x = (1, -1)$. There are two agents with utility functions

$$u^1(c_0, c_1, c_2) = c_0 + 2c_1, \quad \text{and} \quad u^2(c_0, c_1, c_2) = c_0 + c_2, \quad (16.6)$$

and endowments $w^1 = (2, 0, 1)$ and $w^2 = (2, 1, 0)$. Consumption at each state and date is restricted to being positive.

Pareto-optimal allocations are of the form $c^1 = (a, 1, 0)$ and $c^2 = (4 - a, 0, 1)$, where $0 \le a \le 4$. Clearly, markets are effectively complete.

To find all security markets equilibria, we derive the two agents' optimal holdings of the security as functions of its price p. Agent 1's optimal holding is 1 for any price $p < 2$ and 0 for any price $p > 2$. At $p = 2$ any holding greater than or equal to 0 and less than or equal to 1 is optimal for agent 1. Agent 2's optimal holding is 0 for any $p < -1$; it is -1 (short-sale) for any $p > -1$ and any value greater than or equal to -1 and less than or equal to 0 at $p = -1$. The security market clears at any price p such that $-1 \le p \le 2$. The associated equilibrium consumption allocations are $(2 - p, 1, 0)$ for agent 1 and $(2 + p, 0, 1)$ for agent 2. There is a continuum of equilibria and all equilibrium allocations are Pareto optimal.

Now consider complete markets. At state prices $q_1 = 2$ and $q_2 = 1$ consumption plan $(1, 1, 0)$ for agent 1 and consumption plan $(3, 0, 1)$ for agent 2 maximize their respective utilities subject to the budget constraints. Note that agent 1's marginal rate of substitution between consumption at date 0 and in state 1 equals q_1 because his or her consumption at date 0 and in state 1 is interior. Agent 2's marginal rate of substitution between consumption at date 0 and in state 2 equals q_2. Because markets clear, we have an equilibrium. It is easy to verify that there are no other complete markets equilibria.

The set of equilibrium allocations under complete markets is thus a proper subset of the set of equilibrium allocations in security markets. □

16.5 Effectively Complete Markets with No Aggregate Risk

In the rest of this chapter we study examples of effectively complete markets. In all these examples, agents' preferences are assumed to have expected utility representations with strictly increasing von Neumann–Morgenstern utility functions.

The first example arises when there is no aggregate risk, agents are strictly risk averse, and their date-1 endowments lie in the asset span. We refer to such economy as a security markets economy with no aggregate risk.

In a security markets economy with no aggregate risk, agents' date-1 consumption plans at any Pareto-optimal allocation are risk free (Corollary 15.5.2). Because the risk-free payoff lies in the asset span, these consumption plans lie in the asset span and markets are effectively complete. If agents' consumptions are restricted to being positive (so that consumption sets are closed and bounded below), then equilibrium allocations are Pareto optimal (Theorem 16.4.1 and Proposition 16.3.2) and hence risk free. Further, interior equilibrium allocations are the same as with complete markets (Theorems 16.4.2 and 16.4.3). In an interior equilibrium (if it is assumed that agents' utility functions are differentiable) securities are priced fairly:

$$E(r_j) = \bar{r} \quad \forall j \tag{16.7}$$

(see Theorem 13.4.1). If date-0 consumption does not enter agents' utility functions, then equilibrium consumption plans equal the expectations of endowments $E(w^i)$.

Example 16.5.1 There are three states and two securities with payoffs

$$x_1 = (1, 1, 1) \quad \text{and} \quad x_2 = (1, 0, 0). \tag{16.8}$$

There are two agents whose preferences depend only on date-1 consumption and have an expected utility representation with strictly increasing and differentiable von Neumann–Morgenstern utility functions and common probabilities $(1/4, 1/2, 1/4)$. Both agents are strictly risk averse. Their respective endowments are $w^1 = (0, 1, 1)$ and $w^2 = (1, 0, 0)$.

Because each agent's endowment lies in the asset span and there is no aggregate risk, markets are effectively complete. In equilibrium, securities must be priced fairly. Setting $p_1 = 1$, which yields $\bar{r} = 1$, we obtain $p_2 = E(x_2)/\bar{r} = 1/4$. The equilibrium consumption plans of both agents are risk free and equal to the expectations of their endowments. They are $c^1 = (3/4, 3/4, 3/4)$ and $c^2 = (1/4, 1/4, 1/4)$.

Note that no use was made of any particular functional form of the utility functions in computing the equilibrium.   □

16.6 Effectively Complete Markets with Options

The second example arises when all options on the aggregate endowment lie in the asset span, agents are strictly risk averse, and their date-1 endowments lie in the asset span. We refer to such economy as a security markets economy with options on the market payoff because the aggregate endowment is the market payoff.

In a security markets economy with options on the market payoff, agents' date-1 consumption plans at any Pareto-optimal allocation are state independent in every subset of states in which the aggregate endowment is state independent (Corollary 15.5.2). Such consumption plans lie in the span of options on the market payoff, and hence markets are effectively complete. If consumption is restricted to being positive, then all equilibrium allocations are Pareto optimal (Theorem 16.4.1 and Proposition 16.3.2). Every complete markets equilibrium allocation is an equilibrium allocation in security markets with options (Theorem 16.4.2), and interior equilibrium allocations in security markets with options are the same as those with complete markets (Theorem 16.4.3).

Note that if the market payoff is different in every state, then, as observed in Section 15.4, markets are complete in a security markets economy with options on the market payoff. Otherwise, if the market payoff takes the same value in two or more states, markets are effectively complete but not complete.

16.7 Effectively Complete Markets with Linear Risk Tolerance

The third example arises when agents have linear risk tolerance (LRT utilities) with common slope and the risk-free payoff and agents' endowments lie in the asset span. We refer to such economy as a security markets economy with LRT utilities. We assume that date-0 consumption does not enter agents' utility functions.

In a security markets economy with LRT utilities, agents' consumption plans at any Pareto-optimal allocation lie in the span of the risk-free payoff and the aggregate endowment (Theorem 15.6.1). Therefore, they lie in the asset span, and markets are effectively complete. Theorem 16.4.2 implies that every complete markets equilibrium allocation is a security markets equilibrium allocation. To apply Theorem 16.4.3 implying the converse, we need to show that for every feasible allocation in a security markets economy with LRT utilities there exists a Pareto-optimal allocation that weakly Pareto dominates that allocation. Proposition 16.3.2 cannot be applied because consumption sets of agents with LRT utilities (as specified in Section 15.6) are either not closed or unbounded below.

As an inspection of the proof of Theorem 16.4.3 reveals, it suffices to show that for every individually rational allocation (that is, every feasible allocation that weakly Pareto dominates the initial endowment allocation) there exists a Pareto-optimal allocation that weakly Pareto dominates that allocation. In the following proposition we show that a security markets economy with LRT utilities has this property. For LRT utilities with strictly negative slope of risk tolerance we impose an additional condition that assures that individually rational allocations are bounded away from the boundaries of consumption sets. When the slope γ of risk tolerance is strictly negative, the consumption sets are bounded above and unbounded below.

Proposition 16.7.1 *Suppose that each agent's risk tolerance is linear with common slope γ. For $\gamma < 0$ assume that there exists $\epsilon > 0$ such that $\alpha^i + \gamma c_s^i \geq \epsilon$ for every individually rational allocation $\{c^i\}$, every i and s. Then for every individually rational allocation there exists a Pareto-optimal allocation that weakly Pareto dominates that allocation.*

Proof: Let $\{c^i\}$ be an individually rational allocation and let A denote the set of allocations that weakly Pareto dominate allocation $\{c^i\}$. Thus

$$A = \left\{ (\tilde{c}^1, \ldots, \tilde{c}^I) \in \mathcal{R}^{SI} : \sum_i \tilde{c}^i \leq \bar{w}, \tilde{c}^i \in C^i, E[v^i(\tilde{c}^i)] \geq E[v^i(c^i)] \right\}. \quad (16.9)$$

where $C^i = \{c \in \mathcal{R}^S : \alpha^i + \gamma c_s > 0, \text{ for every } s\}$.

With exception of $\gamma = 1$ (logarithmic utility), all LRT utility functions are well defined on the boundary of the set C^i. Assuming first (pending a separate discussion below) that $\gamma \neq 1$, we define the set $\bar{A}$ in the same way as A in 16.9 replacing C^i by its closure $\bar{C}^i = \{c \in \mathcal{R}^S : \alpha^i + \gamma c_s \geq 0, \text{ for every } s\}$. Clearly, $\bar{A}$ is the closure of A and hence is a closed set. It is also nonempty and convex.

Consider the problem of maximizing the social welfare function 15.3 (with strictly positive weights) over all allocations in $\bar{A}$. If $\bar{A}$ is compact, then that problem has a solution. We show that $\bar{A}$ is compact.

A basic criterion for compactness of a closed and convex set is that its only direction of recession (or asymptotic direction) is the zero vector. A vector z is a *direction of recession* of a convex set $Y \in \mathcal{R}^n$ if $y_0 + \lambda z \in Y$ for every $y_0 \in Y$ and $\lambda \geq 0$. It is to be noted that convexity of Y implies that if $y_0 + \lambda z \in Y$ for some $y_0 \in Y$ and every $\lambda \geq 0$, then the same is true for all $y_0 \in Y$. If the set Y is bounded below, then $z \geq 0$ for every direction of recession z of Y.

To show that the only direction of recession of $\bar{A}$ is zero, we consider two cases: when γ is strictly positive and when it is negative. If $\gamma > 0$, then the set $\bar{C}^i$ is bounded below for each i. Consequently, if $z = (z^1, \ldots, z^I) \in \mathcal{R}^{SI}$ is a direction of recession of $\bar{A}$, then $z^i \geq 0$ for each i. The feasibility constraint implies that

$$\sum_i z^i \leq 0, \quad (16.10)$$

for every direction of recession z of $\bar{A}$. It follows from 16.10 and $z^i \geq 0$, that $z = 0$.

If $\gamma \leq 0$, then the set $\bar{C}^i$ is unbounded below, but we prove that the preferred set $\{\tilde{c}^i \in \bar{C}^i : E[v^i(\tilde{c}^i)] \geq E[v^i(c^i)]\}$ is bounded below. The same argument as for $\gamma > 0$ implies that the only direction of recession of $\bar{A}$ is the zero vector.

That the preferred set is bounded below follows from the fact that the LRT utility function with $\gamma \leq 0$ is bounded above and unbounded below (see Section 9.9). A more precise argument is as follows: Let $\bar{v}^i$ be the upper bound on the values that the utility function v^i can take. Denote $E[v^i(c^i)]$ by $\bar{u}^i$. Then

$$E[v^i(\tilde{c}^i)] \geq \bar{u}^i \quad (16.11)$$

implies

$$\pi_s v^i\left(\tilde{c}^i_s\right) \geq \bar{u}^i - \sum_{s' \neq s} \pi_{s'} v^i\left(\tilde{c}^i_{s'}\right) \geq \bar{u}^i - \bar{v}^i. \tag{16.12}$$

Consequently,

$$v^i\left(\tilde{c}^i_s\right) \geq \bar{u}^i - \bar{v}^i. \tag{16.13}$$

or

$$\tilde{c}^i_s \geq (v^i)^{-1}(\bar{u}^i - \bar{v}^i). \tag{16.14}$$

The right hand side of 16.14 (which is well defined since function v^i is strictly increasing and unbounded below) constitutes a lower bound on the preferred set.

Let $\{\tilde{c}^i\}$ be a solution to the problem of maximizing the social welfare function 15.3 over the set $\bar{A}$. We have to show that $\{\tilde{c}^i\}$ is a feasible allocation, that is, that $\{\tilde{c}^i\} \in A$. Consider first the case of $\gamma < 0$. Since allocation $\{c^i\}$ is individually rational, all allocations in A are individually rational and, by the assumption of Proposition 16.7.1, bounded away from the boundaries of sets C^i by ϵ. Therefore, one can replace the set C^i in the definition 16.9 of A by $\{c \in \mathcal{R}^S : \alpha^i + \gamma c_s \geq \epsilon$, for every $s\}$. It follows that A is closed and hence $A = \bar{A}$. For $\gamma = 0$, we also have $A = \bar{A}$ since $C^i = \bar{C}^i = \mathcal{R}^S$. Finally, for $\gamma > 0$ the marginal utility of consumption at the boundary of $\bar{C}^i$ is infinity (Inada condition) implying that the allocation $\{\tilde{c}^i\}$ that solves the social welfare maximization problem cannot lie on the boundary of the set $\bar{A}$, and hence it lies in A.

It remains to consider the case of logarithmic utilities, that is, $\gamma = 1$. The set C^i is not closed but the utility function diverges to negative infinity at the boundary of C^i. This implies that the preferred set $\{\tilde{c}^i \in C^i : E[v^i(\tilde{c}^i)] \geq E[v^i(c^i)]\}$ is closed for each i and hence that A is closed. The same argument as for other strictly positive values of γ implies that A is compact. The welfare maximizing allocation is the desired Pareto optimal allocation. $\qquad\square$

Since all equilibrium allocations in an economy with LRT utilities are interior, Proposition 16.7.1 and Theorems 16.4.2 and 16.4.3 imply that equilibrium allocations in security markets are the same as complete markets equilibrium allocations.

16.8 Multifund Spanning

A common feature of the preceding three examples of effectively complete markets is that agents' date-1 consumption plans at each Pareto-optimal allocation lie in a low-dimensional subspace of the asset span. These cases are usually referred to as *multifund spanning* because equilibrium consumption plans are in the span of payoffs of relatively few portfolios (mutual funds). In an economy with no aggregate risk, each agent's equilibrium consumption plan is risk free and we have *one-fund spanning*. In the case of LRT utilities, each agent's equilibrium consumption plan lies in the span of the market payoff and the risk-free payoff, and we have *two-fund spanning*. In the case of options on the market payoff, each agent's equilibrium consumption plan lies in the span of options, and we have multifund spanning with as many funds as the number of distinct values the market payoff can take.

16.9 A Second Pass at the CAPM

We demonstrated in Section 14.5 that, if there exists at least one agent with quadratic utility function and whose equilibrium consumption is in the span of the market payoff and the risk-free payoff, then the equation of the security market line of the CAPM holds in equilibrium. In particular, the CAPM holds in a representative-agent economy in which the representative agent has a quadratic utility.

Consider a security markets economy with the risk-free payoff in the asset span. If all agents have quadratic utility functions, then their risk tolerance is linear with common slope -1, and the results of Section 16.7 imply that equilibrium consumption plans lie in the span of the market payoff and the risk-free payoff. Consequently, the CAPM holds.

We have thus extended the CAPM to a security markets economy with a risk-free security and with many agents having different quadratic utility functions (Agents' quadratic utility functions can have different parameter α.) A further extension of the CAPM that dispenses with the assumptions of the security markets economy and the presence of a risk-free security will be presented in Chapter 19.

16.10 Notes

The notion of constrained Pareto optimality was introduced by Diamond [3]. A general discussion of the optimality of equilibrium allocations in incomplete markets (with many goods) can be found in Geanakoplos and Polemarchakis [5]. When there is more than one good, or in the multidate model of security markets considered in Part 7, the notion of constrained Pareto optimality is of limited usefulness because of the endogeneity of the asset span (owing to the dependence of security payoffs on future prices). Hart [6] provided an example of an economy with incomplete markets and two goods in which there exist two equilibrium allocations, one of which Pareto dominates the other. Each allocation is constrained optimal with respect to its asset span. Evidently, this cannot happen when there is a single good.

Constrained optimality of a consumption allocation can be viewed as Pareto optimality of the corresponding portfolio allocation when agents' rank portfolios according to the utility of consumption they generate. More precisely, if the utility function u^i is strictly increasing, then one can define the indirect utility of portfolio h and date-0 consumption c_0 by setting $v^i(c_0, h) \equiv u^i(c_0, w_1^i + hX)$. A feasible allocation of portfolios and date-0 consumptions $\{(c_0^i, h^i)\}$ is Pareto optimal if there is no alternative feasible allocation $\{(c'^i_0, h'^i)\}$ such that $v^i(c_0^i, h^i) \geq v^i(c'^i_0, h'^i)$ for every agent i with strict inequality for at least one agent. An allocation $\{(c_0^i, h^i)\}$ is Pareto optimal iff the consumption allocation $\{(c_0^i, c_1^i)\}$ is constrained optimal, where $c_1^i = w_1^i + h^i X$.

The definition of effectively complete markets presented in Section 16.3 is not standard. An alternative definition is that markets are effectively complete if every equilibrium allocation is Pareto optimal (see Elul [4]). Theorem 16.4.1 says that every equilibrium allocation in security markets that are effectively complete in the sense of Section 16.3 is Pareto optimal if agents' utility functions are strictly increasing and their consumption sets are bounded below and closed. Thus, under these assumptions on agents' utility functions and consumption sets, the alternative definition of effectively complete markets is weaker than the definition of Section 16.3.

The analysis of efficient allocation of risk in the case of LRT utilities follows Rubinstein [8]. The case of options on the market payoff originated with Breeden and Litzenberger [2].

An excellent exposition of the concept of direction of recession of a set can be found in Rockafellar [7]. The result that a closed and convex set is compact if its only direction of recession is the zero vector can also be found in Rockafellar [7]. For a characterization of directions of recession of a preferred set of expected utility, see Bertsekas [1].

Bibliography

[1] Bertsekas, D. Necessary and sufficient conditions for existence of an optimal portfolio. *Journal of Economic Theory*, **8**:235–47, 1974.

[2] Breeden, D. T. and Litzenberger, R. Prices of state-contingent claims implicit in option prices. *Journal of Business*, **51**:621–51, 1978.

[3] Diamond, P. The role of a stock market in a general equilibrium model with technological uncertainty. *American Economic Review*, **48**:759–76, 1967.

[4] Elul, R. Effectively complete equilibria – a note. *Journal of Mathematical Economics*, **32**:113–19, 1999.

[5] Geanakoplos, J. and Polemarchakis, H. Existence, regularity, and constrained suboptimality of competitive allocations when the asset markets is incomplete. In Walter Heller and David Starrett, editors, *Essays in Honor of Kenneth J. Arrow, Volume III*. Cambridge University Press, 1986.

[6] Hart, O. On the optimality of equilibrium when the market structure is incomplete, *Journal of Economic Theory*, **11**:418–43.

[7] Rockafellar, R. T. *Convex Analysis*. Princeton University Press, Princeton, NJ, 1970.

[8] Rubinstein, M. An aggregation theorem for securities markets. *Journal of Financial Economics*, **1**:225–44, 1974.

Part Six

Mean-Variance Analysis

17

The Expectations and Pricing Kernels

17.1 Introduction

In Chapter 6 we showed that the payoff pricing functional – and also its extension, the valuation functional – can be represented either by state prices or by risk-neutral probabilities. In this chapter we derive another representation of the payoff pricing functional, the pricing kernel. The existence of the pricing kernel is a consequence of the Riesz representation theorem, which says that any linear functional on a vector space can be represented by a vector in that space.

We begin by introducing the concepts of inner product, orthogonality, and orthogonal projection. These concepts are associated with an important class of vector spaces, the Hilbert spaces, to which the Riesz representation theorem applies. In the finance context, the Riesz representation theorem implies that any linear functional on the asset span can be represented by a payoff. Two linear functionals are of particular interest: the payoff pricing functional and the expectations functional, which maps every payoff into its expectation. Their representations are the pricing kernel and the expectations kernel, respectively.

Hilbert space methods are important for the study of the Capital Asset Pricing Model and factor pricing in the following chapters. Our treatment of these methods here is mathematically superficial, for our interest is in arriving quickly at results that are applicable in finance. In particular, the finite-dimensional contingent claims space $\mathcal{R}^S$ is for us the primary example of a Hilbert space. The most important applications of Hilbert space methods come when the payoff space is infinite-dimensional. Readers who plan to study the infinite-dimensional case are encouraged to read the sources cited at the end of this chapter.

17.2 Hilbert Spaces and Inner Products

An *inner product* on a vector space $\mathcal{H}$ is a function from $\mathcal{H} \times \mathcal{H}$ to $\mathcal{R}$ usually indicated by a dot that obeys the the following properties for all $x, y \in \mathcal{H}$

and all $a, b \in \mathcal{R}$:

- *symmetry:* $x \cdot y = y \cdot x$,
- *linearity:* $x \cdot (ay + bz) = a(x \cdot y) + b(x \cdot z)$,
- *strict positivity:* $x \cdot x > 0$ when $x \neq 0$.

The inner product is also referred to as a scalar product or as a dot product.

The inner product defines a *norm* of a vector in the vector space $\mathcal{H}$ as

$$\|x\| \equiv \sqrt{(x \cdot x)}. \tag{17.1}$$

The norm satisfies the following important properties for all $x, y \in \mathcal{H}$:

- *triangle inequality:* $\|x + y\| \leq \|x\| + \|y\|$,
- *Cauchy–Schwarz inequality:* $|x \cdot y| \leq \|x\| \, \|y\|$.

Further, the norm defines the convergence of a sequence of vectors in $\mathcal{H}$ and therefore the continuity of functionals on $\mathcal{H}$.

A *Hilbert space* is a vector space $\mathcal{H}$ that is equipped with an inner product and is complete with respect to the norm induced by its inner product. In this context, completeness means that any Cauchy sequence of elements of the vector space $\mathcal{H}$ converges to an element of that space.

17.3 The Expectations Inner Product

The space $\mathcal{R}^S$ of state-contingent date-1 consumption plans is a Hilbert space. The most familiar inner product in that space is the Euclidean inner product

$$x \cdot y = \sum_s x_s y_s. \tag{17.2}$$

Another inner product, important in the derivation of the Capital Asset Pricing Model, is the *expectations inner product*

$$x \cdot y = E(xy), \tag{17.3}$$

where, as usual, $E(xy) = \sum_s \pi_s x_s y_s$ for a probability measure π on S. The norm induced by the expectations inner product is

$$\|x\| = \sqrt{E(x^2)} = \sqrt{\text{var}(x) + [E(x)]^2}. \tag{17.4}$$

17.4 Orthogonal Vectors

Two vectors $x, y \in \mathcal{H}$ are *orthogonal*, denoted by $x \perp y$, iff their inner product is zero:

$$x \perp y \text{ iff } x \cdot y = 0. \tag{17.5}$$

A collection of vectors $\{z_1, \ldots, z_n\}$ in a Hilbert space $\mathcal{H}$ is an *orthogonal system* if $z_i \perp z_j$ for all $i \neq j$. If in addition $\|z_i\| = 1$ for every i, then the collection $\{z_1, \ldots, z_n\}$ is an *orthonormal system*. An orthonormal system is an *orthonormal basis* for its linear span.

Pythagorean Theorem 17.4.1 *If $\{z_1, \ldots, z_n\}$ is an orthogonal system in a Hilbert space $\mathcal{H}$, then*

$$\left\|\sum_{i=1}^{n} z_i\right\|^2 = \sum_{i=1}^{n} \|z_i\|^2. \tag{17.6}$$

Proof: Write the left-hand side using the inner product and apply the definition of orthogonality. □

A useful implication of the Pythagorean theorem is the following:

Corollary 17.4.2 *Any orthogonal system of nonzero vectors is linearly independent.*

Proof: Let $\{z_1, \ldots, z_n\}$ be an orthogonal system with $z_i \neq 0$ for each i. Suppose that

$$\sum_{i=1}^{n} \lambda_i z_i = 0 \tag{17.7}$$

for some $\lambda_i \in \mathcal{R}$. Because $\{\lambda_1 z_1, \ldots, \lambda_n z_n\}$ is also an orthogonal system, it follows from Eqs. (17.6) and (17.7) that

$$\sum_{i=1}^{n} \lambda_i^2 \|z_i\| = \left\|\sum_{i=1}^{n} \lambda_i z_i\right\| = 0. \tag{17.8}$$

This implies that $\lambda_i = 0$ for every i and thus that the vectors $z_1, \ldots, z_n$ are linearly independent. □

17.5 Orthogonal Projections

A vector $x \in \mathcal{H}$ is orthogonal to a linear subspace $\mathcal{Z} \subset \mathcal{H}$ iff it is orthogonal to every vector in $z \in \mathcal{Z}$:

$$x \perp \mathcal{Z} \text{ iff } x \cdot z = 0 \quad \forall z \in \mathcal{Z}. \tag{17.9}$$

If the subspace $\mathcal{Z}$ is the linear span of vectors $z_1, \ldots, z_n$, then a vector x is orthogonal to $\mathcal{Z}$ iff it is orthogonal to every z_i for $i = 1, \ldots, n$. The set of all vectors orthogonal to a subspace $\mathcal{Z}$ is the *orthogonal complement* of $\mathcal{Z}$ and is denoted $\mathcal{Z}^\perp$. It is a linear subspace of $\mathcal{H}$.

Projection Theorem 17.5.1 *For any finite-dimensional subspace $\mathcal{Z}$ of a Hilbert space $\mathcal{H}$ and any vector $x \in \mathcal{H}$, there exist unique vectors $x^{\mathcal{Z}} \in \mathcal{Z}$ and $y \in \mathcal{Z}^\perp$ such that $x = x^{\mathcal{Z}} + y$.*[1]

Proof: Let $\{z_1, \ldots, z_n\}$ be an orthogonal system that spans $\mathcal{Z}$, and define

$$x^{\mathcal{Z}} = \sum_{i=1}^{n} \frac{x \cdot z_i}{z_i \cdot z_i} z_i, \tag{17.10}$$

and

$$y = x - x^{\mathcal{Z}}. \tag{17.11}$$

The vector $x^{\mathcal{Z}}$ so defined is in $\mathcal{Z}$. We have

$$y \cdot z_j = \left(x - \sum_{i=1}^{n} \frac{x \cdot z_i}{z_i \cdot z_i} z_i \right) \cdot z_j \tag{17.12}$$

$$= \left(x - \frac{x \cdot z_j}{z_j \cdot z_j} z_j \right) \cdot z_j = 0. \tag{17.13}$$

Therefore $y \perp z_j$ for every $j = 1, \ldots, n$. Hence, $y \in \mathcal{Z}^\perp$.

  To see that $x^{\mathcal{Z}}$ is unique, suppose that $x = x_1^{\mathcal{Z}} + y_1 = x_2^{\mathcal{Z}} + y_2$ for some $x_1^{\mathcal{Z}}, x_2^{\mathcal{Z}} \in \mathcal{Z}$ and $y_1, y_2 \in \mathcal{Z}^\perp$. The Pythagorean Theorem implies

$$\|y_2\|^2 = \|x_1^{\mathcal{Z}} - x_2^{\mathcal{Z}}\|^2 + \|y_1\|^2, \tag{17.14}$$

and

$$\|y_1\|^2 = \|x_1^{\mathcal{Z}} - x_2^{\mathcal{Z}}\|^2 + \|y_2\|^2. \tag{17.15}$$

Equations (17.14) and (17.15) imply that

$$\|x_1^{\mathcal{Z}} - x_2^{\mathcal{Z}}\|^2 = 0; \tag{17.16}$$

thus, by the strict positivity of inner products, $x_1^{\mathcal{Z}} = x_2^{\mathcal{Z}}$. □

  If $\mathcal{Z}$ is a (finite-dimensional) subspace of a Hilbert space $\mathcal{H}$, then Theorem 17.5.1 implies that $\mathcal{H}$ can be decomposed as $\mathcal{H} = \mathcal{Z} + \mathcal{Z}^\perp$, with $\mathcal{Z} \cap \mathcal{Z}^\perp = \{0\}$.

---

[1] The projection theorem holds for every closed (and possibly infinite-dimensional) subspace of $\mathcal{H}$. Our proof applies only in the finite-dimensional case. In the finance applications to be discussed, only the finite-dimensional version of the theorem is needed.

Vector $x^{\mathcal{Z}}$ of the unique decomposition of Theorem 17.5.1 is the *orthogonal projection* of x on $\mathcal{Z}$. If the projection is taken with respect to the expectations inner product, then the coefficients of the representation (17.10) of the orthogonal projection are

$$\frac{x \cdot z_i}{z_i \cdot z_i} = \frac{E(xz_i)}{E(z_i^2)}, \tag{17.17}$$

and we have

$$x^{\mathcal{Z}} = \sum_{i=1}^{n} \frac{E(xz_i)}{E(z_i^2)} z_i. \tag{17.18}$$

Thus, the projection with respect to the expectations inner product is the same as the linear regression. Equation (17.18) is the equation for the predicted value of the dependent variable for given values of the independent variables.

Example 17.5.2 In the Hilbert space $\mathcal{R}^2$ with the expectations inner product given by probabilities $(1/4, 3/4)$, let $\mathcal{Z} = \text{span}\{(1, 1)\}$ and $x = (1, 2)$. The orthogonal projection $x^{\mathcal{Z}}$ is

$$x^{\mathcal{Z}} = \frac{(1, 2) \cdot (1, 1)}{(1, 1) \cdot (1, 1)}(1, 1) = \frac{7}{4}(1, 1) = (7/4, 7/4). \tag{17.19}$$

$\square$

17.6 Diagrammatic Methods in Hilbert Spaces

One of the most appealing features of Hilbert spaces is that they lend themselves well to diagrammatic representations. To see this, consider a two-dimensional Hilbert space in which coordinates are expressed in terms of an orthonormal basis ϵ_1, ϵ_2. The inner product of two vectors x and y is given by

$$x \cdot y = (x_1\epsilon_1 + x_2\epsilon_2) \cdot (y_1\epsilon_1 + y_2\epsilon_2). \tag{17.20}$$

Because ϵ_1 and ϵ_2 are orthonormal, we have

$$x \cdot y = x_1y_1 + x_2y_2, \tag{17.21}$$

and thus we can represent the Hilbert space by the Euclidean plane of ordered pairs of real numbers with the "natural basis" $(1, 0), (0, 1)$ and in which the inner product is the Euclidean inner product. Therefore x and y are orthogonal if they are perpendicular; that is, if $x_1y_1 + x_2y_2 = 0$.

In finance applications, the basis vectors are state claims. Although these are orthogonal under the expectations inner product, they do not constitute an orthonormal basis because they do not have unit norm:

$$e_s \cdot e_s = E(e_s^2) = \pi_s \neq 1. \tag{17.22}$$

If we use state claims as the basis in a diagrammatic representation, then orthogonal payoffs need not be perpendicular (unless probabilities of all states are the same). Orthogonal projections are skewed. For instance, the orthogonal projection $x^{\mathcal{Z}} = (7/4, 7/4)$ of vector $x = (1, 2)$ on $\mathcal{Z} = \text{span}\{(1, 1)\}$ in Example 17.5.2 differs from the perpendicular projection $(3/2, 3/2)$. Of course, it is easy to eliminate this skewness by rescaling the basis vectors.

17.7 Riesz Representation Theorem

A linear and (norm) continuous functional on a Hilbert space has a simple form; it is the inner product with a vector in that space.

Theorem 17.7.1 (Riesz–Frechet) *If* $F : \mathcal{H} \to \mathcal{R}$ *is a continuous linear functional on a Hilbert space* $\mathcal{H}$, *then there exists a unique vector* k_f *in* $\mathcal{H}$ *such that*

$$F(x) = k_f \cdot x \quad \forall x \in \mathcal{H}. \tag{17.23}$$

Proof: If F is the zero functional, then we take $k_f = 0$. Suppose that F is a nonzero functional. Let $\mathcal{N} = \{x \in \mathcal{H} : F(x) = 0\}$ be the null space of F and $\mathcal{N}^\perp$ the orthogonal complement of $\mathcal{N}$. We have $\mathcal{H} = \mathcal{N} + \mathcal{N}^\perp$, and $\mathcal{N}^\perp \neq \{0\}$.

Choose a nonzero vector z in $\mathcal{N}^\perp$. By multiplying z by a scalar we can have $F(z) = 1$. Any vector $x \in \mathcal{H}$ can be written as

$$x = [x - F(x)z] + F(x)z. \tag{17.24}$$

Note that $[x - F(x)z] \in \mathcal{N}$. Because $z \in \mathcal{N}^\perp$, it follows that

$$z \cdot x = z \cdot [F(x)z]. \tag{17.25}$$

Now set

$$k_f = \frac{z}{(z \cdot z)}. \tag{17.26}$$

Then Eq. (17.25) implies

$$k_f \cdot x = \frac{F(x)(z \cdot z)}{z \cdot z} = F(x), \tag{17.27}$$

and thus k_f satisfies Eq. (17.23).

It remains to show that k_f is unique. If there are k_f and k'_f satisfying Eq. (17.23), then

$$(k_f - k'_f) \cdot x = 0 \qquad (17.28)$$

holds for every $x \in \mathcal{H}$; hence, $(k_f - k'_f) = 0$. □

The vector k_f in the representation (17.23) is called the Riesz *kernel* corresponding to F.

17.8 Construction of the Riesz Kernel

Finding the Riesz kernel for a linear functional on the Hilbert space $\mathcal{R}^S$ with the Euclidean inner product is easy. The kernel is obtained from $k_{fs} = F(e_s)$, which implies by linearity that $F(x) = \sum_s k_{fs} x_s$. Obtaining the kernel for the expectations inner product is equally easy. The functional F can first be written $F(x) = \sum_s k_s x_s$. Then $k_{fs} = k_s/\pi_s$ gives the desired representation $F(x) = \sum_s \pi_s k_{fs} x_s = E(k_f x)$.

Any complete subspace of a Hilbert space is a Hilbert space in its own right under the same inner product. The Riesz Representation Theorem can therefore be applied to linear functionals on complete subspaces of a Hilbert space. Thus if $\mathcal{Z}$ is a complete subspace of a Hilbert space $\mathcal{H}$ and F is a continuous linear functional on $\mathcal{Z}$, then there exists a unique kernel k_f in $\mathcal{Z}$ such that $F(z) = k_f \cdot z$ holds for every $z \in \mathcal{Z}$.

If the subspace $\mathcal{Z}$ is a linear span of a finite collection of vectors $\{z_1, \ldots, z_n\}$, then kernel k_f of a linear functional $F : \mathcal{Z} \to \mathcal{R}$ can be constructed as follows:

Let

$$w_i = F(z_i), \qquad (17.29)$$

for $i = 1, \ldots, n$ be the values of F on the basis vectors of $\mathcal{Z}$. The kernel k_f has to satisfy n equations

$$w_i = k_f \cdot z_i \quad i = 1, \ldots, n. \qquad (17.30)$$

Because $k_f \in \mathcal{Z}$, we have $k_f = \sum_{j=1}^{n} a_j z_j$. Substituting in Eq. (17.30), we obtain n equations

$$w_i = \sum_{j=1}^{n} a_j z_j \cdot z_i \quad i = 1, \ldots, n \qquad (17.31)$$

with n unknowns a_j that can be solved using standard methods.

The following example illustrates the preceding construction:

Example 17.8.1 Let $\mathcal{Z} = \text{span}\{(1, 1)\} \subset \mathcal{R}^2$, and let the inner product be the expectations inner product given by probabilities $(1/4, 3/4)$. Let $F : \mathcal{Z} \to \mathcal{R}$ be given by

$$F(z) = 2z_1, \tag{17.32}$$

for $z = (z_1, z_2) \in \mathcal{Z}$.

Vector $(1, 1)$ constitutes a basis of $\mathcal{Z}$. The kernel k_f has to satisfy $k_f = a(1, 1)$ for some scalar a. Because $F(1, 1) = 2$, we can solve for a from the single equation

$$2 = a(1, 1) \cdot (1, 1) = a(1/4 + 3/4). \tag{17.33}$$

Thus $a = 2$ and

$$k_f = (2, 2). \tag{17.34}$$

$\square$

17.9 The Expectations Kernel

The asset span is a subspace of the Hilbert space $\mathcal{R}^S$ with the expectations inner product and hence is a Hilbert space in its own right. Consequently the Riesz Representation Theorem applies to linear functionals defined on the asset span. Two linear functionals on the asset span $\mathcal{M}$ are of particular interest: the expectations functional, discussed in this section, and the payoff pricing functional, discussed in Section 17.10. The probability measure π defining the expectations inner product is taken to be agents' subjective probability measure. If agents' preferences have expected utility representations, then π is the probability measure (assumed common to all agents) of the expected utility.

The *expectations functional E* maps every payoff $z \in \mathcal{M}$ into its expectation $E(z)$. The Riesz kernel k_e associated with the expectations functional is the unique payoff that satisfies

$$E(z) = E(k_e z), \quad \forall z \in \mathcal{M}. \tag{17.35}$$

We emphasize that Eq. (17.35) is valid only when z is in the asset span and need not be valid for contingent claims outside the asset span. The expectations kernel can be constructed using the method of Section 17.8 with security payoffs $x_1, \ldots, x_n$ as the basis of $\mathcal{M}$.

If the risk-free payoff is in the asset span $\mathcal{M}$, then the expectations kernel k_e is risk free and equal to one in every state. If the risk free payoff is not in the asset span, then the kernel k_e is the orthogonal projection of the risk free payoff on $\mathcal{M}$. To see this, observe that

$$E[(e - k_e)z] = 0 \tag{17.36}$$

for every z in $\mathcal{M}$, where e denotes the payoff of one in every state. Therefore $e - k_e$ is orthogonal to $\mathcal{M}$. Because $e = (e - k_e) + k_e$, it follows that k_e is the projection of e onto $\mathcal{M}$.

Example 17.9.1 Assume that there are three states and two securities with payoffs $x_1 = (1, 1, 0)$ and $x_2 = (0, 1, 1)$. The probability of each state is $1/3$.

To find the expectations kernel we consider the following two equations for expected payoffs:

$$\frac{2}{3} = E(k_e x_1) \tag{17.37}$$

and

$$\frac{2}{3} = E(k_e x_2). \tag{17.38}$$

Because the expectations kernel k_e lies in the asset span, we have

$$k_e = h_1 x_1 + h_2 x_2 = (h_1, h_1 + h_2, h_2) \tag{17.39}$$

for some portfolio (h_1, h_2). Substituting Eq. (17.39) in Eqs. (17.37) and (17.38) we obtain

$$\frac{2}{3} = \frac{1}{3}h_1 + \frac{1}{3}(h_1 + h_2), \tag{17.40}$$

and

$$\frac{2}{3} = \frac{1}{3}(h_1 + h_2) + \frac{1}{3}h_2. \tag{17.41}$$

The solution is $h_1 = h_2 = 2/3$, which gives

$$k_e = \left(\frac{2}{3}, \frac{4}{3}, \frac{2}{3} \right). \tag{17.42}$$

Note that k_e is not the risk-free payoff because the the risk-free payoff is not in the asset span. □

17.10 The Pricing Kernel

The Riesz kernel associated with the payoff pricing functional q on the asset span $\mathcal{M}$ is the *pricing kernel* k_q. It is the unique payoff in $\mathcal{M}$ that satisfies

$$q(z) = E(k_q z), \quad \forall z \in \mathcal{M}. \tag{17.43}$$

The pricing kernel can be constructed using the method of Section 17.8 with security payoffs $x_1, \ldots, x_n$ as the basis of $\mathcal{M}$.

The expectation $E(k_q z)$ is well defined for contingent claims z not in the asset span, but it does not in general define a positive valuation functional on $\mathcal{R}^S$. This is so because the pricing kernel need not be positive (or strictly positive) even if there is no strong arbitrage (arbitrage). For example, if there is no portfolio with strictly positive payoff, then the pricing kernel cannot be strictly positive.

If there is no arbitrage (strong arbitrage), then there exists a strictly positive (positive) state price vector $q = (q_1, \ldots, q_S)$ such that

$$q(z) = \sum_s q_s z_s \qquad (17.44)$$

for every $z \in \mathcal{M}$. Consider the vector of state prices rescaled by the probabilities of states denoted by $q/\pi = (q_1/\pi_1, \ldots, q_S/\pi_S)$. We can rewrite Eq. (17.44) as

$$q(z) = E\left(\frac{q}{\pi} z\right). \qquad (17.45)$$

Equations (17.43) and (17.45) imply that

$$E\left[\left(\frac{q}{\pi} - k_q\right) z\right] = 0 \qquad (17.46)$$

for every $z \in \mathcal{M}$ and hence that $q/\pi - k_q$ is orthogonal to $\mathcal{M}$. Because $q/\pi = (q/\pi - k_q) + k_q$, it follows that the pricing kernel k_q is the projection of q/π on $\mathcal{M}$.

The pricing kernel is unique regardless of whether markets are complete or incomplete. If markets are incomplete, then there exist multiple state-price vectors. When rescaled by probabilities, all these vectors have the same projection on the asset span, and that projection is the pricing kernel k_q. If markets are complete, then there exists a unique state-price vector q, and the pricing kernel k_q equals q/π.

If q is an equilibrium payoff pricing functional, then

$$q(z) = E\left(\frac{\partial_1 v}{\partial_0 v} z\right) \qquad (17.47)$$

for every $z \in \mathcal{M}$ (see Eq. (14.1)), where $\partial_1 v/\partial_0 v$ is the vector of marginal rates of substitution of an agent whose utility function has an expected utility representation $E[v(c)]$ and whose equilibrium consumption is interior. The projection of the vector $\partial_1 v/\partial_0 v$ on the asset span $\mathcal{M}$ equals the pricing kernel k_q. If markets are complete, the vector of marginal rates of substitution equals k_q, and this holds for all agents with interior consumption.

Substituting $z = k_e$ in Eq. (17.46), we obtain

$$E\left(\frac{q}{\pi}\right) = E(k_q). \tag{17.48}$$

It follows that if the state-price vector q is positive and nonzero, then the expectation of the pricing kernel is strictly positive. If the risk-free payoff is in the asset span, then

$$E(k_q) = E(k_q k_e) = \frac{1}{\bar{r}}, \tag{17.49}$$

which is used in the following chapter.

Example 17.10.1 In Example 17.9.1, assume that security prices are $p_1 = 1$, $p_2 = 4/3$. To find the pricing kernel, we consider the equations for prices of securities

$$1 = E(k_q x_1) \tag{17.50}$$

and

$$4/3 = E(k_q x_2). \tag{17.51}$$

The pricing kernel k_q lies in the asset span, and thus we have

$$k_q = h_1 x_1 + h_2 x_2 = (h_1, h_1 + h_2, h_2) \tag{17.52}$$

for some portfolio (h_1, h_2). The solution is $h_1 = 2/3$, $h_2 = 5/3$, which gives

$$k_q = \left(\frac{2}{3}, \frac{7}{3}, \frac{5}{3}\right). \tag{17.53}$$

$\square$

17.11 Notes

Comprehensive treatments of the theory of Hilbert spaces can be found in Luenberger [4], Dudley [3], and Young [5]. Hilbert space methods were introduced in financial economics by Chamberlain [1] and Chamberlain and Rothschild [2].

In Section 17.2 we noted without discussion that a space on which an inner product has been defined must be complete to be a Hilbert space. This requirement is innocuous in finite-dimensional spaces with the Euclidean or the expectations inner product but not in infinite-dimensional spaces. For example, let Φ be the space of finitely nonzero sequences of real numbers (i.e., sequences with only a finite number of nonzero terms). The expectations inner product defined by probabilities 1/2, 1/4, 1/8, ... has all the properties of Section 17.2, but the space is not complete and hence is not a Hilbert space. To see this, consider the sequence $\{z_n\}$ of elements of

Φ, where z_n is a sequence of ones in the first n places and zeros thereafter. Sequence $\{z_n\}$ converges in the norm to $(1, 1, \ldots)$ (and hence is a Cauchy sequence), but the limit is not an element of Φ.

Bibliography

[1] Chamberlain, G. Funds, factors and diversification in arbitrage pricing models. *Econometrica*, **51**:1305–23, 1983.

[2] Chamberlain, G. and Rothschild, M. Arbitrage, factor structure and mean variance analysis in large asset markets. *Econometrica*, **51**:1281–1304, 1983.

[3] Dudley, R. M. *Real Analysis and Probability*. Wadsworth and Brooks, Pacific Grove, CA, 1989.

[4] Luenberger, D. G. *Optimization by Vector Space Methods*. Wiley, New York, 1969.

[5] Young, N. *An Introduction to Hilbert Space*. Cambridge University Press, Cambridge, UK, 1988.

18

The Mean-Variance Frontier Payoffs

18.1 Introduction

Although variance does not in general provide an accurate measure of risk (see Chapter 10), the analysis of expected returns and variances of returns plays an important role in the theory and applications of finance. Such analysis leads to identification of returns that have minimal variance for a given expected return.

The analysis relies on Hilbert space methods developed in Chapter 17 – in particular, on the representations of the payoff pricing functional by the pricing kernel and the expectations functional by the expectations kernel. The returns that attain minimum variance for a given expected return lie on a line passing through the returns on the pricing kernel and the expectations kernel. The analysis of expected returns and variances of returns has a simple diagrammatic representation.

18.2 Mean-Variance Frontier Payoffs

A payoff is a *mean-variance frontier payoff* if there is no other payoff with the same price and the same expectation but a smaller variance. In other words, the mean-variance frontier payoffs minimize variance subject to constraints on price and expectation.

Let $\mathcal{E}$ be the subspace of $\mathcal{M}$ spanned by the expectations kernel k_e and the pricing kernel k_q. The central result of this chapter is the following:

Theorem 18.2.1 *A payoff is a mean-variance frontier payoff iff it lies in the span of the expectations kernel and the pricing kernel.*

Proof: Taking the orthogonal projection (with respect to the expectations inner product) of an arbitrary payoff $z \in \mathcal{M}$ onto $\mathcal{E}$ results in

$$z = z^{\mathcal{E}} + \epsilon, \tag{18.1}$$

with $z^{\mathcal{E}} \in \mathcal{E}$ and $\epsilon \in \mathcal{E}^{\perp}$. In particular, ϵ is orthogonal to both k_e and k_q. Therefore ϵ has zero expectation and zero price, implying that z and $z^{\mathcal{E}}$ have the same expectation and the same price. Further, because ϵ is orthogonal to $z^{\mathcal{E}}$ and $E(\epsilon) = 0$, it follows that $\mathrm{cov}(\epsilon, z^{\mathcal{E}}) = E(\epsilon)E(z^{\mathcal{E}}) = 0$. Consequently, $\mathrm{var}(z) = \mathrm{var}(z^{\mathcal{E}}) + \mathrm{var}(\epsilon)$, and thus $\mathrm{var}(z^{\mathcal{E}}) \leq \mathrm{var}(z)$ with strict inequality if $\epsilon \neq 0$. This implies that every mean-variance frontier payoff lies in $\mathcal{E}$.

For the converse, we have to show that every payoff in $\mathcal{E}$ is a mean-variance frontier payoff. Suppose, to the contrary, that there exists a payoff z in $\mathcal{E}$ that is not a mean-variance frontier payoff. Then there must exist another payoff z' with the same price and the same expectation but smaller variance than z. Using the argument of the first part of the proof we can assume that $z' \in \mathcal{E}$. Because z and z' have the same price and the same expectation, we have $E[k_q(z - z')] = 0$ and $E[k_e(z - z')] = 0$. This implies that $z - z' \in \mathcal{E}^{\perp}$. Because also $z - z' \in \mathcal{E}$, it follows that $z = z'$. This is a contradiction to the assumption that z' has smaller variance than z. □

If the expectations kernel and the pricing kernel are collinear (that is, $k_q = \gamma k_e$ for some $\gamma \neq 0$), then the set of mean-variance frontier payoffs $\mathcal{E}$ is a line. The expectations kernel and the pricing kernel are collinear iff all portfolios have the same expected return (equal to $1/\gamma$). If the risk-free payoff lies in the asset span, then k_e and k_q are collinear iff fair pricing holds. Under fair pricing, that is when $E(r_j) = \bar{r}$ for every security j, the kernels are $k_e = e$ and $k_q = (1/\bar{r})e$, where e is the risk-free unit payoff.

Because the case of fair pricing has already been extensively discussed in Sections 13.4 and 16.5, we are more interested in the case when k_e and k_q are not collinear. Then the set of mean-variance frontier payoffs $\mathcal{E}$ is a plane (see Figure 18.1).

If there are only two nonredundant securities, then the asset span is a plane. Further, if the expectations and pricing kernels are not collinear, then the asset span coincides with the set of mean-variance frontier payoffs. Thus, every payoff is a mean-variance frontier payoff if there are two securities. Note that the number of states is irrelevant.

For brevity, "frontier payoff" is often used in place of "mean-variance frontier payoff."

18.3 Frontier Returns

The return associated with any payoff having a nonzero price equals that payoff divided by its price. *Frontier returns* are the returns on the frontier payoffs or, equivalently, frontier payoffs with unit price.

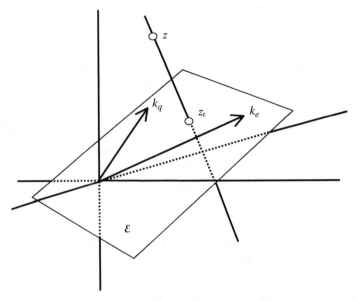

Figure 18.1 The set of frontier payoffs is the plane $\mathcal{E}$ spanned by k_q and k_e. Any payoff z can be projected onto $\mathcal{E}$.

It follows from Theorem 18.2.1 that the return r_q on the pricing kernel and the return r_e on the expectations kernel are frontier returns. They are

$$r_e = \frac{k_e}{E(k_q)} \quad \text{and} \quad r_q = \frac{k_q}{E(k_q^2)}, \tag{18.2}$$

where the pricing kernel was used to derive the prices of k_q and k_e.

If the expectations kernel and the pricing kernel are collinear, then returns r_q and r_e are equal. The set of frontier returns consists of the single return r_e. If the risk-free payoff lies in the asset span, that single return equals the risk-free return $\bar{r}$.

We assume throughout the rest of this chapter that the expectations kernel and the pricing kernel are not collinear. If k_e and k_q are not collinear, then the set of frontier returns is the line passing through the return r_q and the return r_e (see Figure 18.2). This line can be indexed by a single parameter λ, and thus

$$r_\lambda = r_e + \lambda(r_q - r_e), \tag{18.3}$$

where $-\infty < \lambda < \infty$.

Example 18.3.1 Suppose that there are three equally likely states and that three securities are traded. The security returns are

$$r_1 = (3, 0, 0) \tag{18.4}$$

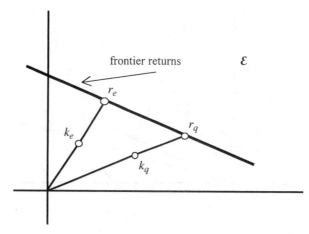

Figure 18.2 The frontier returns consist of the line connecting the return on the expectations kernel and the return on the pricing kernel.

$$r_2 = (0, 6, 0) \tag{18.5}$$

$$r_3 = \left(\frac{6}{7}, \frac{3}{7}, \frac{9}{7}\right). \tag{18.6}$$

We wish to know which, if any, of these returns are on the mean-variance frontier.

To see if any of the security returns are mean-variance frontier returns, we locate the set of frontier returns. We first find the returns on the expectations and pricing kernels. Because markets are complete, the expectations kernel is the risk-free payoff $(1, 1, 1)$, and the pricing kernel is the state-price vector q rescaled by the probabilities of states. The state-price vector is the unique solution to the equations

$$1 = 3q_1 \tag{18.7}$$

$$1 = 6q_2 \tag{18.8}$$

$$1 = \frac{6}{7}q_1 + \frac{3}{7}q_2 + \frac{9}{7}q_3. \tag{18.9}$$

The solution is $q_1 = 1/3, q_2 = 1/6, q_3 = 1/2$. The pricing kernel equals q/π, that is $(1, 1/2, 3/2)$.

The prices of the expectations and pricing kernels are obtained using the pricing kernel. The price of the expectations kernel $(1, 1, 1)$ is 1 and the return r_e is therefore $(1, 1, 1)$. The price of the pricing kernel $(1, 1/2, 3/2)$ is $7/6$, and the return r_q equals r_3. Return r_3 is therefore a frontier return. Returns r_1 and r_2 are not, for they are not on the line generated by r_e and r_q.   □

The expectation of the frontier return r_λ defined by Eq. (18.3) is

$$E(r_\lambda) = E(r_e) + \lambda[E(r_q) - E(r_e)]. \tag{18.10}$$

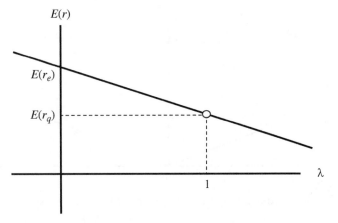

Figure 18.3 Expected returns for frontier returns indexed by λ. The expectations kernel has $\lambda = 0$, and the pricing kernel has $\lambda = 1$.

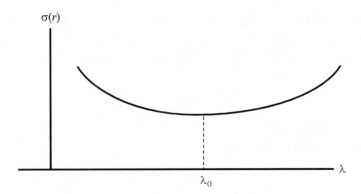

Figure 18.4 Standard deviation of frontier returns when there exists no risk-free return.

The variance of r_λ is

$$\text{var}(r_\lambda) = \text{var}(r_e) + 2\lambda\text{cov}(r_e, r_q - r_e) + \lambda^2\text{var}(r_q - r_e) \qquad (18.11)$$

and its standard deviation $\sigma(r_\lambda)$ is the square root of $\text{var}(r_\lambda)$. The expectations and standard deviations of frontier returns are shown in Figures 18.3 and 18.4.

If the expectations kernel is risk free, then $E(r_e)$ equals the risk-free return $\bar{r}$; and as follows from Eq. (18.10), the expectation of the frontier return r_λ is then

$$E(r_\lambda) = \bar{r} + \lambda[E(r_q) - \bar{r}]. \qquad (18.12)$$

For use later, note that

$$\bar{r} > E(r_q). \qquad (18.13)$$

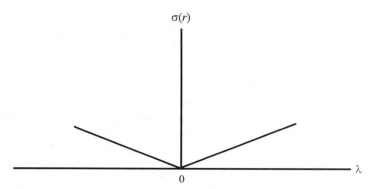

Figure 18.5 Standard deviation of frontier returns when there exists a risk-free return.

To see this, we first observe that

$$E(k_q^2) = [E(k_q)]^2 + \text{var}(k_q) > [E(k_q)]^2, \tag{18.14}$$

because the pricing kernel k_q is not risk free (under the maintained assumption that k_q and k_e are not collinear). Taking expectations in the right-hand equation of (18.2) and using Eq. (18.14) and the fact that $\bar{r} = 1/E(k_q)$ (17.49), we obtain

$$E(r_q) = \frac{E(k_q)}{E(k_q^2)} < \frac{1}{E(k_q)} = \bar{r}. \tag{18.15}$$

If the expectations kernel is risk-free, then, as follows from Eq. (18.11), the variance of the frontier return r_λ is

$$\text{var}(r_\lambda) = \lambda^2 \text{var}(r_q), \tag{18.16}$$

and the standard deviation is

$$\sigma(r_\lambda) = |\lambda|\sigma(r_q) \tag{18.17}$$

(see Figure 18.5).

There always exists a frontier return with minimum variance. Of course, if the risk-free claim lies in the asset span, then the minimum-variance frontier return is the risk-free return. But if the risk-free payoff is not in the asset span, then all returns have strictly positive variances. The minimum-variance frontier return may be obtained by minimizing (18.11) with respect to λ. Because the var(r_λ) of Eq. (18.11) is quadratic in λ, the unique solution λ_0 to that minimization problem can be obtained from the first-order condition. It is given by

$$\lambda_0 = -\frac{\text{cov}(r_e, r_q - r_e)}{\text{var}(r_q - r_e)}. \tag{18.18}$$

Given the preceding results, the set of expected returns and standard deviations of returns are as indicated in Figures 18.6 and 18.7.

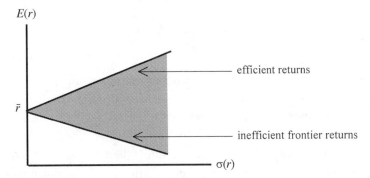

Figure 18.6 The shaded region shows the feasible means and standard deviations of returns when the risk-free return is traded. The upper boundary of the region consists of the efficient frontier returns; the lower boundary consists of the inefficient frontier returns.

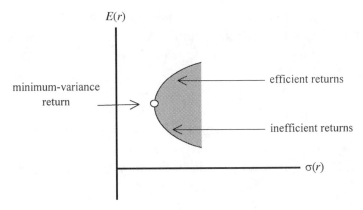

Figure 18.7 The shaded region shows expected returns and standard deviations of returns when the risk-free payoff is not in the asset span.

18.4 Zero-Covariance Frontier Returns

Because the set of frontier returns is a line, any two distinct frontier returns can be used in place of r_e and r_q to describe this line. In deriving the beta pricing relation in the next section we use two frontier returns that are uncorrelated (i.e., have zero covariance). We show here that for every frontier return r_λ, other than the minimum-variance return, there is another frontier return such that it and r_λ have zero covariance.

Consider a frontier return r_λ given by Eq. (18.3). Another frontier return r_μ, given by Eq. (18.3) with index μ, has zero covariance with r_λ and is the zero-covariance frontier return associated with r_λ if

$$\text{cov}(r_\lambda, r_\mu) = \text{var}(r_e) + (\lambda + \mu)\,\text{cov}(r_e, r_q - r_e) + \lambda\mu\,\text{var}(r_q - r_e) = 0. \quad (18.19)$$

Solving for μ results in

$$\mu = \frac{\text{var}(r_e) + \lambda \text{cov}(r_e, r_q - r_e)}{\text{cov}(r_e, r_q - r_e) + \lambda \text{var}(r_q - r_e)}. \qquad (18.20)$$

Thus, μ is well-defined if the denominator is not equal to zero. The denominator of Eq. (18.20) equals zero when $\lambda = \lambda_0$ (see Eq. (18.18)); that is when r_λ is the minimum-variance return. There exists no zero-covariance frontier return associated with the minimum-variance frontier return.

If the risk-free payoff lies in the asset span, then the zero-covariance return associated with every frontier return (other than the risk-free return) is the risk-free return.

18.5 Beta Pricing

Let r_λ be a frontier return other than the minimum-variance return and let r_μ be the associated zero-covariance frontier return. Taking the orthogonal projection (using the expectations inner product) of the return r_j of security j onto the plane of frontier payoffs $\mathcal{E}$ results in

$$r_j = r_j^{\mathcal{E}} + \epsilon_j, \qquad (18.21)$$

with $r_j^{\mathcal{E}} \in \mathcal{E}$ and $\epsilon_j \in \mathcal{E}^\perp$. In particular, ϵ_j is orthogonal to both k_e and k_q and therefore has zero expectation and zero price.

Because ϵ_j has zero price, $r_j^{\mathcal{E}}$ is a frontier return. Using the returns r_λ and r_μ to describe the frontier line, return $r_j^{\mathcal{E}}$ can be written $r_\mu + \beta_j(r_\lambda - r_\mu)$ for some β_j. Consequently,

$$r_j = r_\mu + \beta_j(r_\lambda - r_\mu) + \epsilon_j. \qquad (18.22)$$

Because ϵ_j has zero expectation, taking expectations of both sides of Eq. (18.22), we obtain

$$E(r_j) = E(r_\mu) + \beta_j[E(r_\lambda) - E(r_\mu)]. \qquad (18.23)$$

Taking the covariances of both sides of Eq. (18.22) with r_λ and then solving the resulting equation for β_j, using the facts that r_λ is uncorrelated with r_μ and with ϵ_j, we find

$$\beta_j = \frac{\text{cov}(r_j, r_\lambda)}{\text{var}(r_\lambda)}. \qquad (18.24)$$

Thus β_j is the regression coefficient of r_j on r_λ.

If the risk-free payoff lies in the asset span, Eq. (18.23) becomes

$$E(r_j) = \bar{r} + \beta_j[E(r_\lambda) - \bar{r}]. \qquad (18.25)$$

Relations (18.24) and (18.25) are the *beta pricing* equations. They say that the risk premium on any security is proportional to the covariance of its return with a reference frontier return. It was seen in Chapter 14 that a similar relation, with the market return substituted for the return r_λ, is the equation of the security market line of the Capital Asset Pricing Model (CAPM). In the following chapter we will demonstrate that the market return is a frontier return in CAPM, implying that the equation of the security market line is a special case of beta pricing.

For the arbitrary security markets of this chapter, the market return is generally not a frontier return. There is thus no justification for substituting the market return for r_λ in Eq. (18.25).

Relations (18.24) and (18.25) hold for portfolio returns as well. If the risk-free return lies in the asset span, the expectation $E(r)$ of an arbitrary return r satisfies

$$E(r) = \bar{r} + \beta[E(r_\lambda) - \bar{r}] \tag{18.26}$$

where

$$\beta = \frac{\text{cov}(r, r_\lambda)}{\text{var}(r_\lambda)}. \tag{18.27}$$

18.6 Mean-Variance Efficient Returns

A return is *mean-variance efficient* if there is no other return with the same variance but greater expectation. In other words, the mean-variance efficient returns maximize expected return subject to a constraint on variance.

As Figures 18.6 and 18.7 indicate, the mean-variance efficient returns are the frontier returns that have expected return equal to or greater than that of the minimum-variance return. If the expectations kernel is risk free, then mean-variance efficient returns are all frontier returns r_λ with $\lambda \leq 0$. In that case the return on the pricing kernel is, in view of Eq. (18.13), inefficient.

18.7 Volatility of Marginal Rates of Substitution

In Section 14.4 we derived the following bound on the standard deviation of an agent's marginal rate of substitution:

$$\sigma\left[\frac{\partial_1 v}{E(\partial_0 v)}\right] \geq \sup_r \frac{|E(r) - \bar{r}|}{\bar{r}\sigma(r)}, \tag{18.28}$$

where the supremum is taken over all returns other than the risk-free return. The bound is the greatest absolute value of the Sharpe ratio divided by the risk-free return.

We are now in a position to interpret this inequality at a deeper level. We observe first that the supremum in (18.28) must be attained at a frontier return because for every return that is not a frontier return there exists another return with the same expectation but smaller variance and hence a greater absolute value of the Sharpe ratio. Second, all frontier returns other than the risk-free return have the same absolute value of the Sharpe ratio. For a frontier return r_λ, where $\lambda \neq 0$, Eqs. (18.12) and (18.17) imply that

$$\frac{|E(r_\lambda) - \bar{r}|}{\sigma(r_\lambda)} = \frac{|\lambda(E(r_q) - \bar{r})|}{|\lambda|\sigma(r_q)} = \frac{|E(r_q) - \bar{r}|}{\sigma(r_q)}. \tag{18.29}$$

Therefore, the supremum in inequality (18.28) is attained at any frontier return other than the risk-free return. In particular, it is attained at the return r_q of the pricing kernel.

It turns out that the absolute value of the Sharpe ratio of r_q divided by the risk-free return equals the standard deviation of the pricing kernel k_q. Substituting $r_q = k_q/E(k_q^2)$ and $\bar{r} = 1/E(k_q)$ (see Eq. (18.2)) in the leftmost term below, we have

$$\frac{|E(r_q) - \bar{r}|}{\bar{r}\sigma(r_q)} = \frac{|[E(k_q)]^2 - E(k_q^2)|}{\sigma(k_q)} = \frac{\sigma^2(k_q)}{\sigma(k_q)} = \sigma(k_q). \tag{18.30}$$

In sum, then, we have

$$\sup_r \frac{|E(r) - \bar{r}|}{\bar{r}\sigma(r)} = \sigma(k_q) \tag{18.31}$$

and

$$\sigma\left(\frac{\partial_1 v}{E(\partial_0 v)}\right) \geq \sigma(k_q) \tag{18.32}$$

for any agent. Thus, the standard deviation of the pricing kernel is a lower bound for the volatility of agents' marginal rates of substitution. Equation (18.32) can, of course, be verified directly, for the projection of any agent's marginal rate of substitution onto the asset span is k_q (Figure 18.8).

Example 18.7.1 In Example 18.3.1, the pricing kernel k_q equals $(1, 1/2, 3/2)$, and its standard deviation is

$$\sigma(k_q) = \frac{1}{\sqrt{6}}. \tag{18.33}$$

The risk-free return $\bar{r}$ equals 1, and the Sharpe ratios of returns r_1 and r_2 are

$$\frac{E(r_1) - 1}{\sigma(r_1)} = 0 \tag{18.34}$$

and

$$\frac{E(r_2) - 1}{\sigma(r_2)} = \frac{1}{\sqrt{8}}, \tag{18.35}$$

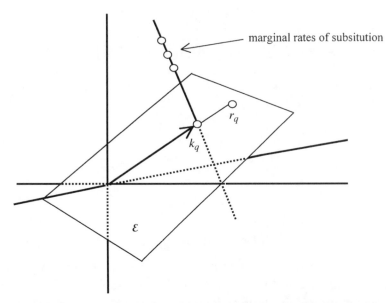

Figure 18.8 The vectors representing agents' marginal rates of substitution all project onto k_q.

respectively. Both numbers are smaller than $\sigma(k_q)$ as they must be given Eq. (18.31). This fact also confirms that the returns r_1 and r_2 are not frontier returns.   □

18.8 Notes

The mean-variance analysis of portfolio returns has been extensively used in finance since its development by Markowitz [1] and [2]. An analytical characterization of the mean-variance frontier was first derived by Merton [3].

Bibliography

[1] Markowitz, H. Portfolio selection. *Journal of Finance*, **7**:77–91, 1952.
[2] Markowitz, H. *Portfolio Selection: Efficient Diversification of Investments*. Wiley, New York, 1959.
[3] Merton, R. C. An analytic derivation of the efficient portfolio frontier. *Journal of Financial and Quantitative Analysis*, **7**:1851–71, 1972.

19

Capital Asset Pricing Model

19.1 Introduction

Beta pricing (see Section 18.5) implies that the risk premium on any security or portfolio is proportional to the covariance of its return with a frontier return. However, beta pricing by itself gives no guidance as to which returns are frontier returns. We will use the term Capital Asset Pricing Model (CAPM) if the market return is a frontier return. Note that the CAPM is here identified with a property of equilibrium security prices, not with a class of models of security markets. Therefore, it will be necessary to determine what restrictions on preferences or payoffs give rise to equilibria that conform to the CAPM definition.

Under the CAPM the market return, being a frontier return, can be taken as the reference portfolio in the beta pricing equation, resulting in the security market line, which relates the risk premium on any security to the covariance between the return on that security and the market return.

In Chapter 14 we derived the equation of the security market line by applying consumption-based security pricing under the assumption that agents have quadratic utilities. The derivation was generalized in Chapter 16. In this chapter we derive the CAPM in an equilibrium under the assumption that agents take variance as a measure of consumption risk (mean-variance preferences). This condition is satisfied when agents' preferences have an expected utility representation with quadratic utilities and also when security payoffs are multivariate normally distributed. We relax two of the assumptions of the Chapter 14 derivation: that agents' endowments lie in the asset span (securities market economy) and that the risk-free payoff is in the asset span.

19.2 Security Market Line

In Chapter 14 we defined the *market payoff* in a securities market economy as the aggregate date-1 endowment $\bar{w}_1$ and the market portfolio as a portfolio with payoff equal to the market payoff. We now extend these definitions to the general case in which agents' endowments, and therefore also the aggregate endowment, need not lie in the asset span.

Each individual's date-1 endowment w_1^i can be decomposed into the sum of two orthogonal components. Using the expectations inner product, we project w_1^i onto the asset span to distinguish the tradable component of the aggregate endowment from a nontradable component that is orthogonal to the asset span. We have

$$w_1^i = w_{1\mathcal{M}}^i + w_{1\mathcal{N}}^i, \tag{19.1}$$

where $w_{1\mathcal{M}}^i \in \mathcal{M}$ is the tradable component of agent i's endowment and $w_{1\mathcal{N}}^i \in \mathcal{N} = \mathcal{M}^\perp$ is the nontradable component. The Projection Theorem 17.5.1 guarantees that there is no ambiguity about this decomposition. The correponding decomposition for the aggregate endowment is

$$\bar{w}_1 = \bar{w}_{1\mathcal{M}} + \bar{w}_{1\mathcal{N}}. \tag{19.2}$$

The *market payoff m* is defined as the tradable component of the aggregate endowment, that is,

$$m = \bar{w}_{1\mathcal{M}}. \tag{19.3}$$

The *market return* r_m is the market payoff m divided by its equilibrium price $q(m)$, which is assumed to be nonzero.

By the definition of the CAPM, the market return r_m is a frontier return. If it is assumed that r_m is not the minimum-variance return, there exists another frontier return, denoted r_{m0}, that has zero covariance with r_m. These two frontier returns can be used in Eq. (18.23) of beta pricing. Thus, we have

Theorem 19.2.1 *If the market return lies on the mean-variance frontier, then*

$$E(r_j) = E(r_{m0}) + \beta_j[E(r_m) - E(r_{m0})], \tag{19.4}$$

for every security j, where $\beta_j = \text{cov}(r_j, r_m)/\text{var}(r_m)$.

Equation (19.4) is the equation of the *security market line*. If the risk-free payoff is in the asset span, then r_{m0} is risk-free and equal to $\bar{r}$, and Eq. (19.4) becomes

$$E(r_j) = \bar{r} + \beta_j[E(r_m) - \bar{r}]. \tag{19.5}$$

Equation (19.5) says that the risk premium $E(r_j) - \bar{r}$ is proportional to the coefficient β_j, the factor of proportionality being the risk premium $E(r_m) - \bar{r}$ on the market return (*market risk premium*). Thus coefficient β_j – the regression coefficient of r_j on the market return – is the appropriate measure of security risk in the CAPM.

The equation of the security market line holds for portfolio returns as well. Substituting r and β for r_j and β_j in Eq. (19.4), we obtain

$$E(r) = E(r_{m0}) + \beta[E(r_m) - E(r_{m0})], \tag{19.6}$$

where β is the regression coefficient of the return r on the market return. For the market return, β equals one; for the zero-covariance return r_{m0}, β equals zero. Return r_{m0} is called the *zero-beta* return.

The following example illustrates the use of Eq. (19.5) for pricing securities.

Example 19.2.2 There are three equally probable states at date 1. The aggregate date-1 endowment is (2,3,4). There are three securities: the first is risk free and has a return $\bar{r} = 1$; the second has a return $r_2 = (0, 3/2, 3)$; the third security has a payoff $x_3 = (0, 0, 1)$. The problem is to find the price p_3 of the third security if the CAPM is assumed.

We observe that the aggregate endowment lies in the span of the first and the second securities. This allows us to find the market return using the prices of those two securities. The price of the third security can be found using the security market line.

The price of the market payoff is 8/3, and its return is $r_m = (3/4, 9/8, 3/2)$. The expected return on the market portfolio is $E(r_m) = 9/8$.

The security market line gives the following:

$$\frac{E(x_3)}{p_3} = \bar{r} + \frac{\text{cov}(x_3, r_m)}{p_3 \text{var}(r_m)}[E(r_m) - \bar{r}] \tag{19.7}$$

or

$$p_3 = \frac{1}{\bar{r}}\left\{E(x_3) - \frac{\text{cov}(x_3, r_m)}{\text{var}(r_m)}[E(r_m) - \bar{r}]\right\}. \tag{19.8}$$

Substituting $E(r_m) = 9/8$, $E(x_3) = 1/3$, $\bar{r} = 1$, $\text{cov}(x_3, r_m) = 1/8$, $\text{var}(r_m) = 3/32$ in Eq. (19.8), we obtain $p_3 = 1/6$.

An alternative way of calculating p_3 is to note that the pricing kernel lies in the frontier plane. Because the market payoff is in the frontier plane, the pricing kernel lies in the span of the market payoff and the risk-free payoff or, equivalently, in the span of r_2 and the risk-free return. By writing the equations (17.30) for pricing the risk-free return and r_2, the pricing kernel can be calculated as $(3/2, 1, 1/2)$. Applying the kernel to x_3 results in $p_3 = 1/6$. □

The simplest case in which Eq. (19.5) (the securities market line) holds is when there are only two securities. We observed in Section 18.2 that with two securities every return is a mean-variance frontier return. In particular, the market return lies on the frontier and the CAPM holds.

19.3 Mean-Variance Preferences

The CAPM obtains in equilibrium when agents have mean-variance preferences. An agent has *mean-variance preferences* if his or her utility function $u(c_0, c_1)$ is strictly increasing and has the representation

$$u(c_0, c_1) = v_0(c_0) + f[E(c_1), \text{var}(c_1)] \tag{19.9}$$

for some functions $v_0 : \mathcal{R} \to \mathcal{R}$ and $f : \mathcal{R} \times \mathcal{R}_+ \to \mathcal{R}$. Under (19.9), agents' preferences are time separable with preferences over date-1 consumption plans depending only on the expectation and variance. The agent therefore takes variance as a measure of consumption risk. An agent with mean-variance preferences is *strictly variance averse* if f in (19.9) is strictly decreasing in variance.

Two important cases that lead to mean-variance preferences – quadratic utilities and normally distributed payoffs and date-1 endowments – are discussed in the next two sections.

Theorem 19.3.1 *If every agent has mean-variance preferences and is strictly variance averse, then in an equilibrium the market return lies on the mean-variance frontier.*

Proof: Let c_1^i be an equilibrium date-1 consumption plan of agent i. We decompose c_1^i into the tradable component and the nontradable component (see Eq. (19.2)) so that

$$c_1^i = c_{1\mathcal{M}}^i + c_{1\mathcal{N}}^i, \tag{19.10}$$

where $c_{1\mathcal{M}}^i \in \mathcal{M}$ and $c_{1\mathcal{N}}^i \in \mathcal{N}$.

It is sufficient to show that the tradable component $c_{1\mathcal{M}}^i$ of each agent's date-1 consumption lies on the mean-variance frontier $\mathcal{E}$ because if that is so, then the tradable component of the aggregate consumption is also a frontier payoff. But the tradable component of aggregate consumption equals the tradable component of the aggregate endowment, which by definition is the market payoff. Therefore, the market return is a frontier return.

To show that $c_{1\mathcal{M}}^i \in \mathcal{E}$, we decompose $c_{1\mathcal{M}}^i$ by projecting it on the frontier plane $\mathcal{E}$ so that

$$c_{1\mathcal{M}}^i = c_{1\mathcal{E}}^i + c_{1\mathcal{I}}^i, \tag{19.11}$$

where $c_{1\mathcal{E}}^i \in \mathcal{E}$ is the frontier component, and $c_{1\mathcal{I}}^i \in \mathcal{E}^\perp$ is the component of $c_{1\mathcal{M}}^i$ orthogonal to the frontier plane (here $\mathcal{I}$ stands for "inefficient" and $\mathcal{E}^\perp$ is the orthogonal complement of $\mathcal{E}$ in $\mathcal{M}$).

Suppose by contradiction that, for some agent i, $c_{1\mathcal{M}}^i$ does not lie on the frontier plane and hence that $c_{1\mathcal{I}}^i \neq 0$. Consider the alternative date-1 consumption plan given by

$$\tilde{c}_1^i \equiv c_{1\mathcal{E}}^i + c_{1\mathcal{N}}^i. \tag{19.12}$$

Note that $\tilde{c}_1^i = c_1^i - c_{1\mathcal{I}}^i$. Because the agent's utility function is strictly increasing, the optimal consumption satisfies the budget constraints with equality, implying that $c_1^i - w_1^i \in \mathcal{M}$. If we use $\tilde{c}_1^i - w_1^i = (c_1^i - w_1^i) - c_{1\mathcal{I}}^i$, it follows that

$$\tilde{c}_1^i - w_1^i \in \mathcal{M}, \tag{19.13}$$

and thus the consumption plan $\tilde{c}_1^i$ can be attained by a net trade in the asset span.

By Theorem 18.2.1 the equilibrium pricing kernel k_q lies in the frontier plane $\mathcal{E}$. Therefore,

$$q(c_{1\mathcal{I}}^i) = E(k_q c_{1\mathcal{I}}^i) = 0, \tag{19.14}$$

and the net trade $\tilde{c}_1^i - w_1^i$ has the same price as $c_1^i - w_1^i$; that is, $q(\tilde{c}_1^i - w_1^i) = q(c_1^i - w_1^i)$. This and (19.13) imply that the date-1 consumption plan $\tilde{c}_1^i$ and the date-0 plan c_0^i satisfy agent i's budget constraint.

Because the expectations kernel also lies in the frontier plane (Theorem 18.2.1), we have

$$E(c_{1\mathcal{I}}^i) = E(k_e c_{1\mathcal{I}}^i) = 0. \tag{19.15}$$

Therefore, $\tilde{c}_1^i$ and c_1^i have the same expectation. Because $c_{1\mathcal{E}}^i, c_{1\mathcal{I}}^i$, and $c_{1\mathcal{E}}^i$ are mutually orthogonal and $E(c_{1\mathcal{I}}^i) = 0$, it follows that $\mathrm{cov}(c_{1\mathcal{E}}^i, c_{1\mathcal{I}}^i) = \mathrm{cov}(c_{1\mathcal{I}}^i, c_{1\mathcal{N}}^i) = 0$. Using Eq. (19.12), we obtain that $\mathrm{cov}(\tilde{c}_1^i, c_{1\mathcal{I}}^i) = 0$ and consequently that

$$\mathrm{var}(c_1^i) = \mathrm{var}(\tilde{c}_1^i) + \mathrm{var}(c_{1\mathcal{I}}^i) > \mathrm{var}(\tilde{c}_1^i), \tag{19.16}$$

where the last strict inequality follows from the assumption that $c_{1\mathcal{I}}^i \neq 0$.

Consumption plan $\tilde{c}_1^i$ has smaller variance than c_1^i, and the two have the same expectation. Because the agent has mean-variance preferences and is strictly variance averse, consumption plan $\tilde{c}_1^i$ is strictly preferred to c_1^i. This contradicts the optimality of c_1^i. Therefore, the tradable component $c_{1\mathcal{M}}^i$ of every agent's equilibrium consumption lies in the mean-variance frontier plane. Because in equilibrium the market payoff equals the sum over agents of the tradable components of agents' consumption plans, the market return lies on the mean-variance frontier as well.

□

It follows from Theorems 19.3.1 and Theorem 19.2.1 that if agents measure consumption risk by variance, then beta, the coefficient of regression of the return on the market return, is the appropriate measure of security risk in equilibrium.

19.4 Equilibrium Portfolios under Mean-Variance Preferences

In the proof of Theorem 19.3.1 we demonstrated that the tradable component of the date-1 equilibrium consumption plan of an agent with mean-variance preferences lies on the mean-variance frontier. The nontradable component of the equilibrium consumption plan is equal to the nontradable component of the endowment. To see this, note that since $c_1^i - w_1^i \in \mathcal{M}$, Eqs. (19.1) and (19.2) imply that

$$c_{1\mathcal{N}}^i = w_{1\mathcal{N}}^i. \tag{19.17}$$

If the risk-free payoff lies in the asset span, then $c_{1\mathcal{N}}^i$ has zero expectation since is orthogonal to the asset span.

Summing up, the equilibrium date-1 consumption plan satisfies

$$c_1^i = c_{1\mathcal{M}}^i + w_{1\mathcal{N}}^i, \quad \text{with} \quad c_{1\mathcal{M}}^i \in \mathcal{E}. \tag{19.18}$$

Let

$$w^i \equiv w_0^i + q(w_{1\mathcal{M}}^i), \tag{19.19}$$

be the agent's wealth at date 0 consisting of his date-0 endowment and the value of the tradable component of his date-1 endowment. Since the mean-variance frontier is spanned by the market return r_m and the zero-covariance return r_{m0}, the tradable component of date-1 equilibrium consumption plan can be written as

$$c_{1\mathcal{M}}^i = a^i r_m + (w^i - c_0^i - a^i) r_{m0}, \tag{19.20}$$

where a^i denotes the amount of date 0 wealth invested in the market portfolio. A simple characterization of the equilibrium investment a^i can be given when the risk-free payoff lies in the asset span. Then $r_{m0} = \bar{r}$ and the expectation and variance of date-1 equilibrium consumption plan can be written using Eqs. (19.18) and (19.20) as

$$E(c_1^i) = (w^i - c_0^i)\bar{r} + a^i[E(r_m) - \bar{r}], \tag{19.21}$$

and

$$\text{var}(c_1^i) = (a^i)^2 \text{var}(r_m) + \text{var}(w_{1\mathcal{N}}^i). \tag{19.22}$$

The equilibrium investment a^i and consumption plan c^i (assumed interior and with strictly positive variance) satisfy the following first-order conditions obtained from substituting Eqs. (19.21) and (19.22) in (19.9) and maximizing with respect to c_0^i and a^i:

$$v_0' = \bar{r}\delta_E f \tag{19.23}$$

$$a^i = -\frac{(E(r_m) - \bar{r})\delta_E f}{2\,\text{var}(r_m)\delta_v f}. \tag{19.24}$$

Here $\delta_E f$ and $\delta_v f$ are the partial derivatives of f with respect to its first and second arguments evaluated at the equilibrium date-1 consumption; v_0' is the derivative of v_0 evaluated at the equilibrium date-0 consumption.

Equation (19.23) states that the marginal rate of substitution between date-0 consumption and the expectation of date-1 consumption equals the risk-free return. Equation (19.24) relates the equilibrium investment in the market portfolio to the risk premium and the variance of the market return, and also to the marginal rate of substitution between expected return and variance of return.

If each agent's mean-variance utility function is strictly increasing in the expectation of date-1 consumption and strictly decreasing in its variance, then all agents whose optimal consumption is not risk-free have investments in the market portfolio that are of the same sign as the risk premium on the market return. It follows that the market risk premium must be strictly positive because otherwise the total wealth invested in the market portfolio would be negative. Thus

$$E(r_m) > \bar{r}. \tag{19.25}$$

Consequently, each agent's investment in the market portfolio is strictly positive or zero implying that the expected return on equilibrium investment exceeds the risk-free return. Because every mean-variance frontier return with expectation that exceeds the risk-free return is mean-variance efficient, returns on agents' equilibrium investments are mean-variance efficient.

The foregoing discussion provides a characterization of an equilibrium portfolio net of the portfolio that generates the tradable component of an agent's date-1 endowment. The agent's equilibrium portfolio is equal to the difference between the portfolio described above and the portfolio that generates $w_{1\mathcal{M}}^i$.

19.5 Quadratic Utilities

If an agent's preferences have an expected utility representation with a quadratic von Neumann–Morgenstern utility function of the form

$$v^i(c_0, c_s) = v_0^i(c_0) + v_1^i(c_s) = v_0^i(c_0) - (c_s - \alpha^i)^2, \quad \text{for} \quad c_s \le \alpha^i, \tag{19.26}$$

then the expected utility of consumption (c_0, c_1) is

$$E[v^i(c_0, c_1)] = v_0^i(c_0) - \{\text{var}(c_1) + [E(c_1) - \alpha^i]^2\}. \tag{19.27}$$

As usual, we assume common probability expectations. The agent's expected utility (Eq. (19.27)) depends only on c_0 and the expectation and variance of c_1. Thus, he or she has mean-variance preferences and is variance averse. Theorem 19.3.1 therefore applies when utility functions are quadratic.

In Chapter 14, with the subsequent generalization in Chapter 16, we derived the equation of the security market line in an equilibrium with quadratic utility functions (19.26) under additional assumptions not appearing in Theorem 19.3.1: that agents' endowments lie in the asset span and that the risk-free payoff is in the asset span. Further, we proved in Chapter 16 that under these assumptions, markets are effectively complete and equilibrium consumption allocations are Pareto optimal. From the analysis of this chapter we conclude that the equation of security market line holds in an equilibrium with quadratic utility functions even when either agents' endowments or the risk-free payoff (or both) lie outside of the asset span. However, the Pareto optimality of equilibrium consumption allocations does not in general hold under the less strict assumptions.

19.6 Normally Distributed Payoffs

If security payoffs and an agent's date-1 endowment are multivariate normally distributed,[1] then his or her date-1 consumption plans that can be generated by portfolios are normally distributed. Because the normal distribution is completely characterized by its expectation and variance, the agent's utility function depends only on date-0 consumption c_0 and the expectation and variance of date-1 consumption plan c_1. If his or her utility functions are time separable and strictly monotone, the agent has mean-variance preferences (19.9).

In particular, if an agent's preferences have an expected utility representation with a time-separable von Neumann–Morgenstern utility function, the mean-variance representation obtains when security payoffs and his or her date-1 endowment are multivariate normally distributed. Further, if the agent is risk averse, then he or she is also variance averse. To see this, recall from Section 10.3 that if two random variables are normally distributed, then the one with strictly greater variance is strictly riskier. Thus, Theorem 19.3.1 applies when security payoffs and agents' date-1 endowments are multivariate normally distributed and agents are risk averse.

Normal payoff distributions can be justified by appeal to the central limit theorem. But that is only if security payoffs are not subject to limited liability. For instance, the payoff of an option is a truncated version of the payoff on the underlying security.

19.7 Notes

A first expression of the risk–return trade-off was given in Theorem 13.3.1. In a world of risk-averse investors, the greater the expected return, the greater is the

---

[1] Strictly, normal distribution of payoffs cannot be incorporated in the model adopted in these book because we assumed that there exist only a finite number of states. However, no harm results if we temporarily trespass into a richer setting.

risk. We observed in Chapter 10 that even if no assumptions about the form of the utility function are made (other than risk aversion), a specific measure of return was available: expected return. We also remarked that variance could not be used as a measure of risk and that it had to be associated with the partial ordering defined in Chapter 10. In the CAPM, in contrast, risk is associated with the complete ordering of return distributions induced by beta, and the security market line implies that the relation between expected return and risk is linear.

If the risk-free payoff and agents' endowments lie in the asset span, the CAPM shares with LRT utilities a property of equilibrium: that date-1 consumption plans lie in the plane spanned by the aggregate endowment and the risk-free payoff. However, the pricing relationship of the CAPM – the security market line – does not apply in the general LRT utilities case (with the exception, of course, of quadratic utilities). Nothing about the assumption that agents have LRT utilities with a common slope of risk tolerance implies that the market payoff is mean-variance efficient. As was shown in Theorem 19.3.1, mean-variance efficiency of the market payoff is a consequence of the assumption that agents measure consumption risk by variance.

In proving Theorem 19.3.1, we assumed that agents' consumption plans were unrestricted. If there are restrictions on consumption (such as positivity), the theorem is still true provided that the equilibrium allocation is interior. But the proof requires a minor modification. Instead of using $\tilde{c}_1^i = c_1^i - c_{1\mathcal{I}}^i$ as an alternative consumption plan, it is necessary to use $\tilde{c}_1^i = c_1^i - \delta c_{1\mathcal{I}}^i$ for small positive δ. Although the first of these consumption plans may not be in the consumption set even if c_1^i is interior, the latter will be for small enough δ.

The portfolio theory under mean-variance preferences originated with Markowitz [3]. The CAPM pricing results were derived independently by Sharpe [10], Lintner, [2], Mossin [5], and Treynor (in unpublished notes).

Derivation of the CAPM without the assumption that the risk-free payoff is traded is from Black [1]. Sufficient conditions for the existence of a CAPM equilibrium when agents have mean-variance preferences, with and without a risk-free security, can be found in Nielsen [6] and [7].

The testable content of the CAPM is the assertion that the market return is mean-variance efficient, which implies the equation of the security market line. In his critique, Roll [8] observed that if one uses a proxy for the market portfolio that is not mean-variance efficient, testing the relation between beta and risk premia is pointless. That is because the CAPM generates a prediction about this relation only when the reference portfolio is mean-variance efficient.

As noted by Ross [9], if the proxy for the market portfolio is mean-variance efficient, the equation of the security market line will be satisfied regardless of whether the CAPM is true. This we showed in Chapter 18.

Milne and Smith [4] analyzed the CAPM in the presence of transactions costs.

Bibliography

[1] Black, F. Capital market equilibrium with restricted borrowing. *Journal of Business*, **45**:444–55, 1972.

[2] Lintner, J. The valuation of risk assets and the selection of risky investments in stock portfolios and capital budgets. *Review of Economics and Statistics*, **47**:13–37, 1965.

[3] Markowitz, H. *Portfolio Selection: Efficient Diversification of Investments*. Wiley, New York, 1959.

[4] Milne, F. and Smith, C. W. Capital asset pricing with proportional transaction cost. *Journal of Financial and Quantitative Analysis*, **XV**:253–66, 1980.

[5] Mossin, J. Equilibrium in a capital asset market. *Econometrica*, **35**:768–83, 1968.

[6] Nielsen, L. T. Equilibrium in CAPM without a riskless asset. *Review of Economic Studies*, **57**:315–24, 1990.

[7] Nielsen, L. T. Existence of equilibrium in CAPM. *Journal of Economic Theory*, **52**:223–31, 1990.

[8] Roll, R. A critique of the asset price theory's tests: Part I. *Journal of Financial Economics*, **4**:129–76, 1977.

[9] Ross, S. A. Risk, return and arbitrage. In Irwin Friend and James Bicksler, editors, *Risk and Return in Finance*. Ballinger, Cambridge, MA, 1976.

[10] Sharpe, W. F. Capital asset prices: A theory of market equilibrium under conditions of risk. *Journal of Finance*, **19**:425–42, 1964.

20

Factor Pricing

20.1 Introduction

In the CAPM, beta is the measure of the sensitivity of a security's return to the market return. The equation of the security market line (19.5) shows that the relation between the risk premium and beta is linear.

The CAPM relies on restrictive assumptions about agents' preferences or security returns, and certainly its empirical implications have not been confirmed by data. In this chapter we consider models of security markets – all with a pricing relation similar to that of the CAPM – but with a factor (or factors) replacing the market return. These factors are typically taken to be proxies for such macroeconomic variables as gross domestic product, the rate of inflation, and so on. The relation between expected return and the measure of the sensitivity of a security's return to factor risk, like the corresponding relation in the case of the CAPM, is linear.

20.2 Exact Factor Pricing

There are K contingent claims $f_1, \ldots, f_K$ called *factors*. Each factor is normalized so as to have zero expectation. The number K of factors is small relative to the number of securities, and the factors may or may not lie in the asset span. The span of the factors and the risk-free claim e is the *factor span*, which is denoted by $\mathcal{F} \equiv \text{span}\{e, f_1, \ldots, f_K\}$. It is assumed that all K factors and the risk-free claim are linearly independent.

Projecting the payoff x_j of each security on the factor span $\mathcal{F}$ (using the expectations inner product) results in the following decomposition:

$$x_j = E(x_j) + \sum_{k=1}^{K} b_{jk} f_k + \delta_j \qquad (20.1)$$

for every j, where δ_j is uncorrelated with f_k for all k and has zero expectation. The coefficient b_{jk} in Eq. (20.1) is the *factor loading* of payoff x_j: it measures the exposure (sensitivity) of that payoff to the factor f_k.

Equation (20.1) can be written using security returns rather than payoffs. If all security prices are nonzero, then

$$r_j = E(r_j) + \sum_{k=1}^{K} \beta_{jk} f_k + \epsilon_j, \tag{20.2}$$

where $\beta_{jk} = b_{jk}/p_j$ and $\epsilon_j = \delta_j/p_j$. Coefficient β_{jk} in Eq. (20.2) is the *factor loading* of return r_j.

Exact factor pricing with factors $f_1, \ldots, f_K$ holds if security prices satisfy

$$p_j = E(x_j)\tau_0 + \sum_{k=1}^{K} b_{jk}\tau_k \quad \forall j \tag{20.3}$$

for some scalars $\tau_0, \ldots, \tau_K$. Equation (20.3) is a linear relation between security prices and factor loadings.

Exact factor pricing can be expressed using expected returns. Dividing Eq. (20.3) by p_j and rearranging terms yields

$$E(r_j) = \gamma_0 + \sum_{k=1}^{K} \beta_{jk}\gamma_k, \tag{20.4}$$

where $\gamma_0 = 1/\tau_0$ and $\gamma_k = -\tau_k/\tau_0$. In this form exact factor pricing is a linear relation between expected returns and factor loadings of returns.

If the risk-free claim and the K factors lie in the asset span, so does the residual δ_j. Then exact factor pricing obtains if the residual δ_j in Eq. (20.1), or equivalently ϵ_j in Eq. (20.2) has zero price; that is, if

$$q(\delta_j) = 0, \tag{20.5}$$

where q is the payoff pricing functional associated with security prices p. To see this, apply the functional q to both sides of Eq. (20.1) and use Eq. (20.5) to obtain Eq. (20.3) with coefficients

$$\tau_0 = \frac{1}{\bar{r}} \quad \text{and} \quad \tau_k = q(f_k) \tag{20.6}$$

equal to factor prices. The coefficients of exact factor pricing for returns are

$$\gamma_0 = \bar{r}, \quad \text{and} \quad \gamma_k = -\bar{r}q(f_k). \tag{20.7}$$

If the risk-free claim and the K factors are payoffs, then the asset span can be decomposed into $\mathcal{M} = \mathcal{F} + \text{span}\{\epsilon_1, \ldots, \epsilon_J\}$. The assumption that each residual δ_j has zero price implies that $k_q \in \mathcal{F}$. It turns out that the condition that the pricing kernel should lie in the factor span is sufficient for exact factor pricing irrespective of whether the risk-free claim and the factors lie in the asset span.

Theorem 20.2.1 *If the pricing kernel k_q lies in the factor span, then exact factor pricing*

$$E(r_j) = \gamma_0 + \sum_{k=1}^{K} \beta_{jk} \gamma_k \qquad (20.8)$$

holds with $\gamma_0 = 1/E(k_q)$ and $\gamma_k = -E(k_q f_k)/E(k_q)$. If in addition the risk-free claim lies in the asset span, then $\gamma_0 = \bar{r}$.

Proof: Multiplying Eq. (20.2) by k_q and taking expectations, we obtain

$$1 = E(r_j)E(k_q) + \sum_{k=1}^{K} \beta_{jk} E(k_q f_k) + E(k_q \epsilon_j). \qquad (20.9)$$

Dividing both sides of Eq. (20.9) by $E(k_q)$ and rearranging, we obtain

$$E(r_j) = \frac{1}{E(k_q)} + \sum_{k=1}^{K} \beta_{jk} \left[-\frac{E(k_q f_k)}{E(k_q)} \right] - \frac{E(k_q \epsilon_j)}{E(k_q)}. \qquad (20.10)$$

Because k_q lies in the factor span $\mathcal{F}$, it is orthogonal to ϵ_j. Thus, $E(k_q \epsilon_j) = 0$ and, as follows from Eq. (20.10),

$$E(r_j) = \frac{1}{E(k_q)} + \sum_{k=1}^{K} \beta_{jk} \left[-\frac{E(k_q f_k)}{E(k_q)} \right]. \qquad (20.11)$$

Therefore, exact factor pricing (20.8) holds with $\gamma_0 = 1/E(k_q)$ and $\gamma_k = -E(k_q f_k)/E(k_q)$. Finally, if the risk-free claim lies in the asset span, then

$$E(k_q) = \frac{1}{\bar{r}}, \qquad (20.12)$$

and $\gamma_0 = \bar{r}$.   □

If the risk-free claim lies in the asset span, then a necessary and sufficient condition for the pricing kernel to lie in the factor span is that the plane of mean-variance frontier payoffs be contained in the factor span. To see this, recall (Theorem 18.2.1) that the mean-variance frontier plane $\mathcal{E}$ is spanned by the risk-free payoff and the pricing kernel. Thus $k_q \in \mathcal{F}$ iff $\mathcal{E} \subset \mathcal{F}$.

20.3 Exact Factor Pricing, Beta Pricing, and the CAPM

Suppose that there is a single factor that is a mean-variance frontier return r normalized so as to have zero expectation,

$$f = r - E(r), \qquad (20.13)$$

for an arbitrary frontier return r other than the risk-free return.

Suppose also that the risk-free claim lies in the asset span. Then the factor f and the risk-free return span the plane of mean-variance frontier payoffs. Consequently, the pricing kernel lies in the factor span. Theorem 20.2.1 implies exact factor pricing:

$$E(r_j) = \bar{r} - \beta_j \bar{r} q(f).\tag{20.14}$$

Because β_j of Eq. (20.14) is the coefficient in the projection of return r_j on the factor span, it is given by

$$\beta_j = \frac{\text{cov}(r_j, f)}{\text{var}(f)} = \frac{\text{cov}(r_j, r)}{\text{var}(r)}\tag{20.15}$$

and hence is the same as the β_j of the beta pricing relation (18.25). Proceeding further, we multiply Eq. (20.13) by k_q and take expectations to get

$$q(f) = E(k_q f) = 1 - \frac{E(r)}{\bar{r}}.\tag{20.16}$$

Using Eq. (20.16), we can rewrite Eq. (20.14) as

$$E(r_j) = \bar{r} + \beta_j [E(r) - \bar{r}].\tag{20.17}$$

This is the beta pricing relation (18.25). Thus, beta pricing with respect to a frontier return r is the same as exact-factor pricing with a single factor equal to return r normalized so as to have zero expectation.

In the CAPM of Chapter 19, the market return r_m lies on the mean-variance frontier. Exact factor pricing with a single factor given by

$$f = r_m - E(r_m)\tag{20.18}$$

is equivalent to the equation of the security market line.

20.4 Factor Pricing Errors

Even if it does not hold exactly, the factor pricing relation (20.4) provides a point of departure for developing a definition of pricing errors.

The *pricing error* of security j is

$$\psi_j \equiv E(r_j) - \gamma_0 - \sum_{k=1}^{K} \beta_{jk} \gamma_k,\tag{20.19}$$

where $\gamma_0 = 1/E(k_q)$ and $\gamma_k = -E(k_q f_k)/E(k_q)$. If pricing errors are zero, then exact factor pricing holds.

Using Eq. (20.10) we can write

$$\psi_j = -\frac{E(k_q \epsilon_j)}{E(k_q)}.\tag{20.20}$$

If the risk-free claim and the K factors lie in the asset span, then $\epsilon_j \in \mathcal{M}$. Thus $E(k_q \epsilon_j) = q(\epsilon_j)$, and, through Eq. (20.12),

$$\psi_j = -\bar{r} q(\epsilon_j), \qquad (20.21)$$

which means that the pricing error equals the price of the residual ϵ_j multiplied by (the negative of) the risk-free return.

A bound on the pricing error can be obtained as follows: projecting k_q on the factor span $\mathcal{F}$, we obtain the following decomposition:

$$k_q = k_q^{\mathcal{F}} + \eta, \qquad (20.22)$$

where $k_q^{\mathcal{F}} \in \mathcal{F}$ and $\eta \perp \mathcal{F}$. Because each ϵ_j is uncorrelated with the factors and has zero expectation, it follows that

$$E(k_q \epsilon_j) = E(\eta \epsilon_j). \qquad (20.23)$$

Applying the Cauchy–Schwarz inequality (Section 17.2), we obtain

$$|E(k_q \epsilon_j)| \leq \|\eta\| \|\epsilon_j\|. \qquad (20.24)$$

Using Eqs. (20.20), (20.22), and $E(\epsilon_j) = 0$, the following bound on the pricing error results:

$$|\psi_j| \leq \frac{1}{E(k_q)} \sigma(\epsilon_j) \|k_q - k_q^{\mathcal{F}}\|. \qquad (20.25)$$

The norm $\|k_q - k_q^{\mathcal{F}}\|$ measures the distance between the pricing kernel k_q and the factor span. Thus, inequality (20.25) indicates that if k_q is close to the factor span, the pricing error on security j is small. When the pricing kernel lies in the factor span, exact factor pricing holds, as seen in Theorem 20.2.1.

20.5 Factor Structure

Security returns have a *factor structure* with factors $f_1, \ldots, f_K$ if the residuals ϵ_j in the decomposition

$$r_j = E(r_j) + \sum_{k=1}^{K} \beta_{jk} f_k + \epsilon_j \qquad (20.26)$$

are uncorrelated with each other,

$$E(\epsilon_i \epsilon_j) = 0 \quad \text{for} \quad i \neq j, \qquad (20.27)$$

in addition to being uncorrelated with factors and having zero expectations. The condition (20.27) is a substantive restriction on security returns and factors. In general, residuals of the projection of security returns on the factor span need not be uncorrelated with each other.

When returns have the factor structure given by Eqs. (20.26) and (20.27), factors are called *systematic risk* because they affect all security returns, while residuals are called *idiosyncratic risk* because each residual is specific to the security in the sense that it is uncorrelated with the factor risk and other security returns. If returns do not have a factor structure (so that the residuals may be correlated with each other), then the terms "systematic risk" and "idiosyncratic risk" are inappropriate: there is no presumption that the residuals are any less pervasive across securities than are the factors.

The term "systematic risk" is sometimes used in the context of the CAPM to mean market risk. This usage is different from systematic risk as defined here. The CAPM does not require that security returns have a factor structure in the sense of (20.26) and (20.27) with the market return as a factor.

A bound on the summed squared pricing errors obtains when security returns have a factor structure.

Theorem 20.5.1 *If security returns have a factor structure, then*

$$\sum_{j=1}^{J} \psi_j^2 \leq \frac{1}{[E(k_q)]^2} \max_j [\sigma^2(\epsilon_j)] \|k_q - k_q^{\mathcal{F}}\|^2. \tag{20.28}$$

Proof: We can assume that all ϵ_j's are nonzero. If some were zero, then the proof to follow would apply to all securities with nonzero ϵ_j. Because the pricing error on a security with zero idiosyncratic risk equals zero (see Eq. (20.20)), inequality (20.28) holds for all securities.

The pricing kernel k_q lies in the asset span $\mathcal{M}$, a subspace of $\mathcal{F} + \text{span}\{\epsilon_1, \ldots, \epsilon_J\}$. Because the residual η of Eq. (20.22) is orthogonal to $\mathcal{F}$, it must lie in $\text{span}\{\epsilon_1, \ldots, \epsilon_J\}$. The assumption of factor structure (20.26) and (20.27) implies (recall Corollary 17.4.2) that the idiosyncratic risks ϵ_j are linearly independent and hence are a basis for $\text{span}\{\epsilon_1, \ldots, \epsilon_J\}$. Consequently, η can be written as

$$\eta = \sum_{j=1}^{J} a_j \epsilon_j, \tag{20.29}$$

for some scalars $a_1, \ldots, a_J$. It follows from Eqs. (20.22) and (20.29) that

$$E(k_q \epsilon_j) = a_j E(\epsilon_j^2). \tag{20.30}$$

Making use of $E(\epsilon_j^2) = \sigma^2(\epsilon_j)$, Eqs. (20.20) and (20.30) imply

$$\psi_j = -\frac{1}{E(k_q)} a_j \sigma^2(\epsilon_j). \tag{20.31}$$

Further, the Pythagorean Theorem 17.6 and Eq. (20.29) imply

$$\sum_{j=1}^{J} a_j^2 E(\epsilon_j^2) = \|\eta\|^2. \tag{20.32}$$

Using $\eta = k_q - k_q^{\mathcal{F}}$ and $E(\epsilon_j^2) = \sigma^2(\epsilon_j)$, Eq. (20.32) can be written as

$$\sum_{j=1}^{J} a_j^2 \sigma^2(\epsilon_j) = \|k_q - k_q^{\mathcal{F}}\|^2. \tag{20.33}$$

Now, if Eq. (20.33) is multiplied by $(1/[E(k_q)]^2) \max_j [\sigma^2(\epsilon_j)]$, and if use is made of $\sigma^2(\epsilon_j) \le \max_j [\sigma^2(\epsilon_j)]$, then

$$\sum_{j=1}^{J} \frac{1}{[E(k_q)]^2} a_j^2 \sigma^4(\epsilon_j) \le \frac{1}{[E(k_q)]^2} \max_j [\sigma^2(\epsilon_j)] \|k_q - k_q^{\mathcal{F}}\|^2. \tag{20.34}$$

The sought-after result (20.28) follows from Eq. (20.31) and inequality (20.34).

$\square$

Theorem 20.5.1 has several important implications. It implies, and hence confirms the finding of Section 20.4, that if the pricing kernel is close to the factor span, then all pricing errors are small. The theorem also implies that if the number of securities is large, then, independent of the location of the pricing kernel, most pricing errors are small. We can be more precise. Let $\rho > 0$ be a small number and let N_ρ be the smallest integer greater than M/ρ, where M denotes the right-hand side of inequality (20.28). If $J > N_\rho$, then at least $J - N_\rho$ securities have squared pricing errors ψ_j^2 smaller than ρ. If not, there is a contradition to inequality (20.28), for then there are more than N_ρ securities with squared pricing errors greater than ρ.

If the number J of securities is so large that $J - N_\rho$ is also large, then for a large number of securities pricing errors must be small. This justifies the term *approximate factor pricing*.

In the limit, if there are infinitely many securities (this specification takes us beyond the finite setting of this book; but see the chapter notes) with a factor structure characterized by bounded variance of idiosyncratic risks, then, as implied by Theorem 20.5.1, all but a finite number of securities have (squared) pricing errors that are arbitrarily small. This is the fundamental conclusion of the Arbitrage Pricing Theory (APT).

20.6 Mean-Independent Factor Structure

Exact factor pricing obtains in a security markets equilibrium under a more restrictive definition of factor structure. This definition is stated in terms of security payoffs.

The residual δ_j determined by the projection of x_j on the factor span,

$$x_j = E(x_j) + \sum_{k=1}^{K} b_{jk} f_k + \delta_j, \tag{20.35}$$

is uncorrelated with the factors. Security payoffs have a *mean-independent factor structure* if uncorrelatedness can be strengthened to mean-independence; that is, to

$$E(\delta_j | f_1, \ldots, f_K) = 0, \tag{20.36}$$

for every j.

In the next theorem we consider securities markets with agents whose preferences have an expected utility representation with common probabilities and with differentiable von Neumann–Morgenstern utility functions.

Theorem 20.6.1 *If security payoffs have a mean-independent factor structure; if the risk-free claim, the factors, and agents' date-1 endowments lie in the asset span; if the aggregate date-1 endowment lies in the factor span; and if agents are strictly risk averse, then exact factor pricing holds in any equilibrium in which the consumption allocation is interior.*

Proof: Let $\{c^i\}$ be a security markets equilibrium consumption allocation, which by Theorem 16.2.1, is constrained optimal. We first prove that the date-1 allocation $\{c_1^i\}$ lies in the factor span $\mathcal{F}$.

Because the risk-free claim and the factors lie in the asset span $\mathcal{M}$, we have that $\mathcal{M} = \mathcal{F} + \text{span}\{\delta_1, \ldots, \delta_J\}$. Further, because all agents' date-1 endowments lie in the asset span $\mathcal{M}$, their date-1 equilibrium consumption plans c_1^i lie in $\mathcal{M}$ as well. Therefore, each c_1^i can be decomposed into

$$c_1^i = \hat{c}_1^i + \Delta^i, \tag{20.37}$$

where $\hat{c}_1^i \in \mathcal{F}$ and $\Delta^i \in \text{span}\{\delta_1, \ldots, \delta_J\}$. It follows that

$$E(\Delta^i | f_1, \ldots, f_K) = 0 \tag{20.38}$$

because the residuals δ_j are mean-independent of the factors. Using Eq. (20.38) and $\hat{c}_1^i \in \mathcal{F}$, we obtain

$$E(\Delta^i | \hat{c}_1^i) = 0. \tag{20.39}$$

Equations (20.37) and (20.39) say that the consumption plan c_1^i is more risky than $\hat{c}_1^i$ (and strictly so if $\Delta^i \neq 0$).

Because

$$\sum_{i=1}^{I} c_1^i = \bar{w}_1 \in \mathcal{F}, \tag{20.40}$$

we have that

$$\sum_{i=1}^{I} \hat{c}_1^i = \bar{w}_1, \quad \text{and} \quad \sum_{i=1}^{I} \Delta^i = 0. \qquad (20.41)$$

Thus, unless $\Delta^i = 0$ holds for every i, allocation $\{\hat{c}^i\}$ Pareto dominates $\{c^i\}$. Therefore, $\Delta^i = 0$, which implies that

$$c_1^i \in \mathcal{F}, \qquad (20.42)$$

for every i.

Because the consumption plan c^i is interior and the von Neumann–Morgenstern utility function is differentiable, the marginal rate of substitution $\partial_1 v^i / \partial_0 v^i$ is well-defined and is a function of date-1 consumption. By Theorem 10.4.1, the marginal rate of substitution is uncorrelated with residuals δ_j; that is

$$E\left(\frac{\partial_1 v^i}{\partial_0 v^i} \delta_j\right) = 0 \qquad (20.43)$$

for every j. We observed in Section 17.10 that the pricing kernel equals the projection of the marginal rate of substitution $\partial_1 v^i / \partial_0 v^i$ on the asset span. Taking into account that $\mathcal{M} = \mathcal{F} + \text{span}\{\delta_1, \ldots, \delta_J\}$ and using Eq. (20.43), we obtain

$$k_q \in \mathcal{F}. \qquad (20.44)$$

Theorem 20.2.1 implies now that exact factor pricing holds.   □

Note that if payoffs have mean-independent factor structure, then the assumption that the δ_i's are uncorrelated with each other is not needed for the proof of exact factor pricing.

20.7 Options as Factors

An important example of contingent claims that form a mean-independent factor structure is the set of payoffs of options on the aggregate endowment. Let n be the number of different values that the aggregate date-1 endowment $\bar{w}_1$ can take. Let $\bar{w}_{1k}$ denote the kth value of the aggregate date-1 endowment (with $\bar{w}_{1k} < \bar{w}_{1,k+1}$, $1 \leq k < n$) and S_k denote the subset of states s such that $\bar{w}_{1s} = \bar{w}_{1k}$.

Suppose that $1 < n$ so that the aggregate date-1 endowment is not risk-free. We consider $K \equiv n - 1$ nonredundant call options on the aggregate date-1 endowment $\bar{w}_1$. That number of options, it should be noted, is one less than the maximal number of nonredundant options. For concreteness, we choose strike prices $a_k = \bar{w}_{1k}$ for $k = 1, \ldots, K$, and we denote by z_k the payoff of the call option with strike price a_k.

We have

$$z_{ks} = \max\{\bar{w}_{1s} - a_k, 0\}, \tag{20.45}$$

so that z_{ks} is nonzero for $s \in S_\ell$ and all $\ell > k$. Define factor f_k by

$$f_k = z_k - E(z_k). \tag{20.46}$$

The aggregate date-1 endowment lies in the span of factors (20.46) and the risk-free payoff (the factor span). To see this, note that $\bar{w}_1 = a_1 + E(z_1) + f_1$ and therefore $\bar{w}_1$ lies in the span of factor f_1 and the risk-free payoff. If the factors and the risk-free payoff lie in the asset span, then the aggregate date-1 endowment lies in the asset span and is the market payoff. Note further that the payoffs of all options on $\bar{w}_1$ lie in the factor span.

Proposition 20.7.1 *Contingent claims (20.46) form a mean-independent factor structure.*

Proof: Let δ_j denote the residual of projection (20.35) of the payoff x_j on the factor span of factors (20.46). We have to show that

$$E(\delta_j | f_1, \ldots, f_K) = 0 \tag{20.47}$$

for every j.

The random vector $(f_1, \ldots, f_K)$ takes the same value in all states within each set S_k and different values across sets S_k. The latter follows from the observation that f_k takes different values in S_k and S_{k+1}. Therefore, Eq. (20.47) is equivalent to

$$E(\delta_j | S_k) = 0 \tag{20.48}$$

for every k. Let e_k denote the contingent claim equal to one in each state of the set S_k and zero in all other states. Then Eq. (20.48) can be written as

$$E(\delta_j e_k) = 0. \tag{20.49}$$

It should be clear that contingent claim e_k lies in the factor span $\mathcal{F}$ (see Section 15.4). Therefore Eq. (20.49) follows from the fact that $\delta_j \in \mathcal{F}^\perp$. $\square$

If the factors and the risk-free claim lie in the asset span, and if all agents are strictly risk averse, then, as follows from Theorem 20.6.1, exact factor-pricing holds in equilibrium. Further, it follows from Section 15.4 that the equilibrium allocation is Pareto optimal.

20.8 Notes

Our analysis of Sections 20.2 and 20.5, based on general Hilbert space methods, can be extended to the case of infinitely many securities with only minor modification. It remains true that exact factor pricing holds iff the pricing kernel lies in the factor span. The approximate factor pricing result says that all but a finite number of securities have arbitrarily small pricing errors. For more discussion, see Chamberlain [2], Chamberlain and Rothschild [3], and Gilles and LeRoy [5].

The first systematic study of factor pricing can be found in Ross [9] and [10] (see also Huberman [6]). Ross developed what he referred to as the Arbitrage Pricing Theory (APT). The term *Arbitrage Pricing Theory* is, however, a misnomer. The absence of arbitrage, or equivalently the strict positivity of the payoff pricing functional, is nowhere needed in the proof of Theorem 20.5.1. Approximate factor pricing holds if security returns have factor structure independent of whether there exists an arbitrage opportunity.

A factor structure with the market return (normalized so as to have zero expectation) as the single factor was first analyzed by Sharpe [11], who referred to it as the *market model*. Exact factor pricing in the market model is equivalent to the security market line of the CAPM.

The model of Section 20.6 originated with Connor [4], who referred to it as the Equilibrium APT (see also Milne [8] and Werner [12]). The model with options on the aggregate endowment derives from Breeden and Litzenberger [1]. The observation that this model is a special case of the Equilibrium APT with mean-independent factor structure was made by Kim [7]. Kim proved that the factor structure of options on the market payoff is in a precise sense minimal.

In Section 20.7 the term "options" was used to describe contingent claims that may or may not lie in the asset span, that is, may or may not be traded. Evidently the term is completely appropriate only in the former case.

The idea of *portfolio diversification* has often been brought up in connection with factor pricing (Ross [9], Chamberlain [2], Chamberlain and Rothschild [3]). One usually thinks of a diversified portfolio as a portfolio that contains small holdings of each of a large number of securities. When security returns have a factor structure (Section 20.5), diversification can be used to reduce idiosyncratic risk in portfolios (that is, the risk in portfolio payoffs that reflects idiosyncratic risk in securities' payoffs). Of course, with a finite number of securities, diversification cannot entirely eliminate idiosyncratic risk, but with an infinite number complete diversification is possible. Portfolios can be constructed that have only factor risk.

When there are infinitely many securities and the security returns have a factor structure, the possibility of constructing portfolios completely free of idiosyncratic risk provides a justification for the assumption that factors lie in the asset span (see Werner [12]).

Note that, as shown, portfolio diversification plays no role in the derivation of approximate factor pricing.

Bibliography

[1] Breeden, D. T. and Litzenberger, R. Prices of state-contingent claims implicit in option prices. *Journal of Business*, **51**:621–51, 1978.

[2] Chamberlain, G. Funds, factors and diversification in arbitrage pricing models. *Econometrica*, **51**:1305–23, 1983.

[3] Chamberlain, G. and Rothschild, M. Arbitrage, factor structure and mean variance analysis in large asset markets. *Econometrica*, **51**:1281–1304, 1983.

[4] Connor, G. A unified beta pricing theory. *Journal of Economic Theory*, **34**:13–31, 1984.

[5] Gilles, C. and LeRoy, S. F. On the arbitrage pricing theory. *Economic Theory*, **1**:213–29, 1991.

[6] Huberman, G. A simple approach to arbitrage pricing theory. *Journal of Economic Theory*, **28**:183–92, 1982.

[7] Kim, C. Stochastic dominance, Pareto optimality, and equilibrium asset pricing. *Review of Economic Studies*, **65**(2):341–56, 1998.

[8] Milne, F. Arbitrage and diversification in a general equilibrium asset economy. *Econometrica*, **56**:815–40, 1988.

[9] Ross, S. A. The arbitrage theory of capital asset pricing. *Journal of Economic Theory*, **13**:341–60, 1976.

[10] Ross, S. A. Risk, return and arbitrage. In Irwin Friend and James Bicksler, editors, *Risk and Return in Finance*. Ballinger, Cambridge, MA, 1976.

[11] Sharpe, W. F. A simplified model of portfolio analysis. *Management Science*, **9**:277–93, 1963.

[12] Werner, J. Diversification and equilibrium in securities markets. *Journal of Economic Theory*, **75**:89–103, 1997.

Part Seven

Multidate Security Markets

21

Equilibrium in Multidate Security Markets

21.1 Introduction

We have thus far limited ourselves to a model of two-date security markets in which securities are traded only once before their payoffs are realized. This model is most suitable for the study of the risk–return relation for securities and the role of securities in the equilibrium allocation of risk.

In the two-date model all uncertainty is resolved at once. It is more realistic to assume that uncertainty is resolved only gradually. As the uncertainty is resolved, agents trade securities again and again. The multidate model of this and the following chapters allows for the gradual resolution of uncertainty and the retrading of securities as new information about security prices and payoffs becomes available.

21.2 Uncertainty and Information

In the multidate model, just as in the two-date model, uncertainty is specified by a set of states S. Each of the states is a description of the economic environment for all dates $t = 0, 1, \ldots, T$. At date 0 agents do not know which state will be realized. But as time passes, they obtain more and more information about the state. Then, at date T, the actual state becomes known to them.

Formally, the information of agents at date t is described by a partition F_t of the set of states S (a *partition* F_t of S is a collection of subsets of S such that each state s belongs to exactly one element of F_t). The interpretation is that at date t agents know the element of the date-t partition to which the actual state belongs. They do not know which state of the known element of the date-t partition is the actual state, but they do know that states that do not belong to that element cannot be realized. The partitions are assumed to be common across agents; that is, all agents have the same information.

At date 0 agents have no information about the state, and thus the date-0 partition is the trivial partition $F_0 = \{S\}$. At date T, agents have full information, and therefore

219

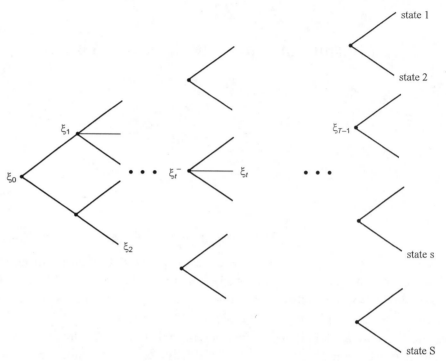

Figure 21.1 An event tree. The initial node is indicated by ξ_0. The nodes at the terminal date coincide with the states. Generic nodes at dates $1, t$ and $T - 1$ are indicated by ξ_1, ξ_t, and ξ_{T-1}, respectively. The precedecessor node to ξ_t is indicated by ξ_t^-.

the date-T partition is the total partition $F_T = \{\{s\} : s \in S\}$. At dates $1, \ldots, T - 1$, agents have intermediate amounts of information. The partition F_{t+1} is finer (but not necessarily strictly finer) than partition F_t; that is, the element of date-$(t + 1)$ partition to which a state belongs is a subset of the element of date-t partition to which it belongs. Equivalently, if two states belong to different elements of the date-t partition, they cannot belong to the same element of the partition at any date after t. Thus, agents never forget anything they once knew; their information about the state is nondecreasing. The $(T + 1)$-tuple of partitions $\{F_0, F_1, \ldots, F_T\}$ is the *information filtration* $\mathcal{F}$.

   Another term for an information filtration (in the finite case studied here) is *event tree* (Figure 21.1). Each element of partition F_t is called a date-t *event* and is a *node* of the event tree. The event $\xi_0 = F_0$ is the *root node*. The *successors* of the event ξ_t are the events $\xi_\tau \subset \xi_t$ for $\tau > t$. The *immediate successors* of ξ_t are the events $\xi_{t+1} \subset \xi_t$. The *predecessors* of ξ_t are the events $\xi_\tau \supset \xi_t$, for $\tau < t$. The unique *immediate predecessor* of ξ_t is the event ξ_{t-1} such that $\xi_{t-1} \supset \xi_t$. Sometimes the immediate predecessor of ξ_t will be denoted ξ_t^-.

The set of all events at all future dates $t = 1, \ldots, T$ is denoted Ξ, and $k = \#(\Xi)$ is the number of events in Ξ. The number of events including ξ_0 is thus $k + 1$.

Example 21.2.1 Suppose that the only relevant information is profit reports of two firms. Each of the reports is either good (G) or bad (B). One firm issues its report at date 1, the other at date 2. The set of states S consists of the four possible outcomes of the two reports: {GG, GB, BG, BB}. The information filtration is

$$F_0 = \{\{GG, GB, BG, BB\}\}, \tag{21.1}$$
$$F_1 = \{\{GG, GB\}, \{BG, BB\}\}, \tag{21.2}$$
$$F_2 = \{\{GG\}, \{GB\}, \{BG\}, \{BB\}\}, \tag{21.3}$$

and thus at date 0 agents know nothing, at date 1 they know the profit report of the first firm, and at date 2 they know the profit reports of both firms.

Because this example will come up again, it is convenient to introduce a compact notation for events. Thus, we let

$$\xi_g \equiv \{GG, GB\}, \qquad \xi_b \equiv \{BG, BB\} \tag{21.4}$$

be the two date-1 events and

$$\xi_{gg} \equiv \{GG\}, \qquad \xi_{gb} \equiv \{GB\}, \qquad \xi_{bg} \equiv \{BG\}, \qquad \xi_{bb} \equiv \{BB\}, \tag{21.5}$$

be the four date-2 events. The set of all future events is $\Xi = \{\xi_g, \xi_b, \xi_{gg}, \xi_{gb}, \xi_{bg}, \xi_{bb}\}$. $\quad\square$

Agents' information about the state has to be reflected properly in all economic variables such as endowments, security prices and dividends, portfolio holdings, consumption plans, and so forth. Specifically, it would not make sense to consider consumption plans or security prices at date t that differ in states that cannot be distinguished based on the information available to agents at date t. One way to specify these variables is to represent them as functions on the set of states S and require that they be *measurable* with respect to the partition F_t. If consumption at date t is represented by a function $c_t : S \to \mathcal{R}$ that takes value $c_t(s)$ in state s, then measurability of c_t with respect to partition F_t requires that $c_t(s) = c_t(s')$ for each s and s' that belong to a common element ξ_t of F_t.

The measurability requirement can be embedded in the notation by using events rather than states to distinguish different values of functions. If c_t is measurable with respect to F_t, then, by definition, $c_t(s) = c_t(s')$ for all s, s' in a given date-t event ξ_t, and we can denote this common value by $c(\xi_t)$.[1]

---

[1] Note that we write $c(\xi_t)$ instead of $c_t(\xi_t)$ to simplify notation.

At times we will use c_t to denote the vector (of dimension equal to the number of events at date t) of values $c(\xi_t)$ for all $\xi_t \in F_t$. Thus, we use the same notation c_t for the consumption plan as an F_t-measurable function and as a vector. The distinction often does not matter; when it does, the intended meaning will always be clear from the context. Similarly, we use c to denote either a $(T+1)$-tuple of F_t-measurable functions c_t or a $(k+1)$-dimensional vector of values $c(\xi)$ for all $\xi \in \Xi$.

The importance of the distinction between functions and vectors will become evident when probabilities are associated with the states (Chapter 25) . When that is done, measurable functions on S will be identified with random variables. To verify conformability for matrix operations, it is necessary to be clear when a scalar random variable (for example) is intended as opposed to the vector of values the random variable takes on.

If every function c_t in the $(T+1)$-tuple c is F_t-measurable, then c is *adapted* to the information filtration $\mathcal{F}$.

21.3 Multidate Security Markets

There exist J securities. Examples of securities include bonds, stocks, options, and futures contracts. Each security is characterized by the dividends it pays at each date. By the dividend we mean any payment to which a security holder is entitled. For stocks, dividends are firms' profit distributions to stockholders; for bonds, dividends are coupon payments and payments at maturity.

The dividend on security j in event ξ_t is denoted by $x_j(\xi_t)$. We use x_{jt} to denote the vector of dividends $x_j(\xi_t)$ in all date-t events ξ_t, and x_t to denote the vector of dividends on all J securities in all date-t events. There are no dividends at date 0. It is possible that a security has nonzero dividend only at a single date. For instance, a zero-coupon bond that matures at date t with face value 1 has dividends equal to 1 in each date-t event and zero dividends at all other dates.

Securities are traded at all dates except the terminal date T. The price of security j in event ξ_t is denoted by $p_j(\xi_t)$. For notational convenience we have date-T prices $p_j(\xi_T)$ even though trade does not take place at date T. These prices are all set equal to zero. We use p_{jt} to denote the vector of prices $p_j(\xi_t)$ in all date-t events ξ_t, and p_t to denote the vector of prices of all J securities in all date-t events.

The holding of security j in event ξ_t is denoted by $h_j(\xi_t)$, and the portfolio of J securities in event ξ_t is denoted by the vector $h(\xi_t)$. The holding of each security may be positive, zero, or (unless a short sales constraint has been imposed) negative. We have again, for notational convenience, a date-T portfolio $h(\xi_T)$, which, though, is set equal to zero. We use h_t to denote the vector of portfolios

$h(\xi_t)$ in all date-t events ξ_t. The $(T + 1)$-tuple $h = (h_0, \ldots, h_T)$ is a *portfolio strategy*.

The *payoff* of a portfolio strategy h in event ξ_t, denoted by $z(h, p)(\xi_t)$, is the cum-dividend payoff of the portfolio chosen at immediate predecessor event ξ_t^- minus the price of the portfolio chosen in ξ_t. Thus,

$$z(h, p)(\xi_t) \equiv [p(\xi_t) + x(\xi_t)]h(\xi_t^-) - p(\xi_t)h(\xi_t). \qquad (21.6)$$

We use $z_t(h, p)$ to denote the vector of payoffs $z(h, p)(\xi_t)$ in all date-t events ξ_t. The price at date 0 of a portfolio strategy h is $p(\xi_0)h(\xi_0)$.

We present two examples of portfolio strategies and their payoffs.

Example 21.3.1 Consider the portfolio strategy that involves buying one share of security j in event ξ_t at date $t \geq 1$ and selling it in every immediate successor event of ξ_t. This portfolio strategy is represented by the vector h, which has 1 in the position associated with the holding of security j in event ξ_t and zeros elsewhere. It has payoff $-p_j(\xi_t)$ in ξ_t, $p_j(\xi_{t+1}) + x_j(\xi_{t+1})$ in each immediate successor event $\xi_{t+1} \subset \xi_t$ and zero elsewhere. The date-0 price of this portfolio strategy is zero.

A *buy-and-hold strategy* involves holding one share of security j in every event of the event tree. It is represented by a vector with 1 in the position associated with the holding of security j in all events except those at the terminal date, and zeros elsewhere. Its payoff equals the dividend $x_j(\xi_t)$ in each event ξ_t for every $t \geq 1$. Its date-0 price equals the date-0 price of security j, $p_j(\xi_0)$. $\square$

As discussed in Section 21.2, date-t dividend x_{jt}, price p_{jt}, portfolio h_t, and payoff $z_t(h, p)$ can also be understood as F_t-measurable functions.

21.4 The Asset Span

The set of payoffs available via trades on security markets is the *asset span* and is defined by

$$\mathcal{M}(p) = \{(z_1, \ldots, z_T) \in \mathcal{R}^k : z_t = z_t(h, p) \text{ for some } h, \text{ and all } t \geq 1\}. \quad (21.7)$$

The payoffs of the portfolio strategies of Example 21.3.1 belong to the asset span. In particular, dividends $(x_{j1}, \ldots, x_{jT})$ of each security j belong to the asset span $\mathcal{M}(p)$ for arbitrary security prices p.

An important distinction between the two-date model and the multidate model is that in the former the asset span is exogenous, depending only on specified security payoffs. In the latter, on the other hand, the asset span depends on security prices, which are endogenous.

Security markets are *dynamically complete* (at prices p) if any consumption plan for future dates (dates 1 to T) can be obtained as the payoff of a portfolio strategy; that is, if $\mathcal{M}(p) = \mathcal{R}^k$. Markets are *incomplete* if $\mathcal{M}(p)$ is a proper subspace of $\mathcal{R}^k$.

21.5 Agents

Measures of consumption $c(\xi_t)$, c_t, and c were defined in Section 21.2.

Agents are assumed to have utility functions defined on the set of all consumption plans $c = (c_0, c_1, \ldots, c_T)$. As in Chapter 1, we assume most of the time that consumption is positive. In that case the utility function of agent i is $u^i : \mathcal{R}_+^{k+1} \to \mathcal{R}$. Utility functions are assumed to be continuous and increasing.[2]

The endowment of agent i is $w^i = (w_0^i, \ldots, w_T^i) \in \mathcal{R}_+^{k+1}$.

21.6 Portfolio Choice and the First-Order Conditions

The consumption-portfolio choice problem of an agent with the utility function u is

$$\max_{c,h} u(c) \tag{21.8}$$

subject to

$$c(\xi_0) = w(\xi_0) - p(\xi_0)h(\xi_0) \tag{21.9}$$

$$c(\xi_t) = w(\xi_t) + z(h, p)(\xi_t) \quad \forall \xi_t \ t = 1, \ldots, T \tag{21.10}$$

and the restriction that consumption be positive, $c \geq 0$, if this restriction is imposed. Budget constraints (21.9) and (21.10) are written as equalities because utility functions are assumed to be increasing.

Budget constraints (21.9) and (21.10) can be written as

$$c_0 = w_0 - p_0 h_0 \tag{21.11}$$

and

$$c_t = w_t + z_t(h, p), \quad t = 1, \ldots, T. \tag{21.12}$$

If the utility function u is differentiable, the necessary first-order conditions for an interior solution to the consumption-portfolio choice problem (21.8) are

$$\partial_{\xi_t} u - \lambda(\xi_t) = 0, \quad \forall \xi_t \ t = 0, \ldots, T, \tag{21.13}$$

$$\lambda(\xi_t)p(\xi_t) = \sum_{\xi_{t+1} \subset \xi_t} [p(\xi_{t+1}) + x(\xi_{t+1})]\lambda(\xi_{t+1}), \quad \forall \xi_t \ t = 0, \ldots, T-1,$$

$$\tag{21.14}$$

---

[2] Utility function u is *increasing at date* t if $u(c_0, \ldots, c_t', \ldots, c_T) \geq u(c_0, \ldots, c_t, \ldots, c_T)$ whenever $c_t' \geq c_t$ for every $(c_0, \ldots, c_T)$; u is *increasing* if it is increasing at every date. Further, u is *strictly increasing at date* t if $u(c_0, \ldots, c_t', \ldots, c_T) > u(c_0, \ldots, c_t, \ldots, c_T)$ whenever $c_t' > c_t$ for every $(c_0, \ldots, c_T)$; and u is *strictly increasing if* it is strictly increasing at every date.

where $\lambda(\xi_t)$ is the Lagrange multiplier associated with budget constraint (21.10). Here $\partial_{\xi_t} u$ denotes the partial derivative of u with respect to $c(\xi_t)$ evaluated at the optimal consumption. If u is quasi-concave, then these conditions together with budget constraints (21.9) and (21.10) are sufficient to determine an optimal consumption-portfolio choice.

If it is assumed that $\partial_{\xi_t} u > 0$, condition (21.14) becomes

$$p(\xi_t) = \sum_{\xi_{t+1} \subset \xi_t} [p(\xi_{t+1}) + x(\xi_{t+1})] \frac{\partial_{\xi_{t+1}} u}{\partial_{\xi_t} u} \qquad (21.15)$$

with typical element

$$p_j(\xi_t) = \sum_{\xi_{t+1} \subset \xi_t} [p_j(\xi_{t+1}) + x_j(\xi_{t+1})] \frac{\partial_{\xi_{t+1}} u}{\partial_{\xi_t} u}. \qquad (21.16)$$

Equation (21.16) says that the price of security j in event ξ_t equals the sum over immediate successor events ξ_{t+1} of cum-dividend payoffs of security j multiplied by the marginal rate of substitution between consumption in event ξ_{t+1} and consumption in event ξ_t. Thus, the relation between the price of a security at any date and its payoff at the next date is the same in the multidate model as in the two-date model.

21.7 General Equilibrium

An *equilibrium* in multidate security markets consists of a vector of security prices p, an allocation of portfolio strategies $\{h^i\}$ and a consumption allocation $\{c^i\}$ such that (1) portfolio strategy h^i and consumption plan c^i are a solution to agent i's choice problem (21.8) at prices p, and (2) markets clear; that is

$$\sum_i h^i = 0, \qquad (21.17)$$

and

$$\sum_i c^i = \sum_i w^i. \qquad (21.18)$$

The portfolio market-clearing condition (21.17) implies, by summing agents' budget constraints, the consumption market-clearing condition (21.18). If there are no redundant securities (that is, if $z(h, p) = 0$ implies $h = 0$), then the converse is also true. If there are redundant securities, then at least one of the multiple portfolio allocations associated with a market-clearing consumption allocation is market-clearing.

As in the two-date model, securities are in zero supply, as seen in the market-clearing condition (21.17). Agents' portfolio holdings are, however, to be viewed as net trades. Hence, securities can be in positive supply. To be more specific, suppose that each agent is endowed with an initial portfolio $\hat{h}_0^i$ but (for simplicity) with no consumption endowments at any future event. The market-clearing condition for optimal portfolio strategies $\bar{h}^i$ under that specification of endowments is

$$\sum_i \bar{h}^i(\xi_t) = \sum_i \hat{h}_0^i, \quad \forall \xi_t. \tag{21.19}$$

This agrees with (21.17) if h^i is interpreted as a net trade: $h^i \equiv \hat{h}_0^i - \bar{h}_0^i$.

21.8 Notes

The event-tree model of gradual resolution of uncertainty is inadequate when time is continuous and the set of states is infinite. In a continuous-time setting agents' information at date t is described by a sigma-algebra (sigma-field) of events instead of a partition.

The notion of general equilibrium in multidate security markets is taken from Radner [5]. Radner referred to the equilibrium of Section 21.7 as an *equilibrium of plans, prices, and price expectations.* This phrase emphasizes that future security prices are to be thought of as agents' price anticipations with rational expectations assumed. All agents have the same price anticipations; these anticipations are correct in the sense that the anticipated prices turn out to be equilibrium prices when an event is realized.

As in the two-date model, our specification is restricted to the case of a single good. The multiple-goods generalization of the model analyzed here is the general equilibrium model with incomplete markets (GEI); see Geanakoplos [3] and Magill and Quinzii [4]. In contradistinction to the two-date model, the existence of a general equilibrium in security markets is not guaranteed under the standard assumptions. The reason is the dependence of the asset span on security prices. As prices change, inducing the asset span may change in dimension, inducing discontinuity of agents' portfolio and consumption demands. For an example of nonexistence of an equilibrium in multidate security markets see Magill and Quinzii [4]. The nonexistence examples are in some sense rare. Results of Duffie and Shafer [2] (see also Duffie [1]) imply that an equilibrium exists for a generic set of agents' endowments and securities' dividends.

Bibliography

[1] Duffie, D. Stochastic equilibria with incomplete financial markets. *Journal of Economic Theory*, **41**:405–16, 1987.

[2] Duffie, D. and Shafer, W. Equilibrium in incomplete markets II: Generic existence in stochastic economies. *Journal of Mathematical Economics*, **15**:199–216, 1986.

[3] Geanakoplos, J. An introduction to general equilibrium with incomplete asset markets. *Journal of Mathematical Economics*, **19**:1–38, 1990.

[4] Magill, M. and Quinzii, M. *Theory of Incomplete Markets*. MIT Press, 1996.

[5] Radner, R. Existence of equilibrium of plans, prices and price expectations in a sequence economy. *Econometrica*, **40**:289–303, 1972.

22

Multidate Arbitrage and Positivity

22.1 Introduction

In multidate security markets, just as in two-date markets, there are two properties of the relation between future payoffs and their current prices that are of special importance: linearity and positivity. We can be brief here because the central concepts of that relation were presented in the two-date model in Chapters 2 and 3.

22.2 Law of One Price and Linearity

The law of one price holds in multidate markets if any two portfolio strategies that have the same payoff have the same date-0 price; that is,

$$\text{if } z(h, p) = z(h', p), \quad \text{then } p_0 h_0 = p_0 h'_0. \tag{22.1}$$

Condition (22.1) holds iff $p_0 h_0 = 0$ for every portfolio strategy h with payoff $z(h, p)$ equal to zero.

As in two-date security markets (recall Theorems 2.4.1 and 2.4.2), the law of one price holds in equilibrium in multidate security markets if agents' utility functions are strictly increasing at date 0.[1]

Henceforth, we assume that the law of one price holds.

The *payoff pricing functional* is a mapping

$$q : \mathcal{M}(p) \to \mathcal{R} \tag{22.2}$$

defined by

$$q(z) = p_0 h_0, \quad \text{where } h \text{ is such that } z = z(h, p), \tag{22.3}$$

for $z \in \mathcal{M}(p)$. The law of one price guarantees that the date-0 price $p_0 h_0$ is the same for every portfolio h that generates payoff z.

---

[1] An alternative sufficient condition is that (1) there exists a portfolio strategy with positive and nonzero payoff, and (2) utility functions are strictly increasing at any date at which that payoff is nonzero.

The payoff pricing functional q assigns to each payoff the date-0 price of a portfolio strategy that generates it. The law of one price implies that q is a linear functional on $\mathcal{M}(p)$.

Because the dividends of each security are generated by a buy-and-hold portfolio strategy (recall Example 21.3.1), we have $x_j \in \mathcal{M}(p)$ for any p. The date-0 price of the buy-and-hold strategy is p_{j0}, and thus

$$q(x_j) = p_{j0}. \tag{22.4}$$

22.3 Arbitrage and Positive Pricing

A *strong arbitrage* in multidate security markets is a portfolio strategy h that has positive payoff $z(h, p)$ and strictly negative date-0 price $p_0 h_0$. An *arbitrage* is a portfolio strategy that either is a strong arbitrage or has a positive and nonzero payoff and zero date-0 price.

As in two-date markets, there can exist a portfolio strategy that is an arbitrage but not a strong arbitrage:

Example 22.3.1 In the context of Example 21.2.1, suppose that there is a single security with dividend equal to 1 in events ξ_{gg} and ξ_{gb} at date 2 and zero otherwise. This security is risky as of date 0, but it becomes risk-free at date 1. If its prices are $p(\xi_0) = 0$, $p(\xi_g) = -1$ and $p(\xi_b) = 0$, then the portfolio strategy of buying the security in event ξ_g and selling it at both subsequent events, with zero holdings at all other events, is an arbitrage but not a strong arbitrage. □

We recall that payoff pricing functional q is positive if $q(z) \geq 0$ for every $z \geq 0$, $z \in \mathcal{M}(p)$. It is strictly positive if $q(z) > 0$ for every $z > 0$, $z \in \mathcal{M}(p)$. The equivalence between positivity (strict positivity) of the payoff pricing functional and the exclusion of strong arbitrage (arbitrage) also holds in multidate security markets (compare Theorems 3.4.2 and 3.4.1).

Theorem 22.3.2 *The payoff pricing functional is strictly positive iff there is no arbitrage.*

Proof: Exclusion of arbitrage means that $p_0 h_0 > 0$ whenever $z(h, p) > 0$. Because $q(z(h, p)) = p_0 h_0$, this is precisely the property of q's being strictly positive on $\mathcal{M}(p)$. □

Theorem 22.3.3 *The payoff pricing functional is positive iff there is no strong arbitrage.*

The following example illustrates the possibility of a payoff pricing functional that is positive but not strictly positive.

Example 22.3.4 The payoff pricing functional associated with the prices of the single security of Example 22.3.1 assigns zero to every payoff. This is a consequence of the security price at date 0 being equal to zero. The zero functional is positive but not strictly positive.   □

22.4 One-Period Arbitrage

The definitions of strong arbitrage and arbitrage of the two-date model can be applied to any nonterminal event of the multidate model. This leads us to the concepts of one-period strong arbitrage and one-period arbitrage, which are closely related to the concepts of Section 22.3.

A *one-period strong arbitrage* in event ξ_t at date $t < T$ is a portfolio $h(\xi_t)$ that has a positive one-period payoff

$$[p(\xi_{t+1}) + x(\xi_{t+1})]h(\xi_t) \geq 0 \quad \text{for every} \quad \xi_{t+1} \subset \xi_t, \tag{22.5}$$

and a strictly negative price

$$p(\xi_t)h(\xi_t) < 0. \tag{22.6}$$

A *one-period arbitrage* in event ξ_t is a portfolio $h(\xi_t)$ that either is a one-period strong arbitrage or has a positive and nonzero one-period payoff and a zero price.

The exclusion of one-period arbitrage at every nonterminal event is equivalent to the exclusion of multidate arbitrage in the sense of Section 22.3. However, only one direction of the corresponding equivalence holds for strong arbitrage. The exclusion of one-period strong arbitrage at every nonterminal event implies the exclusion of multidate strong arbitrage. However, the converse is not true. In Example 22.3.1 there is one-period strong arbitrage at ξ_g, but there is no multidate strong arbitrage.

22.5 Positive Equilibrium Pricing

The payoff pricing functional associated with equilibrium security prices is referred to as the *equilibrium payoff pricing functional*. Under appropriate monotonicity properties of agent's utility functions, there cannot be an arbitrage or a strong arbitrage at equilibrium prices. The equilibrium pricing functional is then strictly positive or positive.

Theorem 22.5.1 *If agents' utility functions are strictly increasing, then there is no arbitrage at equilibrium security prices. Further, the equilibrium payoff pricing functional is strictly positive.*

Proof: Suppose that there exists a portfolio strategy h that is an arbitrage. Thus, $z(h, p) \geq 0$ and $p_0 h_0 \leq 0$ with at least one strict inequality. Let h^i and c^i be agent i's equilibrium portfolio strategy and consumption plan. Then $h^i + h$ and $c^i + [-p_0 h_0, z(h, p)]$ satisfy the budget constraints and, because utility u^i is strictly increasing, the latter consumption plan is strictly preferred to c^i. We obtain a contradiction. Theorem 22.3.2 implies now that the equilibrium payoff pricing functional is strictly positive. □

Theorem 22.5.2 *If agents' utility functions are increasing, and are strictly increasing at date* 0, *then there is no strong arbitrage at equilibrium security prices. Further, the equilibrium payoff pricing functional is positive.*

The proof is similar to that for Theorem 22.5.1.

It is sometimes convenient to assume that consumption in a multidate model takes place only at the initial and terminal dates. Theorem 22.5.1 cannot be applied if that is the case because utility is not strictly increasing at intermediate dates. A variation that does apply is the following:

Theorem 22.5.3 *If agents' utility functions are increasing, and are strictly increasing at date* T, *and if there exists a security the dividends of which are positive at every date and strictly positive at date* T, *then there is no arbitrage at equilibrium security prices. Further, the equilibrium payoff pricing functional is strictly positive.*

Proof: Let security j be such that $x_{jt} \geq 0$ for every $t \geq 1$ and $x_{jT} > 0$. The equilibrium price p_{jt} must be strictly positive at every date $t < T$ in every event, for otherwise an agent could purchase security j in an event in which the price is negative, hold it through date T, and thereby strictly increase his or her consumption at date T.

Let h^i and c^i be agent i's equilibrium portfolio strategy and consumption plan. Suppose that there exists a portfolio strategy h that is an arbitrage. Thus, $z(h, p) \geq 0$ and $p_0 h_0 \leq 0$ with at least one strict inequality. If $z_T(h, p) > 0$, then we obtain a contradiction to the optimality of h^i and c^i in exactly the same way as in the proof of Theorem 22.5.1. If $z_T(h, p) = 0$ but $p_0 h_0 < 0$, then purchasing security j at the cost equal to $-p_0 h_0$ and holding it (and portfolio h) through date T strictly increase an agent's consumption at date T. Specifically, for portfolio $\hat{h} = h + (0, \ldots, \alpha, \ldots, 0)$, where α is the jth coordinate and is defined by $\alpha p_{j0} = -p_0 h_0$, we have that $h^i + \hat{h}$ and $c^i + [-p_0 \hat{h}_0, z(\hat{h}, p)]$ satisfy the budget constraints, and the latter consumption plan is strictly preferred to c^i. If $z_T(h, p) = 0$ and $p_0 h_0 = 0$ but $z(h, p)(\xi_t) > 0$ for some ξ_t, then a similar argument, as in the case of $p_0 h_0 < 0$ applies. Purchasing security j in event ξ_t and holding it (and portfolio h) through date T increases the agent's utility. We have a contradiction. □

Thus, Theorems 3.6.3 and 3.6.1 extend from the two-date to the multidate model. Note that the security prices of Example 22.3.1 could not be equilibrium prices under strictly increasing utility functions.

22.6 Notes

As in two-date security markets, the assumption of no arbitrage plays a central role in multidate markets. Influential articles in which the importance of arbitrage is recognized are Ross [3], Black and Scholes [1], and Harrison and Kreps [2].

Bibliography

[1] Black, F. and Scholes, M. The pricing of options and corporate liabilities. *Journal of Political Economy*, **81**:637–54, 1973.
[2] Harrison, J. M. and Kreps, D. M. Martingales and arbitrage in multiperiod securities markets. *Journal of Economic Theory*, **20**:381–408, 1979.
[3] Ross, S. A. A simple approach to the valuation of risky streams. *Journal of Business*, **51**:453–75, 1978.

23

Dynamically Complete Markets

23.1 Introduction

As defined in Chapter 21, security markets are dynamically complete (at prices p) if any consumption plan for future dates can be obtained as a payoff of a portfolio strategy; that is, if $\mathcal{M}(p) = \mathcal{R}^k$. Security markets are incomplete if $\mathcal{M}(p)$ is a proper subspace of $\mathcal{R}^k$.

In the two-date model of Chapter 1, completeness of security markets requires the existence of at least as many securities as states. In the multidate model the opportunity to trade securities at future dates implies that many fewer securities than events are necessary for markets to be dynamically complete.

In this chapter we provide a characterization of dynamically complete security markets and show that, for such markets, equilibrium consumption allocations are Pareto optimal.

23.2 Dynamically Complete Markets

An example of securities that result in markets that are dynamically complete at arbitrary prices are the *Arrow securities*. The Arrow security for event ξ_t has a dividend of one in event ξ_t at date t and zero in all other events and at all other dates. If all k Arrow securities are traded, then any consumption plan in $\mathcal{R}^k$ can be generated using a buy-and-hold portfolio strategy.

With Arrow securities, markets are dynamically complete even if trading is limited to date 0. As noted in Section 23.1, the opportunity to trade at future dates significantly reduces the number of securities needed for dynamically complete markets. A simple characterization of dynamically complete markets obtains as an extension of the characterization of complete markets in the two-date model (see Chapter 1).

The *one-period payoff matrix* in event ξ_t at date t, $t < T$, is a $J \times k(\xi_t)$ matrix with entries $p_j(\xi_{t+1}) + x_j(\xi_{t+1})$ for all j and all immediate successors ξ_{t+1} of ξ_t. Here, $k(\xi_t)$ is the number of immediate successors of event ξ_t.

Theorem 23.2.1 *Markets are dynamically complete iff the one-period payoff matrix in each nonterminal event ξ_t is of rank $k(\xi_t)$.*

Proof: Markets are dynamically complete iff, for each nonterminal event ξ_t and arbitrary payoffs in immediate successors of ξ_t, there exists a portfolio that generates those payoffs. Such a portfolio exists iff the one-period payoff matrix in ξ_t has rank $k(\xi_t)$. That follows from the characterization of complete security markets for the two-date model, as given in Theorem 1.2.1. $\qquad\square$

It follows that the minimum number of securities required for markets to be dynamically complete equals the maximum number of branches emerging from any node of the event tree. Having that number of securities is not, however, always sufficient; security prices may be such that one-period payoffs of securities are redundant in some events, and thus markets may be incomplete even if there exist the necessary number of securities.

Example 23.2.2 In Example 21.2.1, two branches emerge from each nonterminal node, and thus the necessary condition for market completeness is that there exist at least two securities.

To see that this condition is not sufficient, suppose that there exist two securities with dividends

$$x_1(\xi_g) = x_1(\xi_b) = 0, \quad x_1(\xi_{gg}) = x_1(\xi_{bb}) = 1, \quad x_1(\xi_{gb}) = x_1(\xi_{bg}) = 0, \quad (23.1)$$

and

$$x_2(\xi_g) = x_2(\xi_b) = 0, \quad x_2(\xi_{gg}) = x_2(\xi_{bb}) = 0, \quad x_2(\xi_{gb}) = x_2(\xi_{bg}) = 1. \quad (23.2)$$

The one-period payoff matrix in each date-1 event is of rank 2. However, if the price of each security in the two date-1 events equals $1/2$, then the one-period payoff matrix at date 0 is of rank one. Thus, markets are incomplete. There is no way for agents to trade securities at date 0 so as to obtain different one-period payoffs in the two date-1 events. $\qquad\square$

23.3 Binomial Security Markets

A *binomial event tree* is an event tree with an arbitrary number of dates T such that at every nonterminal date each event has exactly two immediate successors: "up" and "down." The simplest example of a binomial event tree was given in Section 21.2.1. Another example follows.

Example 23.3.1 Suppose that there are two securities traded at every date: a discount bond b maturing at date T and a risky stock a. The dividend of the bond at date T is 1, and its price at date t is $p_b(\xi_t) = (\bar{r})^{-(T-t)}$ for every event ξ_t. The price of the stock at date 0 is $p_{a0} = 1$. In the two possible events at date 1, the price of the stock is u or d $(u > d)$, depending on whether the "up" or "down" event occurs. Stock prices at subsequent dates are defined similarly; the one-period return on the stock is always u or d. The stock price at date t is therefore $p_a(\xi_t) = u^{t-l}d^l$ in an event ξ_t such that the number of "downs" preceding it from date 0 to date t is l where $1 \le l \le t$. The dividend on the stock is nonzero only at the terminal date T and is $x_a(\xi_T) = u^{T-l}d^l$ in an event ξ_T such that the number of "downs" preceding it is l.

Such binomial security markets are dynamically complete. At every date and in every nonterminal event, the one-period return matrix is

$$\begin{bmatrix} \bar{r} & \bar{r} \\ u & d \end{bmatrix},$$

which has full rank 2 because $u > d$ by assumption. Thus, we have dynamically complete markets with two securities and 2^T events at terminal date T.

The particular specifications of stock and bond prices in this example are very restrictive. For instance, there is no reason in general to expect the one-period return on the bond to be the same in every nonterminal event. The property of dynamic completeness does not require this simplification; all that is needed is that the one-period payoff matrix be of full rank at each nonterminal event. □

23.4 Event Prices in Dynamically Complete Markets

If security markets are dynamically complete, then the payoff pricing functional q is a linear functional on the space $\mathcal{R}^k$. It can be identified by its values on the unit vectors in $\mathcal{R}^k$. The event-ξ unit vector, denoted by $e(\xi)$, is the dividend of the Arrow security associated with ξ. We define $q(\xi) \equiv q(e(\xi))$ and refer to $q(\xi)$ as the *event price* of ξ.

Because every $z \in \mathcal{R}^k$ can be written as $z = \sum_{\xi \in \Xi} z(\xi)e(\xi)$, we have

$$q(z) = q\left(\sum_{\xi \in \Xi} z(\xi)e(\xi) \right) = \sum_{\xi \in \Xi} q(e(\xi))z(\xi) = \sum_{\xi \in \Xi} q(\xi)z(\xi). \quad (23.3)$$

Equation (23.3) is the representation of the payoff pricing functional by event prices. If one uses the same notation to denote the functional q and the the k-dimensional vector of event prices $q(\xi)$ for all $\xi \in \Xi$, Eq. (23.3) can be written

$$q(z) = qz. \quad (23.4)$$

Event prices are (strictly) positive iff the payoff pricing functional is (strictly) positive. Theorems 3.4.1 and 3.4.2 allow us to conclude that event prices are strictly positive iff there is no arbitrage and that they are positive iff there is no strong arbitrage. Thus, calculating event prices and determining whether they are strictly positive (positive) is a way of verifying whether security prices exclude arbitrage (strong arbitrage).

The event prices associated with security prices p can be calculated by finding portfolio strategies with payoffs $e(\xi)$ for all ξ. The event price $q(\xi)$ is then the date-0 price of the portfolio strategy with payoff $e(\xi)$. It is more convenient to describe event prices as a solution to a system of linear equations as in two-date security markets (see Chapter 2). The event prices satisfy

$$q(\xi_t)\, p_j(\xi_t) = \sum_{\xi_{t+1} \subset \xi_t} q(\xi_{t+1})[p_j(\xi_{t+1}) + x_j(\xi_{t+1})], \qquad (23.5)$$

for every event ξ_t, $t \geq 0$, and every security j with $q(\xi_0)$ set equal to 1.

To prove this consider the portfolio strategy of buying one share of security j at date $t \geq 1$ in event ξ_t and selling it at the subsequent date $t+1$ in every possible successor event $\xi_{t+1} \subset \xi_t$ (see Example 21.3.1). Denoting this portfolio strategy by $\hat{h}$, we have $z(\hat{h}, p)(\xi_t) = -p_j(\xi_t)$; $z(\hat{h}, p)(\xi_{t+1}) = p_j(\xi_{t+1}) + x_j(\xi_{t+1})$ for $\xi_{t+1} \subset \xi_t$, and $z(\hat{h}, p)(\varsigma) = 0$ in all other events ς. Because $\hat{h}_0 = 0$, we have that $q(z(\hat{h}, p)) = p_0 \hat{h}_0 = 0$. Using the representation (23.4) of the payoff pricing functional by event prices, we obtain Eq. (23.5).

Equation (23.5) for $t = 0$ is derived from the portfolio strategy consisting of buying one share of security j at date 0 and selling it in all date-1 events. This portfolio strategy has the payoff $p_j(\xi_1) + x_j(\xi_1)$ in each date-1 event ξ_1 and zero elsewhere. Its date-0 price is $p_j(\xi_0)$, and thus Eq. (23.5) results.

The system of equations (23.5) can be solved for event prices q under given security prices p. One starts by solving for date-1 event prices. Knowing these, one can solve for date-2 event prices from appropriate versions of Eq. (23.5), and so on. In the case of nonzero event prices, one can alternatively rewrite Eq. (23.5) in terms of relative event prices $q(\xi_{t+1})/q(\xi_t)$, solve for the relative prices, and then calculate event prices from the relative prices. Note that the satisfaction of the rank condition of Theorem 23.2.1 ensures a unique solution for Eq. (23.5).

Results of this section will be extended to incomplete markets in Chapter 24.

23.5 Event Prices in Binomial Security Markets

Event prices in the binomial security markets of Example 23.3.1 can easily be found using Eq. (23.5). We have two equations for the two securities in each event ξ_t:

$$q(\xi_t) = uq(\xi_{t+1}^u) + dq(\xi_{t+1}^d) \qquad (23.6)$$

and

$$q(\xi_t) = \bar{r}q(\xi_{t+1}^u) + \bar{r}q(\xi_{t+1}^d), \qquad (23.7)$$

where ξ_{t+1}^u and ξ_{t+1}^d denote the immediate successor events of event ξ_t.
The solution for relative event prices is

$$\frac{q(\xi_{t+1}^u)}{q(\xi_t)} = \frac{\bar{r} - d}{\bar{r}(u - d)} \qquad (23.8)$$

$$\frac{q(\xi_{t+1}^d)}{q(\xi_t)} = \frac{u - \bar{r}}{\bar{r}(u - d)} \qquad (23.9)$$

for every ξ_t. The event price of event ξ_t at date t such that the number of "downs" preceding it is l is

$$q(\xi_t) = \left(\frac{u - \bar{r}}{\bar{r}(u - d)}\right)^l \left(\frac{\bar{r} - d}{\bar{r}(u - d)}\right)^{t-l}. \qquad (23.10)$$

Event prices $q(\xi_t)$ are strictly positive iff $u > \bar{r} > d$ (i.e., if the one-period risk-free return is between the high and the low one-period returns on the risky security). In that case there is no arbitrage in the binomial security markets. Event prices are positive, and there is no strong arbitrage if $u \geq \bar{r} \geq d$.

23.6 Equilibrium in Dynamically Complete Markets

An agent's consumption-portfolio choice problem in multidate security markets is

$$\max_{c,h} u(c) \qquad (23.11)$$

subject to

$$c_0 = w_0 - p_0 h_0 \qquad (23.12)$$
$$c_t = w_t + z_t(h, p), \quad t \geq 1. \qquad (23.13)$$

Because the price $p_0 h_0$ of portfolio strategy h at date 0 equals the value of its payoff under the payoff pricing functional q, the budget constraint (23.12) can be written as

$$c_0 = w_0 - q(c_{1+} - w_{1+}), \qquad (23.14)$$

where c_{1+} denotes the consumption plan c from date 1 on; that is, $c_{1+} = (c_1, \ldots, c_T)$, and thus $c = (c_0, c_{1+})$. The budget constraint (23.13) can be rewritten as

$$c_{1+} - w_{1+} \in \mathcal{M}(p). \qquad (23.15)$$

Consequently, we can rewrite the optimization problem (23.11) as

$$\max_c u(c) \tag{23.16}$$

subject to Eqs. (23.14) and (23.15). If markets are dynamically complete, then $\mathcal{M}(p) = \mathcal{R}^k$ and restriction (23.15) is vacuous. Moreover, the budget constraint (23.14) can be written as

$$c_0 + q c_{1+} = w_0 + q w_{1+}, \tag{23.17}$$

where q is the vector of event prices associated with security prices p.

The optimization problem (23.16) becomes utility maximization under the single budget constraint (23.17). This latter maximization problem is the consumption choice problem of agent i facing complete contingent commodity markets. At price $q(\xi)$ the agent can purchase one unit of consumption in event ξ. One unit of date-0 consumption has price 1. The first-order condition for an interior solution to the utility maximization under the budget constraint (23.17) is

$$q(\xi) = \frac{\partial_\xi u}{\partial_{\xi_0} u} \tag{23.18}$$

for every event ξ.

The equivalence of the optimization problem (23.11) and utility maximization under the single budget constraint (23.17) tells us that consumption allocation $\{c^i\}$ and security prices p are an equilibrium in security markets that are dynamically complete (under p) if the same allocation $\{c^i\}$ and prices q are an equilibrium in contingent commodity markets. The equilibrium security prices p and the contingent commodity prices q are related via (23.5); that is, q are the event prices associated with p.

23.7 Pareto-Optimal Equilibria

As in the two-date model, a consumption allocation is *Pareto optimal* if it is impossible to reallocate the total endowment so as to make some agent strictly better off without making any other agent strictly worse off. That is, allocation $\{c^i\}$ is Pareto optimal if there does not exist an alternative allocation $\{c'^i\}$ which is feasible

$$\sum_{i=1}^{I} c'^i = \sum_{i=1}^{I} w^i, \tag{23.19}$$

weakly preferred by every agent,

$$u^i(c'^i) \geq u^i(c^i), \tag{23.20}$$

and strictly preferred by at least one agent (so that (23.20) holds with strict inequality for at least one i).

The first welfare theorem states that an equilibrium allocation in commodity markets is Pareto optimal under the same assumptions as those of the two-date model.

Theorem 23.7.1 *If security markets are dynamically complete under equilibrium security prices and agents' utility functions are strictly increasing, then every equilibrium consumption allocation is Pareto optimal.*

Proof: The proof is the same as that for Theorem 15.3.1. If markets are dynamically complete, then each equilibrium consumption allocation is also an equilibrium allocation of complete contingent commodity markets (see Section 23.6). By the first welfare theorem, the latter allocation is Pareto optimal. □

The first-order conditions for an interior Pareto-optimal allocation are that marginal rates of substitution $\partial_\xi u / \partial_{\xi_0} u$ are the same for all agents. In an interior equilibrium under dynamically complete markets, marginal rates of substitution are equal to event prices (see Eq. (23.18)).

23.8 Notes

The concept of dynamically complete markets has its origins in the literature on option pricing; see Black and Scholes [2], Cox and Ross [3], Rubinstein [9], and Harrison and Kreps [6]. The Pareto optimality of equilibrium allocations in complete security markets was first pointed out by Arrow [1] in the two-date model. The analysis was extended by Guesnerie and Jaffray [5] and Kreps [7], [8] to dynamically complete markets in the multidate model. Binomial security markets were first studied by Cox, Ross, and Rubinstein [4].

Bibliography

[1] Arrow, K. J. The role of securities in the optimal allocation of risk bearing. *Review of Economic Studies*, **31**:91–6, 1964.
[2] Black, F. and Scholes, M. The pricing of options and corporate liabilities. *Journal of Political Economy*, **81**:637–54, 1973.
[3] Cox, J. C. and Ross, S. A. The valuation of options for alternative stochastic processes. *Journal of Financial Economics*, **3**:145–66, 1976.
[4] Cox, J. C., Ross, S. A., and Rubinstein, M. Option pricing: A simplified approach. *Journal of Financial Economics*, **7**:229–63, 1979.
[5] Guesnerie, R. and Jaffray, J.-Y. Optimality of equilibrium of plans, prices, and price expectations. In J. Drèze, editor, *Allocation Under Uncertainty*. MacMillan, London, 1974.
[6] Harrison, J. M. and Kreps, D. M. Martingales and arbitrage in multiperiod securities markets. *Journal of Economic Theory*, **20**:381–408, 1979.

[7] Kreps, D. M. Multiperiod securities and the efficient allocation of risk: A comment on the Black–Scholes option pricing model. In John McCall, editor, *The Economics of Uncertainty and Information*. University of Chicago Press, Chicago, 1982.

[8] Kreps, D. M. Three essays on capital markets. *Revista Espanola de Economia*, **4**:111–146, 1987.

[9] Rubinstein, M. The valuation of uncertain income streams and the pricing of options. *Bell Journal of Economics*, **7**:407–25, 1976.

24

Valuation

24.1 Introduction

Whether for two-date security markets (see Chapter 5) or for multidate security markets, it is useful to have valuation defined on the entire contingent claim space $\mathcal{R}^k$, not just on the asset span $\mathcal{M}(p)$.

The *valuation functional* is a linear functional

$$Q : \mathcal{R}^k \to \mathcal{R} \qquad (24.1)$$

that extends the payoff pricing functional from the asset span $\mathcal{M}(p)$ to the contingent claim space $\mathcal{R}^k$; that is,

$$Q(z) = q(z) \quad \text{for every } z \in \mathcal{M}(p). \qquad (24.2)$$

The valuation functional assigns a value to every multidate contingent claim. We are interested in valuation functionals that are strictly positive (positive) because this property reflects the absence of arbitrage (strong arbitrage). A strictly positive (positive) valuation functional will be used in Chapter 25 to derive event prices and risk-neutral probabilities in the multidate model.

24.2 The Fundamental Theorem of Finance

The fundamental theorem of finance asserts the existence of a strictly positive (positive) valuation functional. Because the asset span and the payoff pricing functional of the multidate model have exactly the same properties as the asset span and the payoff pricing functional of the two-date model, the existence and properties of the valuation functional are the same as well.

Theorem 24.2.1 (Fundamental Theorem of Finance) *Security prices exclude arbitrage iff there exists a strictly positive valuation functional.*

241

Theorem 24.2.2 (Fundamental Theorem of Finance, Weak Form) *Security prices exclude strong arbitrage iff there exists a positive valuation functional.*

As already noted, the proofs of these theorems given in Chapter 5 for the two-date model carry over to the multidate model. In the proofs of the necessity parts, the payoff pricing functional is extended one dimension at a time. We choose a contingent claim z^* that is not in the asset span and extend the payoff pricing functional to the subspace spanned by $\mathcal{M}(p)$ and z^*. The value of z^* is selected from an interval defined by the bounds

$$q_u(z^*) \equiv \min_h \{p_0 h_0 : z(h, p) \geq z^*\} \tag{24.3}$$

and

$$q_\ell(z^*) \equiv \max_h \{p_0 h_0 : z(h, p) \leq z^*\}. \tag{24.4}$$

If security prices exclude strong arbitrage, then the bounds define an interval $[q_\ell(z^*), \ q_u(z^*)]$ such that assigning to z^* a value drawn from this interval leads to a positive linear extension of the payoff pricing functional. If security prices exclude arbitrage, the interval has nonempty interior, and each value in the interior leads to a strictly positive extension.

The following example illustrates the bounds:

Example 24.2.3 In Example 21.2.1, suppose that there are two securities, a discount bond maturing at date 1 (security 1) and a discount bond maturing at date 2 (security 2). Thus, the dividends of the one-period bond are $x_1(\xi_g) = x_1(\xi_b) = 1$ at date 1 and $x_1(\xi) = 0$ for all events $\xi \in F_2$ at date 2. For the two-period bond the dividends are $x_2(\xi_g) = x_2(\xi_b) = 0$ at date 1 and $x_2(\xi) = 1$ for all events $\xi \in F_2$ at date 2. Let the price at date 0 for the one-period bond be $p_1(\xi_0) = 0.9$ and the prices for the two-period bond be $p_2(\xi_0) = 0.75$, $p_2(\xi_g) = 0.9$, and $p_2(\xi_b) = 0.8$.

Markets are incomplete, for the rank condition of Theorem 23.2.1 fails in both events at date 1. The asset span $\mathcal{M}(p)$ is four-dimensional, whereas the contingent claim space is six-dimensional. In fact, the contingent claim

$$z = [z(\xi_g), z(\xi_b), z(\xi_{gg}), z(\xi_{gb}), z(\xi_{bg}), z(\xi_{bb})] \tag{24.5}$$

can be generated by a portfolio strategy iff $z(\xi_{gg}) = z(\xi_{gb})$, and $z(\xi_{bg}) = z(\xi_{bb})$.

Consider the contingent claim z^* given by $z_1^* = (0, 0)$ and $z_2^* = (2, 1, 1, 0)$. Clearly, $z^* \notin \mathcal{M}(p)$. The upper bound on the value of z^* is determined by solving the minimization problem (24.3). We have

$$\min_h p_1(\xi_0) h_1(\xi_0) + p_2(\xi_0) h_2(\xi_0) \tag{24.6}$$

subject to

$$z(h, p) \geq z^*. \tag{24.7}$$

Constraint (24.7) implies that

$$h_2(\xi_g) \geq 2, \qquad h_2(\xi_g) \geq 1, \qquad h_2(\xi_b) \geq 1, \qquad h_2(\xi_b) \geq 0, \tag{24.8}$$

$$h_1(\xi_0) + 0.9[h_2(\xi_0) - h_2(\xi_g)] \geq 0, \quad \text{and} \quad h_1(\xi_0) + 0.8[h_2(\xi_0) - h_2(\xi_b)] \geq 0. \tag{24.9}$$

The solution to the linear programming problem (24.6) calls for a date-1 holding of two 2-period bonds if the first corporate report is good $[h_2(\xi_g) = 2]$ and one 2-period bond if the first report is bad $[h_2(\xi_b) = 1]$. These holdings have to be financed by a date-0 portfolio. Purchasing ten 2-period bonds $[h_2(\xi_0) = 10]$ and selling 7.2 one-period bonds $[h_1(\xi_0) = -7.2]$ at date 0 generates a date-1 payoff of 1.8 if the first report is good and 0.8 if the first report is bad, as needed to finance the date-1 holdings. The date-0 price of this portfolio strategy is 1.02.

The payoff of this portfolio strategy is $(0, 0)$ at date 1, and $(2, 2, 1, 1)$ at date 2. It is the smallest contingent claim in the asset span that exceeds z^*. Because security prices exclude arbitrage, the date-0 price of 1.02 of this portfolio strategy must be minimal.

In this example the optimal portfolio strategy could have been determined by simply finding the smallest contingent claim that lies in the asset span and satisfies inequality (24.7) and then identifying the portfolio strategy that generates that contingent claim. This solution method does not work in general, for usually the smallest element of the asset span does not exist. In general, it is necessary to solve the linear programming problem explicitly, either as one large linear program, or, using backward induction, as several smaller programs.

The lower bound on the value of z^* is determined by solving the maximization problem (24.4). We have

$$\max_h \ p_1(\xi_0)h_1(\xi_0) + p_2(\xi_0)h_2(\xi_0) \tag{24.10}$$

subject to

$$z(h, p) \leq z^*. \tag{24.11}$$

The solution to this problem is identical to the minimization problem (24.6) except that nine, not ten, units of the two-period bond are purchased at date 0. The date-0 price of this portfolio strategy is 0.27. It generates a payoff of $(0, 0, 1, 1, 0, 0)$, which is the greatest payoff that is less than or equal to z^*. $\square$

As in two-date security markets, a strictly positive (positive) valuation functional associated with an equilibrium payoff pricing functional is given by an agent's marginal rates of substitution between consumption at date 0 and at future dates. If the agent's equilibrium consumption is interior and his or her utility function is strictly increasing (increasing), then the vector of marginal rates of substitution $\{\partial_\xi u/\partial_{\xi_0} u\}$ defines a strictly positive (positive) valuation functional that assigns the value $\sum_{\xi \in \Xi} z(\xi)\,(\partial_\xi u/\partial_{\xi_0} u)$ to a contingent claim $z \in \mathcal{R}^k$.

24.3 Uniqueness of the Valuation Functional

Extension of the payoff pricing functional to a valuation functional is in general not unique. When markets are incomplete, there exists a continuum of values for any contingent claim not in the asset span, and each value defines a strictly positive extension of the payoff pricing functional. When markets are dynamically complete, the asset span $\mathcal{M}(p)$ equals the contingent claim space $\mathcal{R}^k$, and the payoff pricing functional and the valuation functional are one and the same. Thus, we have

Theorem 24.3.1 *Suppose that security prices exclude arbitrage. Then security markets are dynamically complete iff there exists a unique strictly positive valuation functional.*

We pointed out in Section 24.2 that if security prices are equilibrium prices, then the marginal rates of substitution of an agent define a valuation functional. If markets are incomplete, those marginal rates may differ among agents, and multiple valuation functionals result. If markets are dynamically complete, then there is a unique valuation functional given by marginal rates of substitution, which are the same for all agents.

24.4 Notes

The valuation functional was introduced in the setting of multidate security markets (including continuous-time markets) by Harrison and Kreps [2]. The derivation of the valuation functional in this chapter follows the method of Chapter 5 and originated with Clark [1].

Bibliography

[1] Clark, S. A. The valuation problem in arbitrage price theory. *Journal of Mathematical Economics*, **22**:463–78, 1993.
[2] Harrison, J. M. and Kreps, D. M. Martingales and arbitrage in multiperiod securities markets. *Journal of Economic Theory*, **20**:381–408, 1979.

Part Eight

Martingale Property of Security Prices

25

Event Prices, Risk-Neutral Probabilities, and the Pricing Kernel

25.1 Introduction

In this chapter we present two closely related representations of the valuation functional – one by event prices and the other by risk-neutral probabilities – and a representation of the payoff pricing functional by the pricing kernel. These representations are the analogues of those of the valuation functional and the payoff pricing functional of the two-date model of Chapters 6 and 17.

Event prices are the multidate counterpart of state prices in the two-date model. The existence of strictly positive (positive) event prices indicates the absence of arbitrage (strong arbitrage). The uniqueness of event prices indicates that markets are dynamically complete. Event prices can be calculated as a solution to linear equations. Once event prices are known, the price of any payoff can be found without identifying a portfolio strategy that generates that payoff.

Risk-neutral probabilities are event prices rescaled by discount factors. The existence of a pricing kernel is a consequence of the Riesz Representation Theorem.

25.2 Event Prices

If security markets are dynamically complete, then the payoff pricing functional q is defined on the entire contingent claim space $\mathcal{R}^k$, and the event price $q(\xi)$ is defined as the price $q(e(\xi))$ of the Arrow security $e(\xi)$ (see Chapter 23). If security markets are incomplete, then the asset span is a proper subspace of the contingent claim space, and some Arrow securities cannot be priced using the payoff pricing functional. The fundamental theorem of finance 24.2.1 (24.2.2) implies that if security prices exclude arbitrage (strong arbitrage), then the payoff pricing functional can be extended to a strictly positive (positive) valuation functional defined on the entire contingent claim space. Event prices can then be defined using a valuation functional.

Let Q be a valuation functional and let

$$q(\xi) \equiv Q(e(\xi)), \tag{25.1}$$

for every $\xi \in \Xi$, where $e(\xi)$ is the event-ξ unit vector in $\mathcal{R}^k$, that is, the dividend of the Arrow security associated with ξ. The value $q(\xi)$ is the *event price* of event ξ under the valuation functional Q. If Q is a strictly positive (positive) functional, then each event price is strictly positive (positive).

Because every contingent claim $z \in \mathcal{R}^k$ can be written as $z = \sum_{\xi \in \Xi} z(\xi) e(\xi)$, we have

$$Q(z) = \sum_{\xi \in \Xi} Q(e(\xi)) z(\xi) = qz, \tag{25.2}$$

where q is now a vector of event prices. The equation

$$Q(z) = qz \tag{25.3}$$

is the representation of the valuation functional by event prices. For a payoff $z \in \mathcal{M}(p)$, we have

$$q(z) = qz. \tag{25.4}$$

Thus, the price of a payoff can be obtained using event prices without determining a portfolio strategy that generates that payoff.

As when markets are dynamically complete (Section 23.4), event prices in incomplete markets can be identified as a positive solution to the linear equations (23.5). To see this, consider a portfolio strategy of buying one share of security j at date $t \geq 1$ in event ξ_t and selling it in every successor event $\xi_{t+1} \subset \xi_t$ at date $t + 1$. Denoting that portfolio strategy by $\hat{h}$, we have $z(\hat{h}, p)(\xi_t) = -p_j(\xi_t)$, $z(\hat{h}, p)(\xi_{t+1}) = p_j(\xi_{t+1}) + x_j(\xi_{t+1})$ for $\xi_{t+1} \subset \xi_t$, and $z(\hat{h}, p)(\varsigma) = 0$ for all other events ς. Because $\hat{h}(\xi_0) = 0$, we have that $q(z(\hat{h}, p)) = p(\xi_0)\hat{h}(\xi_0) = 0$. Applying Eq. (25.4) to the payoff $z(\hat{h}, p)$, we obtain

$$q(\xi_t) p_j(\xi_t) = \sum_{\xi_{t+1} \subset \xi_t} q(\xi_{t+1})[p_j(\xi_{t+1}) + x_j(\xi_{t+1})]. \tag{25.5}$$

Equation (25.5) holds for every $t \geq 1$, every $\xi_t \in F_t$, and every security j. A similar argument shows that Eq. (25.5) holds also at date 0 with $q(\xi_0)$ set equal to one.

Equations (25.5) are the same as Eqs. (23.5) for dynamically complete markets. There are now J equations with $k(\xi_t)$ unknowns $q(\xi_{t+1})/q(\xi_t)$. We just argued that event prices associated with a valuation functional are a solution to Eq. (25.5). A positive valuation functional defines a positive solution, and a strictly positive functional defines a strictly positive solution. If markets are incomplete, there are many valuation functionals (see Theorem 24.3.1), and Eqs. (25.5) have many solutions.

Theorem 25.2.1 *There exists a strictly positive valuation functional iff there exists a strictly positive solution to Eqs. (25.5). Each strictly positive solution q defines a strictly positive valuation functional Q by $Q(z) = qz$.*

Proof: Necessity was proved above. Suppose that q is a strictly positive solution to Eq. (25.5). Then the functional Q defined by $Q(z) = qz$ is linear and strictly positive. Applying Eq. (25.5), one can show that if $z \in \mathcal{M}(p)$ so that $z = z(h, p)$ for some portfolio strategy h, then $qz = p_0 h_0$. Thus, $Q(z) = p_0 h_0$; that is, Q coincides with the payoff pricing functional on $\mathcal{M}(p)$. Therefore, Q is a valuation functional. □

Similarly,

Theorem 25.2.2 *There exists a positive valuation functional iff there exists a positive solution to equations (25.5). Each positive solution q defines a positive valuation functional Q by $Q(z) = qz$.*

Theorems 25.2.1 and 25.2.2 say that Eqs. (25.5) provide a complete characterization of event prices. Thus, event prices can be equivalently defined as a positive or strictly positive solution to those equations. The fundamental theorem of finance can be restated as saying that security prices exclude arbitrage (strong arbitrage) iff there exists a strictly positive (positive) solution to Eqs. (25.5).

If security prices are equilibrium prices, the vector of marginal rates of substitution of each agent whose consumption is interior defines a (generally distinct) vector of event prices (see Section 24.2).

Example 25.2.3 In Example 24.2.3, Eqs. (25.5) take the following form:

$$q(\xi_{gg}) + q(\xi_{gb}) = 0.9q(\xi_g) \tag{25.6}$$
$$q(\xi_{bg}) + q(\xi_{bb}) = 0.8q(\xi_b) \tag{25.7}$$
$$q(\xi_g) + q(\xi_b) = 0.9 \tag{25.8}$$
$$0.9q(\xi_g) + 0.8q(\xi_b) = 0.75. \tag{25.9}$$

These equations uniquely identify date-1 event prices as $q(\xi_g) = 0.3$ and $q(\xi_b) = 0.6$, but leave date-2 event prices as an arbitrary positive (or strictly positive) solution to the following equations obtained from Eqs. (25.6) and (25.7):

$$q(\xi_{gg}) + q(\xi_{gb}) = 0.27, \tag{25.10}$$
$$q(\xi_{bg}) + q(\xi_{bb}) = 0.48. \tag{25.11}$$

The existence of strictly positive event prices indicates that there exist no arbitrage. Nonuniqueness of event prices indicates that markets are incomplete. □

25.3 Risk-Free Return and Discount Factors

The *one-period return* on security j in event ξ_{t+1} is its one-period (cum-dividend) payoff in ξ_{t+1} divided by its price in the immediate predecessor event ξ_t (where $\xi_t \equiv \xi_{t+1}^-$),

$$r_j(\xi_{t+1}) \equiv \frac{p_j(\xi_{t+1}) + x_j(\xi_{t+1})}{p_j(\xi_t)}. \tag{25.12}$$

We use $r_{j,t+1}$ to denote the one-period return on security j at date $t+1$.

A one-period return at date $t+1$ is *risk-free* if it takes the same value for any two date-$t+1$ events that have a common predecessor at date t. We denote the one-period risk-free return realized in event ξ_{t+1} by $\bar{r}(\xi_{t+1})$. By definition, the return $\bar{r}(\xi_{t+1})$ does not depend on the event ξ_{t+1} as long as $\xi_{t+1} \subset \xi_t$ for some ξ_t but, of course, may depend on ξ_t. In other words, $\bar{r}_{t+1}$ as a function on states is measurable with respect to F_t.

Examples of securities with one-period risk-free returns at date $t+1$ include the one-period risk-free bond issued at date t and a discount bond issued at date 0 and maturing at date $t+1$. We will frequently assume that at every date and in every event a security (or a portfolio) exists with a risk-free one-period return.

If at every date and in every event a security (or portfolio) with a strictly positive risk-free, one-period return exists, then we can define the *discount factor* in event ξ_t as the reciprocal of the cumulated risk-free return:

$$\rho(\xi_t) \equiv \prod_{\tau=1}^{t} [\bar{r}(\xi_\tau)]^{-1}, \quad t = 1, \dots, T, \tag{25.13}$$

where ξ_τ is the date-τ predecessor event of ξ_t, that is $\xi_\tau \supset \xi_t$. Note that $\rho(\xi_t)$ is the same for any two date-t events that have a common predecessor at date $t-1$; that is ρ_t is F_{t-1} measurable. We also set $\rho(\xi_0) \equiv 1$. For use later, note that Eq. (25.13) implies

$$\rho(\xi_t) = \bar{r}(\xi_{t+1})\rho(\xi_{t+1}). \tag{25.14}$$

25.4 Risk-Neutral Probabilities

We define the *risk-neutral probability* of an event ξ_T at date T as the ratio of its event price and the discount factor,

$$\pi^*(\xi_T) \equiv \frac{q(\xi_T)}{\rho(\xi_T)}, \tag{25.15}$$

and the risk-neutral probability of an event ξ_t at date t for $t < T$ by

$$\pi^*(\xi_t) \equiv \sum_{\xi_T \subset \xi_t} \pi^*(\xi_T). \tag{25.16}$$

Risk-neutral probabilities are strictly positive (positive) iff event prices are strictly positive (positive).

The risk-neutral probability of any event ξ_t satisfies

$$\pi^*(\xi_t) = \frac{q(\xi_t)}{\rho(\xi_t)}. \tag{25.17}$$

To see this, we note first that Eq. (25.17) holds for date-T events by definition (25.15). Next, we substitute Eq. (25.15) in the right-hand side of Eq. (25.16) to obtain

$$\pi^*(\xi_t) = \sum_{\xi_T \subset \xi_t} \frac{q(\xi_T)}{\rho(\xi_T)}. \tag{25.18}$$

Equation (25.5), when applied to the risk-free security in event ξ_t, implies

$$q(\xi_t) = \sum_{\xi_{t+1} \subset \xi_t} \bar{r}(\xi_{t+1}) q(\xi_{t+1}). \tag{25.19}$$

Substituting $\rho(\xi_t)/\rho(\xi_{t+1})$ for $\bar{r}(\xi_{t+1})$ (see Eq. (25.14)) in Eq. (25.19) and using Eq. (25.19) recursively, we obtain

$$q(\xi_t) = \sum_{\xi_T \subset \xi_t} \frac{\rho(\xi_t)}{\rho(\xi_T)} q(\xi_T). \tag{25.20}$$

Equations (25.18) and (25.20) imply Eq. (25.17).

For date-0 event ξ_0, Eq. (25.17) says that

$$\pi^*(\xi_0) = \frac{q(\xi_0)}{\rho(\xi_0)} = 1. \tag{25.21}$$

Because $\pi^*(\xi_0) = \sum_{\xi_T \subset \xi_0} \pi^*(\xi_T)$, Eq. (25.21) implies that π^* is indeed a probability measure.

Equation (25.17) indicates that risk-neutral probabilities are rescaled event prices. The existence of strictly positive (positive) risk-neutral probabilities is equivalent to security prices excluding arbitrage (strong arbitrage). These are restatements of the fundamental theorems of finance. Further, the risk-neutral probabilities are unique iff markets are dynamically complete.

If risk-neutral probabilities are strictly positive, conditional probabilities can be defined as

$$\pi^*(\xi_{t+1}|\xi_t) \equiv \frac{\pi^*(\xi_{t+1})}{\pi^*(\xi_t)} \tag{25.22}$$

for $\xi_{t+1} \subset \xi_t$. It follows from Eqs. (25.17) and (25.14) that

$$\pi^*(\xi_{t+1}|\xi_t) = \frac{q(\xi_{t+1})}{q(\xi_t)} \bar{r}(\xi_{t+1}). \tag{25.23}$$

Substituting Eq. (25.23) in Eq. (25.5) yields

$$p_j(\xi_t) = [\bar{r}(\xi_{t+1})]^{-1} \sum_{\xi_{t+1} \subset \xi_t} \pi^*(\xi_{t+1}|\xi_t)[p_j(\xi_{t+1}) + x_j(\xi_{t+1})] \qquad (25.24)$$

for every nonterminal event ξ_t and every security j. Equations (25.24) provide a complete characterization of risk-neutral probabilities. They can be used to calculate conditional risk-neutral probabilities. Marginal risk-neutral probabilities can then be obtained recursively from Eq. (25.22) as $\pi^*(\xi_{t+1}) = \pi^*(\xi_{t+1}|\xi_t) \cdot \pi^*(\xi_t)$, with $\pi^*(\xi_0) = 1$.

25.5 Expected Returns under Risk-Neutral Probabilities

When equipped with risk-neutral probabilities, the set of states S can be regarded as a probability space, just as in the two-date case. All measurable functions on S, such as date-t consumption plans, portfolio strategies, security prices, dividends, and so forth (see Section 21.2) can be regarded as random variables.

The expected value of a random variable, say the one-period return r_{jt} on security j at date t with respect to the risk-neutral probabilities π^* is denoted by $E^*(r_{jt})$. The asterisk indicates that the expectation is taken with respect to π^*. In the following sections we will also be using $E(r_{jt})$ to denote the expectation taken with respect to "natural probabilities" π that reflect agents' subjective beliefs about the states.

We write $E^*(r_{j,t+1}|\xi_t)$ to denote the expectation of $r_{j,t+1}$ under probabilities π^* conditional on event ξ_t, a scalar. Thus,

$$E^*(r_{j,t+1}|\xi_t) \equiv \sum_{\xi_{t+1} \subset \xi_t} \pi^*(\xi_{t+1}|\xi_t) r_j(\xi_{t+1}). \qquad (25.25)$$

We use $E_t^*(r_{j,t+1})$ to denote the expectation of $r_{j,t+1}$ conditional on F_t, that is, an F_t-measurable random variable that takes value $E^*(r_{j,t+1}|\xi_t)$ in event ξ_t.

Using the notation for conditional expectations, Eq. (25.24) is written

$$p_{jt} = (\bar{r}_{t+1})^{-1} E_t^*(p_{j,t+1} + x_{j,t+1}). \qquad (25.26)$$

Thus, the date-t price of security j equals the conditional expectation of its one-period payoff discounted by the one-period risk-free return, where the expectation is taken with respect to risk-neutral probabilities. Equation (25.26) can be written in terms of returns as

$$\bar{r}_{t+1} = E_t^*(r_{j,t+1}). \qquad (25.27)$$

Thus, the conditional expected one-period return on each security equals the risk-free one-period return, where the expectation is taken with respect to risk-neutral probabilities.

Example 25.5.1 In Example 24.2.3, one-period risk-free returns are $\bar{r}_1(\xi_0) = 1/p(\xi_0) = 1.11$, $\bar{r}_2(\xi_g) = 1/p(\xi_g) = 1.11$, $\bar{r}_2(\xi_b) = 1/p(\xi_b) = 1.25$. The discount factors are $\rho(\xi_{gg}) = \rho(\xi_{gb}) = 0.81$, $\rho(\xi_{bb}) = \rho(\xi_{bg}) = 0.72$, $\rho(\xi_g) = \rho(\xi_b) = 0.9$.

Risk-neutral probabilities can be obtained from Eqs. (25.24). Because we have already calculated event prices in Example 25.2.3, we derive risk-neutral probabilities from event prices using Eq. (25.24). One set of event prices is $q(\xi_{gg}) = 0.05$, $q(\xi_{gb}) = 0.22$, $q(\xi_{bg}) = 0.18$, $q(\xi_{bb}) = 0.3$, $q(\xi_g) = 0.3$ and $q(\xi_b) = 0.6$. The associated risk-neutral probabilities are

$$\pi^*(\xi_g) = \frac{q(\xi_g)}{\rho(\xi_g)} = 0.33, \qquad \pi^*(\xi_b) = \frac{q(\xi_b)}{\rho(\xi_b)} = 0.67, \tag{25.28}$$

$$\pi^*(\xi_{gg}) = \frac{q(\xi_{gg})}{\rho(\xi_{gg})} = 0.061, \qquad \pi^*(\xi_{gb}) = \frac{q(\xi_{gb})}{\rho(\xi_{gb})} = 0.272, \tag{25.29}$$

$$\pi^*(\xi_{bg}) = \frac{q(\xi_{bg})}{\rho(\xi_{bg})} = 0.25, \qquad \pi^*(\xi_{bb}) = \frac{q(\xi_{bb})}{\rho(\xi_{bb})} = 0.417. \tag{25.30}$$

Note that

$$\pi^*(\xi_{gg}) + \pi^*(\xi_{gb}) + \pi^*(\xi_{bg}) + \pi^*(\xi_{bb}) = 1, \tag{25.31}$$

and

$$\pi^*(\xi_{gg}) + \pi^*(\xi_{gb}) = \pi^*(\xi_g), \qquad \pi^*(\xi_{bg}) + \pi^*(\xi_{bb}) = \pi^*(\xi_b). \tag{25.32}$$

$\square$

25.6 Risk-Neutral Valuation

Substituting risk-neutral probabilities (25.24) in Eq. (25.3) yields

$$Q(z) = \sum_{t=1}^{T} E^*(\rho_t z_t) \tag{25.33}$$

for every contingent claim $z = (z_1, \ldots, z_T) \in \mathcal{R}^k$. Equation (25.33) is the representation of the valuation functional by risk-neutral probabilities. The value of a contingent claim equals the sum of discounted expected payoffs with respect to the risk-neutral probabilities. In particular,

$$q(z) = \sum_{t=1}^{T} E^*(\rho_t z_t) \tag{25.34}$$

for $z \in \mathcal{M}(p)$.

Example 25.6.1 (Binomial Option Pricing) We saw in Example 22.3.1 that the event price of an event at date t that has l "downs" between dates 0 and t is $(\frac{u-\bar{r}}{\bar{r}(u-d)})^l(\frac{\bar{r}-d}{\bar{r}(u-d)})^{t-l}$. The date-$t$ discount factor $\rho_t = (\bar{r})^{-t}$ is deterministic. Equation (25.17) implies that the risk-neutral probability is $(\frac{u-\bar{r}}{u-d})^l(\frac{\bar{r}-d}{u-d})^{t-l}$. Because there are $\binom{t}{l}$ states that have l "downs" between dates 0 and t, and because

$$\sum_{l=0}^{t} \binom{t}{l} \left(\frac{u-\bar{r}}{u-d}\right)^l \left(\frac{\bar{r}-d}{u-d}\right)^{t-l} = 1, \tag{25.35}$$

the risk-neutral probabilities for all events at date t sum to one for every t.

Because binomial security markets are dynamically complete, every contingent claim lies in the asset span and can be priced by the payoff pricing functional. A European call option on the stock with maturity T and exercise price k has a payoff $\max\{u^{T-l}d^l - k, 0\}$ at date T (which depends on the number of "downs" between dates 0 and T) and zero payoff at all other dates. Applying Eq. (25.34) with the risk-neutral probabilities from Example 18.4.2, we obtain the price of the option at date 0:

$$\sum_{l=0}^{T} \binom{T}{l} \frac{1}{(\bar{r})^T} \max\{u^{T-l}d^l - k, 0\} \left(\frac{u-\bar{r}}{u-d}\right)^l \left(\frac{\bar{r}-d}{u-d}\right)^{T-l}. \tag{25.36}$$

This is the binomial option pricing formula.   □

25.7 Value Bounds

The upper and the lower bounds on the value of a multidate contingent claim (see Eqs. (24.3) and (24.4)) can be derived using event prices or risk-neutral probabilities. For a contingent claim $z \in \mathcal{R}^k$, we have

$$q_u(z) = \max_q \{qz\} \tag{25.37}$$

and

$$q_\ell(z) = \min_q \{qz\}, \tag{25.38}$$

where the maximum and minimum are taken over all positive event-price vectors; that is, over all positive solutions to Eq. (25.5). If z lies in the asset span $\mathcal{M}(p)$, then the value qz is the same for all positive event-price vectors q and the bounds $q_u(z)$ and $q_\ell(z)$ are both equal to the price $q(z)$.

Using risk-neutral probabilities instead of event prices, the bounds can be written as

$$q_u(z) = \max_{\pi^*} \sum_{t=1}^{T} E^*(\rho_t z_t) \tag{25.39}$$

and

$$q_\ell(z) = \min_{\pi^*} \sum_{t=1}^{T} E^*(\rho_t z_t), \tag{25.40}$$

where the minimum and maximum are taken over all risk-neutral probabilities. These representations are the analogues of those of the two-date model (see Section 6.5).

25.8 The Pricing Kernel

In Chapter 17, the Riesz Representation Theorem was used to show that in the two-date model there exists a unique payoff k_q, the pricing kernel, such that the price of any payoff z equals $E(k_q z)$, where the expectation is taken with respect to natural probabilities π. The natural probabilities reflect agents' subjective beliefs about the states and, in particular, can be derived from the axioms of expected utility.

Let π denote the natural probabilities of the states in the multidate model, and let E denote the expectation with respect to the natural probabilities. The pricing kernel in multidate security markets is obtained as the Riesz representation of the payoff pricing functional q on the asset span $\mathcal{M}(p)$ under the inner product $z \cdot y = \sum_{t=1}^{T} E(z_t y_t)$. Thus, the pricing kernel is a payoff $k_q \in \mathcal{M}(p)$ such that

$$q(z) = \sum_{t=1}^{T} E(k_{qt} z_t) \tag{25.41}$$

for every $z \in \mathcal{M}(p)$. Displaying events explicitly, Eq. (25.41) can be written as

$$q(z) = \sum_{\xi \in \Xi} \pi(\xi) k_q(\xi) z(\xi) \tag{25.42}$$

for every $z \in \mathcal{M}(p)$.

Applying Eq. (25.42) to the payoff of the portfolio strategy consisting of buying one share of security j in event ξ_t and selling it in every successor event ξ_{t+1} (see Section 25.2) shows that the pricing kernel satisfies the following equations:

$$k_q(\xi_t) p_j(\xi_t) = \sum_{\xi_{t+1} \subset \xi_t} \pi(\xi_{t+1}|\xi_t) k_q(\xi_{t+1})[p_j(\xi_{t+1}) + x_j(\xi_{t+1})] \tag{25.43}$$

for every j and every ξ_t. As usual, Eq. (25.43) can be written as

$$k_{qt} p_{jt} = E_t[k_{q,t+1}(p_{j,t+1} + x_{j,t+1})]. \tag{25.44}$$

In terms of one-period returns, Eq. (25.44) can be written as

$$k_{qt} = E_t(k_{q,t+1} r_{j,t+1}) \tag{25.45}$$

for any security j. In particular, if a security (or a portfolio) with one-period, risk-free return $\bar{r}_{t+1}$ exists, then

$$k_{qt} = \bar{r}_{t+1} E_t(k_{q,t+1}).$$ (25.46)

The pricing kernel in dynamically complete markets is given by

$$k_q(\xi) = \frac{q(\xi)}{\pi(\xi)}.$$ (25.47)

To see this, substitute Eq. (25.47) in the right-hand side of Eq. (25.42) to obtain $\sum_{\xi \in \Xi} q(\xi) z(\xi)$, which equals $q(z)$. Thus, under dynamically complete markets the pricing kernel equals event prices rescaled by the probabilities.

25.9 Notes

Whether prices of payoffs are calculated using event prices, risk-neutral probabilities, or the pricing kernel is entirely a matter of convenience. In pricing derivative securities it is often most convenient to use risk-neutral probabilities. That is because risk-neutral probabilities can be calculated directly from the prices of the securities used to construct the replicating payoffs. In contrast, in empirical work the pricing kernel is often the choice. Financial data can be used to construct estimates of, for example, the variances and covariances of returns under the natural probabilities, implying that it is more convenient to work with those rather than the risk-neutral probabilities.

Sometimes the pricing kernel is replaced by its reciprocal, in which case the payoff being priced is divided in each event by this new payoff rather than multiplied. The term *deflator* is used for the reciprocal of the pricing kernel. Some authors, such as Duffie [3], define the pricing kernel as we have defined it (rather than as its reciprocal), but nonetheless referred to it as a deflator.

Risk-neutral probabilities and event prices were first analyzed by Harrison and Kreps [4], Cox and Ross [1], Cox, Ross, and Rubinstein [2], and Rubinstein [5].

The assumption that there is a portfolio with one-period, risk-free return at every date (see Section 25.4) is inessential. When there is no portfolio with risk-free return, one can use any other security (or portfolio strategy) that has positive one-period (risky) returns in the construction of Section 25.4. Then, instead of rescaling event prices by cumulated risk-free returns, it is possible to define a *deflator* as a portfolio strategy that has strictly positive payoffs at all events and then use the deflator to rescale event prices. Each deflator defines a set of generally distinct risk-neutral probabilities.

Bibliography

[1] Cox, J. C. and Ross, S. A. The valuation of options for alternative stochastic processes. *Journal of Financial Economics*, **3**:145–66, 1976.

[2] Cox, J. C., Ross, S. A., and Rubinstein, M. Option pricing: A simplified approach. *Journal of Financial Economics*, **7**:229–63, 1979.

[3] Duffie, D. *Dynamic Asset Pricing Theory,* Second Edition. Princeton University Press, Princeton, NJ, 1996.

[4] Harrison, J. M. and Kreps, D. M. Martingales and arbitrage in multiperiod securities markets. *Journal of Economic Theory*, **20**:381–408, 1979.

[5] Rubinstein, M. The valuation of uncertain income streams and the pricing of options. *Bell Journal of Economics*, **7**:407–25, 1976.

26

Security Gains as Martingales

26.1 Introduction

Dividends on securities and portfolios may be very complex. If we consider stocks as an example, corporate managers have a strong aversion to dividend reductions. This suggests that they are likely to increase dividends only when they are confident that the increase can be sustained. Typically this means that dividends will be increased only after an extended period of higher earnings. Complex dividend patterns such as this result in complex intertemporal dependence in security and portfolio prices.

We show in this chapter that if gains (defined below) from holding securities or portfolios are considered instead of their prices, the complexity of the intertemporal dependence disappears: the gains are martingales.

By definition, a sequence $\{y_t\}_{t=0}^{T}$ of random variables on S such that each y_t is measurable with respect to partition F_t is a *martingale* under probability measure π if

$$E_t(y_\tau) = y_t \quad \forall \tau \geq t, \tag{26.1}$$

where E_t is the expectation conditional on F_t under π.

There are two martingale representations of gains on securities and portfolios: one with respect to risk-neutral probabilities, and the other with respect to natural probabilities and the pricing kernel.

We assume in this chapter that at every event there exists a security or a portfolio with a strictly positive one-period, risk-free return.

26.2 Gain and Discounted Gain

The buy-and-hold strategy for security j terminated at t generates a payoff equal to the dividend $x_{j\tau}$ at each date $\tau < t$ and a payoff of $p_{jt} + x_{jt}$ at date t. The gain from holding security j from date 0 to date t is measured in units of date-t consumption and is defined as the sum of the date-t payoff of the buy-and-hold strategy and the

258

values of payoffs prior to date t when they are successively reinvested so as to earn one-period, risk-free returns. The value at date t of dividend $x_{j\tau}$ reinvested to earn one-period risk-free returns is $(\rho_\tau/\rho_t)x_{j\tau}$ where ρ_τ is the discount factor at τ.

Formally, the *gain* $g_j(\xi_t)$ on security j in event ξ_t, $t \geq 1$, is defined by

$$g_j(\xi_t) \equiv p_j(\xi_t) + [\rho(\xi_t)]^{-1} \sum_{\tau=1}^{t} \rho(\xi_\tau)x_j(\xi_\tau), \qquad (26.2)$$

where ξ_τ is the predecessor event of ξ_t at τ. The gain $g_j(\xi_0)$ at date 0 equals the price $p_j(\xi_0)$. When the notation for events is suppressed, Eq. (26.2) becomes

$$g_{jt} = p_{jt} + \rho_t^{-1} \sum_{\tau=1}^{t} \rho_\tau x_{j\tau}, \qquad (26.3)$$

$t \geq 1$, and $g_{j0} = p_{j0}$.

The *discounted gain* on security j at date t is the gain measured in units of date-0 consumption instead of date-t consumption:

$$d_{jt} \equiv \rho_t g_{jt}. \qquad (26.4)$$

The discounted gain equals the sum of discounted date-t price and discounted dividends from date 0 through t:

$$d_{jt} = \rho_t p_{jt} + \sum_{\tau=1}^{t} \rho_\tau x_{j\tau}. \qquad (26.5)$$

The discounted gain at date 0 equals p_{j0}.

Equation (26.5) implies that

$$d_{j,t+1} - d_{jt} = \rho_{t+1}(x_{j,t+1} + p_{j,t+1}) - \rho_t p_{jt}. \qquad (26.6)$$

Thus, the change in the discounted gain over one period equals the discounted current dividend plus the change in the discounted price. For the (undiscounted) gain, we have

$$g_{j,t+1} - \bar{r}_{t+1} g_{jt} = x_{j,t+1} + p_{j,t+1} - \bar{r}_{t+1} p_{jt}. \qquad (26.7)$$

The gain on a security with nonzero dividend only at the terminal date T equals the price at any nonterminal date and the dividend at the terminal date. The discounted gain equals the discounted price at any nonterminal date and the discounted dividend at the terminal date.

The definitions of gain and discounted gain for portfolio strategies are the analogues of the definitions for securities. Thus, the gain at date $t \geq 1$ on a portfolio strategy equals the sum of the date-t payoff and the values of payoffs at prior dates reinvested to earn risk-free returns; that is,

$$g_t(h) \equiv p_t h_t + \rho_t^{-1} \sum_{\tau=1}^{t} \rho_\tau z_\tau(h, p). \qquad (26.8)$$

The discounted gain on a portfolio strategy is

$$d_t(h) \equiv \rho_t p_t h_t + \sum_{\tau=1}^{t} \rho_\tau z_\tau(h, p). \tag{26.9}$$

The gain and discounted gain at date 0 are $g_0(h) = d_0(h) = p_0 h_0$.

In the presence of risk-neutral probabilities or natural probabilities, gains and discounted gains are random variables adapted to the information filtration $\{F_t\}$.

26.3 Discounted Gains as Martingales

Discounted gains on securities and portfolio strategies are martingales:

Theorem 26.3.1 *The discounted gain on any security is a martingale under risk-neutral probabilities. That is*

$$E_t^*(d_{j\tau}) = d_{jt}, \quad \forall \tau \geq t, \quad \forall j. \tag{26.10}$$

Further, the discounted gain on any portfolio strategy is a martingale under risk-neutral probabilities.

Proof: Multiplying both sides of Eq. (25.26) by the discount factor ρ_t, we obtain

$$\rho_t p_{jt} = \rho_{t+1} E_t^*(x_{j,t+1} + p_{j,t+1}). \tag{26.11}$$

Because $E_t^*(\rho_t p_{jt}) = \rho_t p_{jt}$, Eq. (26.11) implies

$$E_t^*[\rho_{t+1}(x_{j,t+1} + p_{j,t+1}) - \rho_t p_{jt}] = 0. \tag{26.12}$$

It follows from Eqs. (26.6) and (26.12) that

$$E_t^*(d_{j,t+1} - d_{jt}) = 0 \tag{26.13}$$

or, because $E_t^*(d_{jt}) = d_{jt}$, that

$$E_t^*(d_{j,t+1}) = d_{jt}, \tag{26.14}$$

for every $t < T$. By recursive substitution, Eq. (26.14) implies Eq. (26.10).

The derivation of Eq. (26.10) goes through for any portfolio strategy, not just for a single security. □

Because E_0^* is the unconditional expectation E^* with respect to π^*, the martingale property (26.10) implies that

$$E^*(d_{j\tau}) = d_{j0} = p_{j0} \tag{26.15}$$

for every τ. Thus, the expected discounted gain on any security at every date equals its date-0 price when the expectation is taken with respect to the risk-neutral probabilities. The same is true for the gain on any portfolio strategy.

For a security with nonzero dividend only at the terminal date T, Eq. (26.10) says that the discounted price has the martingale property for $\tau < T$; that is, $\rho_t p_{jt} = E_t^*(\rho_\tau p_{j\tau})$ for every $\tau \geq t$, $\tau < T$. Further, $\rho_t p_{jt} = E_t^*(\rho_T x_{jT})$ for every $t < T$.

Example 26.3.2 The discounted gains on security 1 (date-1 bond) in Example 24.2.3 are $d_1(\xi_g) = d_1(\xi_b) = 0.9$ in the two events at date 1 and $d_{12} = 0$ at date 2. For security 2 (date-2 bond), the discounted gains are $d_2(\xi_{gg}) = d_2(\xi_{gb}) = 0.81$, $d_2(\xi_{bg}) = d_2(\xi_{bb}) = 0.72$, and $d_2(\xi_g) = 0.81$, $d_2(\xi_b) = 0.72$. One can check that both discounted gains satisfy the martingale property (26.14) under the risk-neutral probabilities found in Example 25.5.1. □

26.4 Gains as Martingales

The product of the gain on a security or portfolio strategy and the pricing kernel is a martingale:

Theorem 26.4.1 *The product of the gain on any security and the pricing kernel is a martingale under the natural probabilities:*

$$E_t(g_{j\tau}k_{q\tau}) = g_{jt}k_{qt}, \quad \forall \tau \geq t, \quad \forall j. \tag{26.16}$$

Further, the product of the gain on any portfolio strategy and the pricing kernel is a martingale under the natural probabilities.

Proof: Equations (25.44) and (25.46) imply

$$E_t[k_{q,t+1}(x_{j,t+1} + p_{j,t+1} - \bar{r}_{t+1}p_{jt})] = 0. \tag{26.17}$$

Using Eqs. (26.7) and (26.17), we obtain

$$E_t[k_{q,t+1}(g_{j,t+1} - \bar{r}_{t+1}g_{jt})] = 0, \tag{26.18}$$

which, by Eq. (25.46), implies that

$$E_t(g_{j,t+1}k_{q,t+1}) = g_{jt}k_{qt}. \tag{26.19}$$

By recursive substitution, we obtain Eq. (26.16).

The derivation of Eq. (26.16) goes through for any portfolio strategy, not just for a single security. □

The martingale property (26.16) implies that

$$E(k_{q\tau}g_{j\tau}) = g_{j0} = p_{j0} \tag{26.20}$$

for every τ. Because $E(k_{q\tau} g_{j\tau})$ is the date-0 price of the gain $g_{j\tau}$, Eq. (26.20) says that the date-0 price of the gain on any security at any date equals the date-0 price of that security. The same is true for the gain on any portfolio strategy.

26.5 Notes

The proposition that discounted gains are martingales under risk-neutral probabilities originated with Harrison and Kreps [7]. That the product of the pricing kernel and the gain is a martingale under the natural probabilities is generally attributed to Hansen and Richard [6].

In the early literature on the efficiency of capital markets it was stated that capital markets are informationally efficient – prices "fully reflect available information" – iff discounted gains are martingales (see, for example, Samuelson [12], Fama [4]). Discounted gains are martingales under natural probabilities only if natural probabilities coincide with risk-neutral probabilities. This is the case under fair pricing and, hence, if agents are risk neutral. In the cited articles the restriction to risk neutrality was not clearly stated. LeRoy [8] presented an example in which agents are risk averse and security gains are not martingales under the natural probabilities. Lucas [10] stated the same conclusion in a more general setting.

For recent surveys of the literature on the efficiency of capital markets, see Fama [5] and LeRoy [9].

It may not be apparent why it is instructive to view security and portfolio prices as martingales. In discrete time there is in fact no particular advantage in doing so. In continuous time, however, martingales become central. To see this, consider that in continuous time the gain on a portfolio is modeled as the outcome of an infinite number of trades, where the trades themselves depend on security prices in general. The gain is computed using stochastic integration, which in turn is based on the fact that, in the absence of arbitrage, security prices are, after a change of measure, martingales.

For a rigorous treatment of stochastic integration see Chung and Williams [2]. For continuous-time finance, the authoritative text is Duffie [3]. Merton's collected papers [11] are also a good introduction to continuous-time finance. Baxter and Rennie [1] is an exceptionally clear and intuitive introductory text.

Bibliography

[1] Baxter, M. and Rennie, A. *Financial Calculus*. Cambridge University Press, Cambridge, UK, 1996.

[2] Chung, K. L. and Williams, R. J. *Introduction to Stochastic Calculus*. Birkhauser, Boston, 1990.

[3] Duffie, D. *Dynamic Asset Pricing Theory*, Second Edition. Princeton University Press, Princeton, NJ, 1996.

[4] Fama, E. F. Efficient capital markets: A review of theory and empirical work. *Journal of Finance*, **25**:283–417, 1970.

[5] Fama, E. F. Efficient capital markets: II. *Journal of Finance*, **46**:1575–1617, 1991.

[6] Hansen, L. P. and Richard, S. F. The role of conditioning information in deducing testable restrictions implied by dynamic asset pricing models. *Econometrica*, **55**:1269–86, 1987.

[7] Harrison, J. M. and Kreps, D. M. Martingales and arbitrage in multiperiod securities markets. *Journal of Economic Theory*, **20**:381–408, 1979.

[8] LeRoy, S. F. Risk aversion and the martingale model of stock prices. *International Economic Review*, **14**:436–46, 1973.

[9] LeRoy, S. F. Efficient capital markets and martingales. *Journal of Economic Literature*, **17**:1583–1621, 1989.

[10] Lucas, R. E. Asset prices in an exchange economy. *Econometrica*, **46**:1429–45, 1978.

[11] Merton, R. C. *Continuous-Time Finance*. Basil Blackwell, Cambridge, UK, 1990.

[12] Samuelson, P. A. Proof that properly anticipated prices fluctuate randomly. *Industrial Management Review*, **6**:41–9, 1965.

27

Conditional Consumption-Based Security Pricing

27.1 Introduction

Consumption-based security pricing relates the risk premium on each security (or portfolio) to the covariance of the security return with an agent's intertemporal marginal rate of substitution. In Chapter 14 we derived consumption-based security pricing in the two-date model for agents whose utility functions have an expected utility representation. Here we again derive the relation in the multidate model for agents whose utility functions have an expected utility representation.

27.2 Expected Utility

With multidate consumption, an agent's utility function $u : \mathcal{R}^{k+1} \to \mathcal{R}$ has a state-independent *expected utility representation* if there exists a function $V : \mathcal{R}^{T+1} \to \mathcal{R}$ and a probability measure π on S such that

$$u(c) \geq u(c') \text{ iff } \sum_{s=1}^{S} \pi_s V(c(s)) \geq \sum_{s=1}^{S} \pi_s V(c'(s)), \tag{27.1}$$

where consumption plan c in Eq. (27.1) is understood as a $(T + 1)$-tuple of F_t-measurable functions c_t with realization $c(s) = [c_0(s), \ldots, c_T(s)]$.

The probabilities π of the expected utility representation are referred to as the natural probabilities. Every measurable function on the set of states S can be regarded as a random variable on S with probability measure π. The expectation with respect to π is denoted by E.

Expected utility (27.1) is written

$$E[V(c)] \equiv \sum_{s=1}^{S} \pi_s V(c(s)). \tag{27.2}$$

Function V is the von Neumann–Morgenstern utility function for multidate

264

consumption. A frequently used time-separable form of V is

$$V(y) = \sum_{t=0}^{T} \delta^t v(y_t) \tag{27.3}$$

for $y = (y_0, \ldots, y_T) \in \mathcal{R}^{T+1}$, and where $v : \mathcal{R} \to \mathcal{R}$ is a time-invariant period utility function and δ a time-invariant discount factor, $0 < \delta$ and usually $\delta < 1$. The expected utility with time-separable von Neumann–Morgenstern utility is

$$E[V(c)] = \sum_{t=0}^{T} \sum_{s \in S} \pi(s) \delta^t v(c_t(s)) \tag{27.4}$$

and can be written as

$$E[V(c)] = \sum_{t=0}^{T} \delta^t E[v(c_t)]. \tag{27.5}$$

We can also write Eq. (27.4) as

$$E[V(c)] = \sum_{t=0}^{T} \sum_{\xi_t \in F_t} \pi(\xi_t) \delta^t v(c(\xi_t)), \tag{27.6}$$

where $\pi(\xi_t) = \sum_{s \in \xi_t} \pi_s$ is the probability of event ξ_t.

Axiomatization of the expected utility representation of preferences over multidate consumption plans is similar to the axiomatization over two-date plans discussed in Section 8.8.

27.3 Risk Aversion

An agent with expected utility function (27.1) is *risk averse* if

$$E[V(c)] \leq V(E(c)) \tag{27.7}$$

for every consumption plan c, where $E(c)$ denotes a deterministic multidate consumption plan $[c_0, E(c_1), \ldots, E(c_T)]$.

An agent is *risk neutral* if

$$E[V(c)] = V(E(c)), \tag{27.8}$$

for every consumption plan c.

An agent is *strictly risk averse* if

$$E[V(c)] < V(E(c)), \tag{27.9}$$

for every nondeterministic consumption plan c.

In Section 9.10 it was shown that for the von Neumann–Morgenstern utility function of two-date consumption, risk aversion is equivalent to concavity in consumption at date 1 for each fixed consumption at date 0. That result generalizes. For the von Neumann–Morgenstern utility function of multidate consumption, risk aversion is equivalent to concavity in consumption at dates 1 through T for each fixed consumption at date 0. Throughout the remaining chapters, risk aversion is taken as meaning that V as a function of multidate consumption plans (which include consumption at date 0) is concave in all its arguments.

Similarly, risk neutrality, which is equivalent to linearity of $V(y_0, \cdot)$ for every y_0, will be taken to mean linearity in all arguments. Therefore, the von Neumann–Morgenstern utility function of a risk-neutral agent is of the form

$$V(y) = \sum_{t=0}^{T} \alpha_t y_t \tag{27.10}$$

for $y \in \mathcal{R}^{T+1}$, where $\alpha_t > 0$ for all t. In the special case of a time-invariant discount factor, we have $\alpha_t = \delta^t$.

27.4 Conditional Covariance and Variance

Consumption-based security pricing in multidate markets involves conditional co-variances and conditional variances of returns. The conditional covariance between, say, one-period returns $r_{j,t+1}$ and $r_{k,t+1}$ on two securities j and k is the conditional expectation of the product of these two terms minus the product of their conditional expectations:

$$\text{cov}_t(r_{j,t+1}, r_{k,t+1}) \equiv E_t(r_{j,t+1}r_{k,t+1}) - E_t(r_{j,t+1})E_t(r_{k,t+1}). \tag{27.11}$$

Conditional covariance between $r_{j,t+1}$ and itself is the conditional variance of $r_{j,t+1}$ denoted $\text{var}_t(r_{j,t+1})$. The corresponding conditional standard deviation is denoted $\sigma_t(r_{j,t+1})$.

27.5 Conditional Consumption-Based Security Pricing

The marginal utility of consumption in event ξ_t of an agent with expected utility function (27.1) is

$$\sum_{s \in \xi_t} \pi_s \partial_t V(c(s)), \tag{27.12}$$

where $\partial_t V(c(s))$ denotes the partial derivative of the von Neumann–Morgenstern utility function V with respect to date-t consumption. This expression indicates that without time separability the marginal expected utility of consumption at any date depends on consumption at all dates. Expression (27.12) can be rewritten as

$$\pi(\xi_t)E[\partial_t V|\xi_t],\tag{27.13}$$

where $\partial_t V$ is understood to be a random variable that takes values $\partial_t V(c(s))$.

Using (27.13), the first-order condition (21.16) of the consumption-portfolio choice problem under expected utility takes the form

$$p_j(\xi_t)E(\partial_t V|\xi_t) = E[(p_{j,t+1} + x_{j,t+1})\partial_{t+1} V|\xi_t],\tag{27.14}$$

for each security j and each event ξ_t, $t < T$. In the notation that suppresses events, Eq. (27.14) appears as

$$p_{jt}E_t(\partial_t V) = E_t[(p_{j,t+1} + x_{j,t+1})\partial_{t+1} V].\tag{27.15}$$

In terms of returns, Eq. (27.15) can be written as

$$E_t(\partial_t V) = E_t(r_{j,t+1}\partial_{t+1} V)\tag{27.16}$$

for every security j.

Suppose that in every event at date t $(0 \le t < T)$ there exists a security (or portfolio) with a one-period, risk-free return $\bar{r}_{t+1}$. Applying Eq. (27.16) to the risk-free security, we obtain

$$\bar{r}_{t+1} = \frac{E_t(\partial_t V)}{E_t(\partial_{t+1} V)}.\tag{27.17}$$

This expression is the exact analogue of expression (14.3) for the risk-free return in the two-date model.

We now derive an expression for the *conditional one-period risk premium* $E_t(r_{j,t+1}) - \bar{r}_{t+1}$ on security j. Following the derivation for the two-date model, we begin by writing the conditional covariance between $r_{j,t+1}$ and $\partial_{t+1} V$ as

$$\text{cov}_t(r_{j,t+1}, \partial_{t+1} V) = E_t(r_{j,t+1}\partial_{t+1} V) - E_t(r_{j,t+1})E_t(\partial_{t+1} V).\tag{27.18}$$

It follows (see Section 14.3) from Eqs. (27.16) and (27.17) that the conditional expected one-period return on security j satisfies

$$E_t(r_{j,t+1}) = \bar{r}_{t+1} - \bar{r}_{t+1}\frac{\text{cov}_t(r_{j,t+1}, \partial_{t+1} V)}{E_t(\partial_t V)}.\tag{27.19}$$

Equation (27.19), which extends Eq. (14.6) to multidate security markets, is the equation of *conditional consumption-based security pricing*. It says that the conditional one-period risk premium $E_t(r_{j,t+1}) - \bar{r}_{t+1}$ on each security j is proportional to the negative of the conditional covariance of the one-period return on that security with the marginal rate of substitution between consumption at date t and at date $t+1$. As in Chapter 14, the expression $\partial_{t+1} V/E_t(\partial_t V)$ is, to be precise, not the marginal rate of substitution under expected utility; the two differ by a conditional probability (see the chapter notes).

Just as in the two-date model, a security that pays off primarily in successor events in which consumption is high relative to current consumption has an expected one-period return greater than the risk-free one-period return.

If the agent's consumption is deterministic at every date, then marginal utility $\partial_t V$ is deterministic for every t. Consumption-based pricing (27.19) implies *fair pricing*, that is, that the one-period expected return on every security equals the risk-free return.

27.6 Security Pricing under Time Separability

That intertemporal marginal rates of substitution depend on consumption at all dates renders expressions (27.17) and (27.19) inconvenient for applied work. Therefore, time-separable expected utility (27.6) is generally used.

Under specification (27.6), the marginal expected utility of consumption in event ξ_t is

$$\pi(\xi_t)\delta^t v'(c(\xi_t)), \tag{27.20}$$

where v' denotes the derivative of v, a function of a single variable. Through Eq. (27.20), the first-order condition (21.16) for the consumption-portfolio choice problem becomes

$$p_j(\xi_t)v'(c(\xi_t)) = \delta \sum_{\xi_{t+1} \subset \xi_t} [p_j(\xi_{t+1}) + x_j(\xi_{t+1})]\frac{\pi(\xi_{t+1})}{\pi(\xi_t)}v'(c(\xi_{t+1})). \tag{27.21}$$

This can be written in a form similar to Eq. (27.14) as

$$p_j(\xi_t)v'(c(\xi_t)) = \delta E[(p_{j,t+1} + x_{j,t+1})v'(c_{t+1})|\xi_t], \tag{27.22}$$

where $v'(c_{t+1})$ is understood as a random variable with realizations $v'(c(\xi_{t+1}))$ for $\xi_{t+1} \in F_t$. If explicit recognition of events is suppressed, Eq. (27.22) is written

$$p_{jt}v'(c_t) = \delta E_t[(p_{j,t+1} + x_{j,t+1})v'(c_{t+1})]. \tag{27.23}$$

The expression for the one-period, risk-free return specializes to

$$\bar{r}_{t+1} = \delta^{-1}\frac{v'(c_t)}{E_t[v'(c_{t+1})]}. \tag{27.24}$$

Finally, under time separability the equation of consumption-based security pricing (27.19) becomes

$$E_t(r_{j,t+1}) = \bar{r}_{t+1} - \delta\bar{r}_{t+1}\frac{\text{cov}_t[v'(c_{t+1}), r_{j,t+1}]}{v'(c_t)}. \tag{27.25}$$

If the agent is risk neutral (and his or her consumption is interior), then consumption-based pricing (27.25) implies fair pricing. Further, if the agent's discount factor is time invariant, then the one-period, risk-free return equals the inverse of the discount factor.

27.7 Volatility of Intertemporal Marginal Rates of Substitution

As was demonstrated in Section 14.4 for the two-date model, consumption-based security pricing can be used to derive a lower bound on the standard deviation of agents' intertemporal marginal rates of substitution. Here we derive the analogue for the multidate model.

Equation (27.15) can be written in terms of one-period returns as

$$E_t(\partial_t V) = E_t[r_{j,t+1} \, \partial_{t+1} V], \tag{27.26}$$

for every security j. Using expression (27.17) for the one-period, risk-free return, we obtain

$$0 = E_t[(r_{j,t+1} - \bar{r}_{t+1}) \, \partial_{t+1} V]. \tag{27.27}$$

Writing an expression for the conditional correlation ρ_t between the marginal utility $\partial_{t+1} V$ and the excess one-period return $r_{j,t+1} - \bar{r}_{t+1}$ and using the fact that $|\rho_t| \le 1$ (compare Section 14.4), we obtain

$$\sigma_t \left(\frac{\partial_{t+1} V}{E_t(\partial_t V)} \right) \ge \frac{|E_t(r_{j,t+1}) - \bar{r}_{t+1}|}{\bar{r}_{t+1}\sigma_t(r_{j,t+1})}. \tag{27.28}$$

Inequality (27.28) says that the conditional volatility of the marginal rate of substitution between consumption at dates t and $t + 1$ in equilibrium is higher than (the absolute value of) the Sharpe ratio of each security divided by the risk-free return.

Inequality (27.28) holds for one-period return on a portfolio as well as return on a security. Taking the supremum over all one-period returns yields for the multidate model a lower bound on the conditional volatility of the intertemporal marginal rates of substitution, the analogue of Eq. (14.16) of Section 14.4.

27.8 Notes

Strictly, the term $\partial_{t+1} V / E_t(\partial_t V)$ in Eqs. (27.19) and (27.28) is not the marginal rate of substitution between consumption at date t and at date $t + 1$. The marginal rate of substitution between consumption in event ξ_t and a successor event ξ_{t+1}, being a ratio of marginal utilities, is

$$\frac{\pi(\xi_{t+1})E(\partial_{t+1} V|\xi_{t+1})}{\pi(\xi_t)E(\partial_t V|\xi_t)}, \tag{27.29}$$

(see Eq. (27.13)). Thus, the term appearing in Eqs. (27.19) and (27.28) lacks the event probabilities and the conditional expectation in the numerator.

The absence of the conditional expectation is a matter of notation only. Because $r_{j,t+1}$ is F_{t+1}-measurable, the conditional covariance between $r_{j,t+1}$ and $\partial_{t+1}V$ is equal to that between $r_{j,t+1}$ and $E_{t+1}(\partial_{t+1}V)$. The explicit argument, which makes use of the rule of iterated expectations, is as follows:

$$\operatorname{cov}_t[r_{j,t+1}, \partial_{t+1}V] = E_t(r_{j,t+1}\partial_{t+1}V) - E_t(r_{j,t+1})E_t(\partial_{t+1}V) \quad (27.30)$$

$$= E_t[E_{t+1}(r_{j,t+1}\partial_{t+1}V)] - E_t(r_{j,t+1})E_t[E_{t+1}(\partial_{t+1}V)] \quad (27.31)$$

$$= E_t[r_{j,t+1}E_{t+1}(\partial_{t+1}V)] - E_t(r_{j,t+1})E_t[E_{t+1}(\partial_{t+1}V)] \quad (27.32)$$

$$= \operatorname{cov}_t[r_{j,t+1}, E_{t+1}(\partial_{t+1}V)]. \quad (27.33)$$

Similarly, we have

$$\sigma_t\left(\frac{\partial_{t+1}V}{E_t(\partial_t V)}\right) = \sigma_t\left(\frac{E_{t+1}(\partial_{t+1}V)}{E_t(\partial_t V)}\right). \quad (27.34)$$

The absence of probabilities indicates a slight inaccuracy of terminology. The corresponding inaccuracy in the case of the two-date model was pointed out in Section 14.3.

The first clear formulations of consumption-based security pricing in multi-date security markets can be found in Lucas [4] and Breeden [2]. Several authors anticipated, with varying degrees of clarity, the ideas of consumption-based security pricing; Beja [1] and Rubinstein [5] are examples. The bound on the volatility of marginal rates of substitution of consumption originated with Hansen and Jagannathan [3].

Bibliography

[1] Beja, A. The structure of the cost of capital under uncertainty. *Review of Economic Studies*, **38**:359–69, 1971.

[2] Breeden, D. T. An intertemporal asset pricing model with stochastic consumption and investment opportunities. *Journal of Financial Economics*, **7**:265–96, 1979.

[3] Hansen, L. P. and Jagannathan, R. Implications of security market data for models of dynamic economies. *Journal of Political Economy*, **99**:225–62, 1991.

[4] Lucas, R. E. Asset prices in an exchange economy. *Econometrica*, **46**:1429–45, 1978.

[5] Rubinstein, M. The valuation of uncertain income streams and the pricing of options. *Bell Journal of Economics*, **7**:407–25, 1976.

28

Conditional Beta Pricing and the CAPM

28.1 Introduction

In this chapter we discuss the counterparts in the multidate setting of the results of Chapter 18 deriving beta pricing and of Chapter 19 deriving the Capital Asset Pricing Model, each in the two-date setting.

The counterpart of the beta pricing relation of Chapter 18 is the conditional beta pricing relation. The derivation of conditional beta pricing is based on the observation that each nonterminal event and its immediate successor events are formally indistinguishable from the two-date model. Accordingly, the pricing relation can be derived in the same way in the multidate case as in the two-date case.

In the derivation of the Conditional CAPM we restrict our attention to the case with quadratic utilities.

28.2 Two-Date Security Markets at a Date-*t* Event

We want to construct two-date security markets associated with nonterminal event ξ_t by viewing variables at ξ_t and the immediate successor events of ξ_t as the analogues of the corresponding variables at date 0 and date 1, respectively, of the two-date model.

The first step is to note that some terms that have a clear meaning in the two-date model have several possible distinct analogues in the multidate model. For example, consider portfolio payoffs. In the two-date model the payoff of a portfolio h is xh. In Chapter 21 we defined the multidate payoff in event ξ_{t+1} of a portfolio strategy h as $[p(\xi_{t+1}) + x(\xi_{t+1})]h(\xi_t) - p(\xi_{t+1})h(\xi_{t+1})$. The two are analogues because the counterpart in the two-date model of p_{t+1} in the multidate model is zero. However, the one-period payoff as defined in Chapter 23, $[p(\xi_{t+1}) + x(\xi_{t+1})]h(\xi_t)$ in event ξ_{t+1}, is also an analogue in the multidate model for the payoff xh in the two-date model. It is this analogue that we will use below. We will see below that, similarly, the market portfolio has two possible analogues in the multidate setting.

271

J securities are traded in the two-date security markets associated with event ξ_t. Each agent chooses a portfolio at ξ_t and a consumption plan for ξ_t and for each of its immediate successors. As noted, the payoff of portfolio $h(\xi_t)$ in two-date security market associated with ξ_t is the one-period payoff in the successor events.

Agent i's utility function over consumption at ξ_t and its immediate successors is defined as follows. We assume that each agent's utility function over multidate consumption plans has an expected utility representation with a time-separable von Neumann–Morgenstern utility function (27.3). That is, we specify

$$V^i(y) = \sum_{t=0}^{T}(\delta_i)^t v^i(y_t), \tag{28.1}$$

for $y = (y_0, \dots, y_T) \in \mathcal{R}^{T+1}$, where $\delta_i > 0$. Agents have common probabilities of events, implying that the expected utility of multidate consumption plan c for agent i can be written $E[V^i(c)]$. The utility function over consumption at ξ_t and its immediate successors is defined by

$$v^i(c(\xi_t)) + \delta_i E[v^i(c_{t+1})|\xi_t]. \tag{28.2}$$

Consider now an equilibrium in multidate security markets given by a vector of security prices p, an allocation of portfolio strategies $\{h^i\}$ and a consumption allocation $\{c^i\}$. Set agent i's endowment at ξ_t in two-date security markets equal to $w^i(\xi_t) + [p(\xi_t) + x(\xi_t)]h^i(\xi_t^-)$ and the endowment at each immediate successor of ξ_t as $w^i(\xi_{t+1}) - p(\xi_{t+1})h^i(\xi_{t+1})$. These endowments are taken as given in analyzing the two-date security markets associated with ξ_t. Note that, since $\sum_i h^i = 0$, the aggregate endowment at ξ_t is equal to $\bar{w}(\xi_t)$ in the two-date security markets. Similarly, the aggregate endowment at each $\xi_{t+1} \subset \xi_t$ is equal to $\bar{w}(\xi_{t+1})$.

The security price vector $p(\xi_t)$, the portfolio allocation $\{h^i(\xi_t)\}$ and the consumption allocations $\{(c^i(\xi_t)\}$ and $\{c^i(\xi_{t+1})\}$ for each $\xi_{t+1} \subset \xi_t$ are an equilibrium for the two-date security markets associated with ξ_t. Each agent will choose the same portfolio at ξ_t and the same consumption plan for ξ_t and each of its immediate successors in the two-date markets as in multidate markets.

28.3 Conditional Beta Pricing

In this section we show that, as one would expect, beta pricing of Section 18.5 carries over to the two-date security markets associated with each date-t event. We call this *conditional beta pricing*.

The set of one-period payoffs of portfolios chosen at ξ_t is the *one-period asset span* associated with ξ_t. It is denoted $\mathcal{M}_{\xi_t}(p)$ and is a subspace of $\mathcal{R}^{k(\xi_t)}$ where, as in Chapter 23, $k(\xi_t)$ denotes the number of immediate successor events of ξ_t.

Formally,

$$\mathcal{M}_{\xi_t}(p) \equiv \{z \in \mathcal{R}^{k(\xi_t)} : z(\xi_{t+1}) = [p(\xi_{t+1}) + x(\xi_{t+1})]h(\xi_t),$$

$$\forall \xi_{t+1} \subset \xi_t, \text{ for some } h(\xi_t) \in \mathcal{R}^J\}. \tag{28.3}$$

The *one-period payoff pricing functional* assigns to each one-period payoff z in the one-period asset span $\mathcal{M}_{\xi_t}(p)$ the price at ξ_t of a portfolio that generates z. Assuming that the law of one price holds at ξ_t, the functional $q_{\xi_t} : \mathcal{M}_{\xi_t}(p) \to \mathcal{R}$ is defined by

$$q_{\xi_t}(z) \equiv p(\xi_t)h(\xi_t) \tag{28.4}$$

for $z \in \mathcal{M}_{\xi_t}(p)$, where $h(\xi_t)$ is a portfolio such that $z(\xi_{t+1}) = [p(\xi_{t+1}) + x(\xi_{t+1})] h(\xi_t)$ for every $\xi_{t+1} \subset \xi_t$.

The asset span $\mathcal{M}_{\xi_t}(p)$ is a Hilbert space when equipped with the *conditional-expectations inner product*

$$y \cdot z \equiv E(yz|\xi_t) \tag{28.5}$$

for $y, z \in \mathcal{M}_{\xi_t}(p)$, where $E(yz|\xi_t) = \sum_{\xi_{t+1} \subset \xi_t} \pi(\xi_{t+1}|\xi_t) y(\xi_{t+1}) z(\xi_{t+1})$. By the Riesz representation theorem there exists a *one-period pricing kernel* $k_{\xi_t}^q \in \mathcal{M}_{\xi_t}(p)$ that represents the one-period payoff pricing functional:

$$q_{\xi_t}(z) = E(k_{\xi_t}^q z|\xi_t) \tag{28.6}$$

for every $z \in \mathcal{M}_{\xi_t}(p)$. Similarly, let $k_{\xi_t}^e \in \mathcal{M}_{\xi_t}(p)$ be the kernel associated with the conditional expectations operator:

$$E(z|\xi_t) = E(k_{\xi_t}^e z|\xi_t) \tag{28.7}$$

for every $z \in \mathcal{M}_{\xi_t}(p)$. We call $k_{\xi_t}^e$ the *conditional expectations kernel*. If there exists a security or portfolio strategy at ξ_t with one-period risk-free payoff, then the conditional expectations kernel is the one-period risk-free payoff equal to one.

Let $\mathcal{E}_{\xi_t} \subset \mathcal{M}_{\xi_t}(p)$ be *the conditional frontier plane*; that is, the subspace that consists of the one-period payoffs that minimize conditional variance subject to a constraint on price and conditional expectation. As in the two-date case, $\mathcal{E}_{\xi_t}$ is the plane spanned by the kernels $k_{\xi_t}^q$ and $k_{\xi_t}^e$ (assumed not collinear).

The returns on the one-period pricing and the conditional expectations kernels are

$$r_{\xi_t}^q \equiv \frac{k_{\xi_t}^q}{q_{\xi_t}(k_{\xi_t}^q)}, \qquad r_{\xi_t}^e \equiv \frac{k_{\xi_t}^e}{q_{\xi_t}(k_{\xi_t}^e)}. \tag{28.8}$$

The set of one-period conditional frontier returns associated with ξ_t is the line passing through $r_{\xi_t}^q$ and $r_{\xi_t}^e$. Therefore each one-period return in that set can be written as

$$r_\lambda = r_{\xi_t}^e + \lambda(r_{\xi_t}^q - r_{\xi_t}^e) \tag{28.9}$$

for some λ. As long as the return r_λ is not the minimum-conditional-variance return, there exists a one-period conditional frontier return r_μ that has zero conditional covariance with r_μ. Using two such conditional frontier returns, the conditional beta pricing relation for the one-period return $r_{j,t+1}$ on security j is

$$E(r_{j,t+1}|\xi_t) = E(r_\mu|\xi_t) + \beta_j(\xi_t)[E(r_\lambda|\xi_t) - E(r_\mu|\xi_t)], \qquad (28.10)$$

where

$$\beta_j(\xi_t) = \frac{\text{cov}(r_{j,t+1}, r_\lambda|\xi_t)}{\text{var}(r_\lambda|\xi_t)}. \qquad (28.11)$$

Suppressing the notation for events, Eq. (28.10) becomes

$$E_t(r_{j,t+1}) = E_t(r_\mu) + \beta_{tj}[E_t(r_\lambda) - E_t(r_\mu)]. \qquad (28.12)$$

This is the conditional beta pricing relation (see Section 18.5).

28.4 Conditional CAPM with Quadratic Utilities

In Sections 28.4 and 28.5 we consider a multidate security markets equilibrium in which markets are dynamically complete, and hence one-period complete at every nonterminal event ξ_t. Then the aggregate endowment lies in the one-period asset span and consequently there exists a portfolio $\tilde{h}(\xi_t)$ at ξ_t the one-period payoff of which equals the aggregate endowment. That is

$$[(p(\xi_{t+1}) + x(\xi_{t+1})]\tilde{h}(\xi_{t+1}) = \bar{w}(\xi_{t+1}), \qquad (28.13)$$

for each $\xi_{t+1} \subset \xi_t$. We call portfolio $\tilde{h}(\xi_t)$ the *aggregate endowment portfolio*. The one-period return on the aggregate endowment portfolio at ξ_{t+1} is

$$r_{\bar{w}}(\xi_{t+1}) = \frac{[p(\xi_{t+1}) + x(\xi_{t+1})]\tilde{h}(\xi_t)}{p(\xi_t)\tilde{h}(\xi_t)}, \qquad (28.14)$$

and can be equivalently written using the one-period payoff pricing functional as

$$r_{\bar{w}}(\xi_{t+1}) = \frac{\bar{w}(\xi_{t+1})}{q_{\xi_t}(\bar{w}_{t+1})}. \qquad (28.15)$$

Suppose that agents' utility functions are of the form (28.1) with quadratic Neumann–Morgenstern utility functions

$$v^i(y_t) = -(y_t - \alpha^i)^2 \qquad (28.16)$$

for $y_t < \alpha^i$, for each t. The resulting utility function (28.2) over consumption in event ξ_t and its immediate successors is

$$-[c(\xi_t) - \alpha^i]^2 - E[(c_{t+1} - \alpha^i)^2|\xi_t], \qquad (28.17)$$

and depends only on the expectation and variance of c_{t+1} conditional on event ξ_t. Specifically, we can write Eq. (28.17) as

$$-[c(\xi_t) - \alpha^i]^2 - \text{var}(c_{t+1}|\xi_t) - [E(c_{t+1}|\xi_t) - \alpha^i]^2. \tag{28.18}$$

Theorem 19.3.1, when applied to the two-date security markets associated with event ξ_t, implies that the one-period return $r_{\tilde{w},t+1}$ is a conditional frontier return. Therefore it can be used as the reference return in the conditional beta pricing relation (28.10). It is assumed that the one-period risk-free return lies in the one-period asset span; we thus have the *conditional security market line*:

$$E(r_{j,t+1}|\xi_t) = \bar{r}(\xi_{t+1}) + \beta_j(\xi_t)[E(r_{\tilde{w},t+1}|\xi_t) - \bar{r}(\xi_{t+1})]. \tag{28.19}$$

Equation (28.19) says that the conditional one-period risk premium $E(r_{j,t+1}|\xi_t) - \bar{r}(\xi_{t+1})$ is proportional to the coefficient $\beta_j(\xi_t)$ which measures the conditional covariance between the one-period return $r_{j,t+1}$ and the return $r_{\tilde{w},t+1}$. Suppressing the notation for events, Eq. (28.19) becomes

$$E_t(r_{j,t+1}) = \bar{r}_{t+1} + \beta_{tj}[E_t(r_{\tilde{w},t+1}) - \bar{r}_{t+1}]. \tag{28.20}$$

The specification (28.16) of quadratic utility functions can be extended to include time-dependent parameter α^i, as well as time-dependent discount factors. None of the arguments above would be affected.

28.5 Multidate Market Return

The aggregate endowment portfolio $\tilde{h}(\xi_t)$ defined by Eq. (28.13) is one analogue of the market portfolio of the two-date model. Another analogue is the portfolio strategy $\hat{h}$ that generates the aggregate endowment as its multidate payoff, that is

$$(p_{t+1} + x_{t+1})\hat{h}_t - p_{t+1}\hat{h}_{t+1} = \bar{w}_{t+1}, \tag{28.21}$$

for each $t < T$. The existence of such portfolio strategy follows from the assumption of dynamically complete markets. The portfolio strategy $\hat{h}$ is termed the *multidate market portfolio strategy*. Note that the aggregate endowment portfolio and the multidate market portfolio coincide at each event at date $T - 1$. In particular, if $T = 1$ the two are the same as each other, and also the same as the market portfolio in the two-date model.

The one-period return on the multidate market portfolio strategy is

$$r_{m,t+1} = \frac{(p_{t+1} + x_{t+1})\hat{h}_t}{p_t\hat{h}_t} = \frac{\bar{w}_{t+1} + p_{t+1}\hat{h}_{t+1}}{p_t\hat{h}_t}, \tag{28.22}$$

where we used Eq. (28.21). Because of the presence of the right-most term in Eq. (28.22), the return $r_{m,t+1}$ does not in general lie on the conditional frontier, implying that it cannot be substituted for the return on the aggregate endowment in the conditional security market line (28.20).

28.6 Conditional CAPM with Incomplete Markets

In the two-date CAPM of Chapter 19 we did not assume market completeness. In the multidate setting of this chapter we did assume dynamic completeness, so as to make the point that the one-period return on the multidate market portfolio strategy does not in general lie on the conditional frontier regardless of whether markets are dynamically complete or incomplete.

In the derivation of the conditional security market line in incomplete markets, it is necessary to replace the aggregate endowment by its projection on the one-period asset span. Let $\bar{w}_{t+1}^{\mathcal{M}}$ denote the projection of the aggregate endowment $\bar{w}_{t+1}$ on the one-period asset span $\mathcal{M}_{\xi_t}(p)$. The one-period return $r_{\bar{w},t+1}$ is defined by $r_{\bar{w},t+1} \equiv \bar{w}_{t+1}^{\mathcal{M}}/q_{\xi_t}(\bar{w}_{t+1}^{\mathcal{M}})$. If agents' utility functions are of the quadratic form (28.16), then in equilibrium the return $r_{\bar{w},t+1}$ lies on the conditional frontier and Eq. (28.20) obtains.

28.7 Notes

The derivation of the Conditional CAPM of Section 28.4 can be extended to more general time-separable conditional-mean-variance preferences. The use of the normal distribution to generate the conditional CAPM is problematic since the assumption of normally distributed dividends does not in general imply that security prices, and therefore also one-period portfolio payoffs, are normally distributed.

The observation that the one-period return on the market portfolio strategy cannot be used in the conditional CAPM Eq. (28.20) is due to Duffie and Zame [2].

Coefficient beta in Eq. (28.20) is both time-dependent and event-dependent. Date-t conditional beta may very well be correlated with conditional risk premium $E_t(r_{\bar{w},t+1}) - \bar{r}_{t+1}$. For empirical investigations of the conditional CAPM see Fama and French [3], Jagannathan and Wang [4], and Campbell, Lo, and MacKinlay [1].

Bibliography

[1] Campbell, J. Y., Lo, A. W., and MacKinlay, A. C. *The Econometrics of Financial Markets*. Princeton University Press, Princeton, NJ, 1969.

[2] Duffie, D. and Zame, W. The consumption-based capital asset pricing model. *Econometrica*, **57**:1279–97, 1989.

[3] Fama, E. F. and French, K. R. The cross section of expected stock returns. *Journal of Finance*, **47**:427–66, 1992.

[4] Jagannathan R. and Wang Z. The conditional CAPM and the cross-section of expected returns. *Journal of Finance*, **51**:3–53, 1996.

Index